NATIONAL LAW AND INTERNATIONAL HUMAN RIGHTS LAW

National Law and International Human Rights Law

Cases of Botswana, Namibia and Zimbabwe

ONKEMETSE TSHOSA
University of Botswana, Botswana

DARTMOUTH

Aldershot • Burlington USA • Singapore • Sydney

Published by
Dartmouth Publishing Company
Ashgate Publishing Limited
Gower House
Croft Road
Aldershot
Hampshire GU11 3HR
England

Ashgate Publishing Company
131 Main Street
Burlington, VT 05401-5600 USA

British Library Cataloguing in Publication Data
Tshosa, Onkemetse
    National law and international human rights : cases of
    Botswana, Namibia and Zimbabwe. - (Law, social change and
    development)
    1. Human rights - Botswana 2. Human rights - Namibia 3. Human
    rights - Zimbabwe
    I. Title
    341.4'81

Library of Congress Control Number: 2001086754

ISBN 0 7546 2175 8

Contents

Abbreviations

AC	Appeal Cases
ACHPR	African Charter on Human and People's Rights
ACHR	American Convention on Human Rights
AJ	Acting Judge
AJA	Acting Judge of Appeal
ALL ER	All England Law Reports
BLR	Botswana Law Reports
CA	Court of Appeal
CJ	Chief Justice
CPEA	Criminal Procedure and Evidence Act
DTA	Democratic Turnhalle Alliance
EA	East African Law Reports
ECHR	European Convention on Human Rights and Fundamental Freedoms
ECtHR	European Court of Human Rights
EHRR	European Human Rights Reports
Ex. D	Exchequer Division
HC	High Court
HCTLR	High Commissioner Territory Law Reports
HRC	Human Rights Committee
ICCPR	International Covenant on Civil and Political Rights
ICESCR	International Covenant on Economic, Social and Cultural rights
ICJ	International Court of Justice
IHRR	International Human Rights Reports
ILM	International Legal Materials
ILO	International Labour Organisation
IR	Irish Law Reports
JA	Justice of Appeal
JP	Judge President
KB	King's Bench Division
LRC	Law Reports of the Commonwealth
NLP	National Land Policy
NmHC	Namibian High Court
NmSC	Namibian Supreme Court

NR	Namibian Law Reports
OAU	Organisation of African Unity
PCIJ	Permanent Court of International Justice
PLAN	People's Liberation Army of Namibia
QB	Queen's Bench Division
RLR	Rhodesian Law Reports
SA	South African Law Reports
SADC	Southern African Development Community
SLR	Scottish Law Reports
SR	Southern Rhodesia
SWA	South West Africa
SWAPO	South West African Peoples' Organisation
Swazi. LR	Swaziland Law Reports
UDI	Unilateral Declaration of Independence
UDHR	Universal Declaration of Human rights
UN Charter	United Nations Charter
UNITA	National Union for the Total Independence of Angola
UNTS	United Nations Treaty Series
WLR	Weekly Law Reports
ZAPU	Zimbabwe African Peoples' Unity
ZHC	Zimbabwean High Court
ZLR	Zimbabwe Law Reports
ZSC	Zimbabwean Supreme Court

Author's Note

International legal norms generally and especially international human rights law play a pivotal role in the protection of national human rights law. In particular, rules and principles of international human rights law have an enriching and enhancing effect on national norms. This enrichment can be assessed through an examination of various judicial pronouncements of national courts. The enterprise is well exemplified by an analysis of case law from the three jurisdictions that form the basis of the book. This book is based on my Ph. D thesis submitted to the Faculty of Law of the University of Edinburgh. The degree was awarded in July 1999.

In writing this book I received assistance and encouragement from many individuals and institutions. First and foremost, my gratitude goes to Professor Tiyanjana Maluwa of University of Cape Town, formerly of the Department of Law at the University of Botswana, who initially helped me to develop a general interest in international law and its interplay with national legal systems. I am also deeply indebted to Dr Stephen Neff, my principal supervisor, for his guidance, encouragement and invaluable advice, and allocating me a lot of his time, often, at the expense of his busy schedule. Similarly, my gratitude extends to Professor William Gilmore, my second supervisor, for his invaluable suggestions and support. Also, I am greatly indebted to Professor Alan Boyle for his advice on the work and financial support which enabled me to conduct research in universities in the United Kingdom especially SOAS and University of London. I should also express my thanks to my fellow research students particularly those in the Department of Public International Law for their encouragement. I benefited much from the discussion I had with them. Of these, David Berry was particularly helpful.

Additionally, I wish to express my sincere thanks and appreciation to the staff of the Edinburgh University Law Library and George Square Library for their much needed assistance. Also, I wish to express my deep thanks to the staff of the Legal Assistance Centre, and the libraries of the University of Botswana and the Faculty of Law of the University of Zimbabwe for allowing me access to their library facilities.

It would be remiss of me if I did not register my deep gratitude to the Government of Botswana for affording me the opportunity, through the University of Botswana, to commence and complete my studies at the University of Edinburgh by granting me the scholarship. Without the scholarship, I would not have been able to embark upon and finish my studies, and hence the production of this book.

Last but by no means the least, I must thank my friends and family, who encouraged me to complete this work. Most deeply I thank my fiancée, Maureen Modiradilo for her warm support and resolve to stand by my side while I was busy trying to bring this work to fruition.

Onkemetse Tshosa
University of Botswana

Part I:
Introduction

1 Theoretical Issues: Monism and Dualism

The theoretical standpoints that have been advanced with an endeavour to explain and clarify the relationship between international law and municipal law are monism and dualism. Treatises on these theories are copious and such an analysis can only be brief.[1] These theories provide the background of, and philosophical clarity to, the analysis. They help to articulate the precise status and role of international human rights law in municipal law. The study, however, demonstrates that, in reality, an examination of the inter-relation of international law to municipal law purely on the basis of these theories is an over-simplification. It does not accord with actual State practice.

Dualist Theory

In its general form, dualism, also known as the transformation or adoption theory, perceives international law and municipal law as two distinct and independent legal orders each having an intrinsically and structurally distinct character.[2] The two legal orders are two separate and self-contained spheres of legal action, and theoretically there should be no point of conflict between them. Because the two are

---

[1]   See for instance, Jennings and Watts, *Oppenheim's International law*, at 53-54; Brownlie, *Principles*, at 32-5; Shearer, *Starke's International Law*, at 63-7; Shaw, *International law*, at 98-102; Dugard, *International Law*, at 36-7; Maluwa, "International Human Rights Norms," at 18-24; Butler, "Comparative Approaches," at 49-51; Umozurike, *The African Charter*, at 107-9.

[2]   Literature on this philosophical standpoint is extensive. Some of the earliest work include O'Connell, *International Law*, at 42; Morgenstern, "Supremacy of international law," 42-92; Brierly, *Law of Nations*, 1963. The latest literature include Brownlie, *Principles*, at 32-33; Shearer, *Starke's International Law*, at 64-65; Jennings and Watts, *Oppenheim's International law*, at 53-54; Shaw, *International law*, at 102-4; Van Dijk and Van Hoof, *The European Convention*, at 11-15; Umozurike, *The African Charter*, at 108-9.

3

separate systems, international law would not as such form part of municipal law of the state: to the extent that in particular instances rules of international law may apply within a state they do so by virtue of their adoption by the internal law of the state and apply as part of the internal law and not as international law.[3]

The dualist school begins its argument with the proposition that law is an act of state will. Thus municipal law can be differentiated from international law in that it is a manifestation of this will internally directed, as distinct from the participation in a collective act of will by which the sovereign powers undertake obligations with respect to other sovereign powers.[4] By emphasising the sovereignty of state will, dualism reveals the influence of the rise in modern states of legislatures with complete internal sovereignty.

Dualism has benefited from the influence of several positivist theorists. The foremost exponents of this theory were Hegel, Anzilotti and Triepel.[5] These theorists adopted the notion of *consent* as an important factor in investigating the relation of international law to municipal law. Because they held the view that international law was based on the consent of sovereign states, it was as such a distinct and independent legal system from municipal law. Triepel, for instance, treats the two legal systems of municipal law and international law as entirely distinct in nature. He asserts firstly, that the two legal systems differ in the particular social relations they govern; state law deals with the social relations between individuals and international law regulates

---

[3] Jennings and Watts, *Oppenhiem's International law*, at 53; Schaffer, "International Law and the Law of South Africa," at 277-9.

[4] Schaffer, "International Law and the Law of South Africa", at 278; O'Connell, *International law*, at 42. According to Umozurike, "The sovereign manifests its will through legislation internally and does so externally in international law with other sovereigns with their common will." See Umozurike, *The African Charter*, at 108.

[5] Cassese, "Modern Constitutions," at 341. Cassese argues that international law received its theoretical foundation and strong practical support when the "dualist" conception of the relationship of international and municipal law was developed by Triepel and subsequently vigorously expanded by Anzilotti. According to this doctrine, it was a logical necessity that States should decide for themselves if and under what conditions to incorporate international rules into their own legal systems. Id, at 356. See also Umozurike, *The African Charter*, at 108.

the social relations between states, who alone are subject to it.[6] In the second sense, Triepel argues, a view widely held by other dualists, that the two systems have different juridical origins. The source of municipal law is the will of the state itself and the source of international law is the common will of states (*gemeinwille*).[7]

Thirdly, according to Anzilotti, the two legal systems are differentiated by the fundamental principles by which each system is conditioned. Municipal law is conditioned by the norm that legislation is to be obeyed whereas international law is conditioned by the *pacta sunt servanda* principle.[8] The latter principle commands that agreements between states are to be respected. This principle is at the heart of modern international law especially conventional international law and underlies the basis for performance of treaty obligations.[9] Because of this conditioning factor, Anzilotti concludes that the two systems are so distinct that no conflict between them is possible.

The Hegelians therefore stress that international law and municipal law exist separately and each is supreme in its own sphere. In cases of conflict, the Hegelians view international law as inferior to and hence weaker than municipal law. The predominance of municipal law is predicated on the notion that a state has a sovereign right to determine which rules of international law are to have effect in municipal sphere. Consequently, international law, including international human rights law, may create rights for individual citizens and be applied by municipal courts only if it has been adopted by such courts or transformed into municipal law through a legislative process.

---

[6] Starke, "The Theory," at 70. See further Morgenstern, "The Supremacy of International Law," at 48-57; Jennings and Watts, *Oppenheim's International Law*, at 53-4. Lindholt observes that the classical dualist theory is "based on the perception that the two types of law regulate different subjects, where national law operates with individual subjects while international law has the states as its subjects." See Lindholt, *Universality of Human Rights*, at 84-5.

[7] Shearer, *Starke's International law*, at 64; Umozurike, *The African Charter*, at 108; Lindholt, *Universality of Human Rights*, at 85.

[8] Umozurike, *The African Charter*, at 108.

[9] See the Vienna Convention of Law of Treaties of 1969, Article, 26 which provides that "Every treaty in force is binding on the parties to it and must be performed by them in good faith." The text of this Convention is reprinted in 8 ILM 679 (1969).

Thus the internal validity and application of international human rights norms is conditioned by a positive legislative enactment or judicial adoption.

Monist Theory

Monism, or alternatively the doctrine of automatic incorporation, maintains that international law and municipal law constitute aspects of a single universal system. This school of thought posits that all rules of law ultimately regulate the behaviour of the individual. The only difference is that in the international sphere the consequences of such behaviour are attributed to the state and in the municipal law sphere they are attributed to the individual citizen.[10]

Proponents of monistic construction of the relation of international law to municipal law view all law as a single system composed of binding rules, whether those rules are obligatory on states or entities other than states. The two systems, as systems of legal rules, are inter-related parts of one single legal structure and the various national systems of law are derived by way of delegation from the international legal system.[11] They are manifestations of one single concept of law binding human beings.

Monism is a feature of the natural law school. One of its leading theorists was Hugo Grotius, a Dutch scholar and diplomat, and the father of the rationalist school of natural law. In Prolegomenon 16 of his *De jure Belli ac Pacis* (1625) Grotius constructs a kind of a "geneacological tree with human nature as the mother of natural law at

---

[10] O'Connell, *International law*, at 39; Starke, "The Theory," at 74-5; Kelsen, *Principles*, at 553-84; Schaffer, "The Law of South Africa," at 279; Brownlie, *Principles*, at 33-4; Jennings and Watts, *Oppenheim's International Law*, at 54; Umozurike, *The African Charter*, at 107-8; Lindholt, *Universality of Human Rights*, at 85.

[11] Kelsen, *Principles,* at 553; Id, *General Theory* , at 363; Jennings and Watts, *Oppenheim's International Law*, at 54. Jennings and Watts note that, "Since international law can thus be seen as essentially part of the same legal order as municipal law, and as superior to it, it can be regarded as incorporated in municipal law, giving rise to no difficulty of principle in its application as international law within states." Id.

the head."[12] He proceeded to represent consent as the mother of the *ius civile* and the *jus gentium*, adding that consent itself derives its force from natural law, so that human nature turns out to be the great grandmother of the *ius civile* and the *ius gentium*. In its origins the monist doctrine owed much to this rationalist construction of a universal legal order.

The main exponents of monism are Kelsen and Lauterpacht. The former, at least, before later aligning himself towards positivism in his later writings,[13] argued that the international legal order is significant only as part of a universal legal order which comprises also the national legal orders of various states.[14] Starke has articulated Kelsen's position thus:

> For him, (Kelsen) jurisprudence is a science, and the object of a science is formed by a cognition and its unity. Unity of cognition connotes unity of object, and this unity must be found in the relation between municipal law and international law. Dualism is inconsistent with the axiomatic unity of science. Any construction other than monism is bound to constitute a denial of the legal character of international law.[15]

Kelsen predicates his argument on what he calls the "basic norm" or the *grundnorm* and argues that both systems of law derive their legal validity from the basic norm and as such they belong to the same system of legal norms.[16]

---

[12] Sanders, "Customary International Law," at 147.

[13] Kunz, *Law of Nations*, at 69-80. Kunz argues that whereas Kelsen in his first writings underlined mostly the contrast between the science of law and sociology, between the normative and natural sciences, it has become more and more important in his work to delimit the science of law *within* the domain of normative sciences versus ethics, morals; hence his struggle against natural law. The pure science of law is and cannot be anything else but the theory of positive law. Ibid., at 69.

[14] Kelsen, *Principles* , at 553. See also Starke, "The Theory," at 75-7.

[15] Starke, "The Theory," at 75.

[16] Kelsen, *General Theory*, at 110-11.

Lauterpacht asserts that it is ultimately the conduct of the individuals which is regulated by law, whether international or national, the only difference being that in the international sphere the consequences of such conduct are attributed to the State. The fact that municipal courts may be bound by the law of their States to enforce statutes which are contrary to international law merely shows that because of the weakness of international law, States admit and tolerate what is actually a conflict of duties within the same legal system, a phenomenon not altogether unknown in other spheres of national law. In any case, from the viewpoint of international law the validity of a pronouncement of a national court is in such cases purely provisional. It leaves intact the international responsibility of a state since it is a well recognised rule that a state is internationally responsible for the decisions of its courts, even if in conformity with the law of the state concerned, whenever that law happens to be contrary to international law.[17]

The monists argue that not only do international legal rules and various national legal orders constitute a single universal system but in cases of conflict national legal orders take subordinate position.[18] A domestic tribunal faced with a problem involving a rule of international law is obliged to apply a rule of international law. In fact, according to monism, the international legal order determines the territorial and temporal spheres of validity of the national legal orders, thus, making possible for the co-existence of a multitude of states.[19] However, inverted monism concedes primacy to municipal law.[20]

The naturalists, and also modern monists, believe that individual citizens, not states, are the real subjects of international law. International law is not by its nature inapplicable to individuals. It recognises individuals as bearers of legal rights and duties of the international legal system. According to Morgenstern:

---

[17] Jennings and Watts, *Openheim's International Law*, at 52-6; Oppenheim, *International Law,* at 38; Shaw, *International Law*, at 102-3; Umozurike, *The African Charter*, at 107-8; Lindholt, *Universality of Human rights*, at 85.

[18] Brownlie, *Principles* , at 33; Shaw, *International Law* , at 100-1.

[19] Kelsen, *Principles* , at 553.

[20] Umozurike, *The African Charter*, at 108.

The essence of the monist view of the relation of international law and national law is that rules of law, international and municipal law alike, are applicable to individuals, and that international law can thus be directly operative in the municipal sphere. Modern decisions have affirmed that individuals can derive rights directly from treaties.[21]

Thus, a specific act of transformation of each individual rule of international law is not required before it can be applied to legal relations within the state.[22] Municipal courts can invoke and apply rules of international law directly even in matters affecting individual citizens. In its advisory opinion on the *Jurisdiction of the Courts of Danzig,* the Permanent Court of International Justice held:

> It may be readily admitted that, according to a well established principle of international law, the *Beamtenabkommen,* being an international agreement, cannot, as such, create direct rights and obligations for the private individuals. But it cannot be disputed that the very object of an international agreement, according to the intention of the contracting parties, may be the adoption by the parties of some rules creating individual rights and obligations and enforceable by the national courts.[23]

The naturalist approach is mainly posited on a strong ethical position and a sense of moral purpose and justice founded upon respect for human rights norms and the general welfare of individuals.

Harmonisation Approach

Despite the merits of monism and dualism, these theories need to be approached with caution. In practical terms, the relationship between

---

[21] Morgenstern, "The Supremacy of International Law," at 50. Also, see Shaw, *International Law* , at 101.

[22] Morgenstern, "The Supremacy of International Law," at 58.

[23] P.C.I.J., (1928) Series B, No. 15, 17; Lauterpacht, *International Law*, at 27-47; See also Nottebohm Case I.C.J. Pep. 1955, p.5.

international law and municipal law of States may not be purely determinable by these theories. This is posited on a number of reasons. First, the internal applicability of international law in general and particularly treaties will always be conditioned by a rule of municipal law. The basic principle in most legal systems is that the internal application of treaties is governed by domestic constitutional law. Secondly, a neat distinction between monist and dualist systems may conceal the practice of courts. Even in monistic countries, courts sometimes fail to effectuate treaties which are binding under international law, for instance, non-self-executing treaties in United States law. Conversely, in dualist systems the courts may sometimes give limited effect even to unincorporated treaties, for example, British courts' use of the European Convention on Human Rights (hereafter the ECHR) before its incorporation into United Kingdom municipal law. In these countries courts rely on the principle that legislation should, wherever possible, be so construed as not to conflict with the international obligations of the state.[24]

Lastly, between the two extreme versions of monism and dualism there lies a whole range of intermediate relationships which do not easily recommend themselves to classification. This means that alternative doctrines have to be proposed to describe these intermediate positions.[25] In the final analysis, the theories are relevant only in the specific context of customary, and not conventional, international law.

The real concern is how international law standards can be infused, or rather incorporated into municipal law to reinforce the effectiveness of the national legal system. This is particularly significant in the general area of human rights protection where rules are sometimes not well defined and inadequate to address practical questions. But this is not to say that these theories are insignificant. They continue to illuminate the interaction between international law and municipal law. Most significantly, they will increasingly have

---

[24] Maluwa, "International Human Rights Norms," at 29; Collier, "The Law of England," at 925; Jackson, "Status of Treaties," at 310; Erasmus, "Namibian Constitution," at 91-7. See also Attorney General of Botswana v. Unity Dow [1992] L.R.C. (Const) 623; Mharapara v. The State [1986] L.R.C. (Const) 234.

[25] Jackson, "Status of Treaties," at 310-11; Maluwa, "International Human Rights Norms," at 29; Brownlie, *Principles*, at 34-5.

some impact on efforts to find practical solutions on the role of international law in municipal legal sphere.

The problem with invoking the monist-dualist arguments to address the relationship between municipal law and international law has therefore resulted in the emergence of the harmonisation or co-ordination approach. This approach posits that, if contradictory rules exist, it does not follow that one of them must necessarily be void. Nor does it follow that the systems which give rise to them are mutually incompatible. One of the functions of juristic reasoning is to eliminate the contradiction by harmonising the points of collision, not by pretending that they do not exist, nor by crushing the one with the other. The harmonisation approach endeavours to avoid situations whereby one system is treated as a derivation of, or superior to, the other, and ignoring the social realities which detach the two legal orders.[26] It is based on the assumption that each system is superior in its own sphere of operation thereby making it possible to treat both systems in the same way.

The harmonisation approach postulates that rules of international law and municipal law should be treated as concordant bodies of doctrine, each autonomous in the sense that it is directed to a specific area and, to some extent, an exclusive area of human conduct, but harmonious in that in their entirety the various rules aim at a basic human good.[27] Both systems derive from the social good and are not pure whim. They are an expression of human need and conviction. In other words, legal rules should be made well-suited to the solution of practical human problems whether emanating from the international or municipal level.

---

[26] O'Connell, *International Law*, at 44; Schaffer, "The Law of South Africa," at 280. Further, see Shearer, *Starke's International Law*, at 65-6, particularly at 66 where he remarks, "To resolve conflicts of obligation by adhering to a theory that asserts the automatic superiority of the one legal order over the other does not reflect the reality, on the one hand, of legal rules that compel national judges to follow the law commanded by national authority, and on the other hand the leeways of judicial choice open to judges in some circumstances to apply international law as part of national law. What should rather be the approach is to harmonise wherever possible the two competing legal prescriptions so as to avoid a conflict of obligations."

[27] O'Connell, *International Law*, at 43.

This approach further assumes that a rule of international law, as a body of rules of human behaviour, forms part of municipal law. It enjoins the municipal judge to exercise a judicial choice and apply international law as part of municipal law. In cases of conflict between the two regimes, the judge should harmonise the two conflicting legal prescriptions so as to avoid a clash of obligations. He should aim at harmonising rules which have different points of formal origins but overlap in operation. At the practical level, the harmonisation or co-ordination approach assists to infuse international standards, couched in general terms, into municipal legal orders by a process of adaptation to local cultures, institutions and laws, including human rights law.[28]

In sum, at a theoretical level, the invocation and application of a particular rule of international law in a given case may depend on whether a State adheres to classical monist or dualist theory. In practice, however, the legal position is different for even under a monist system, an express and unambiguous legislation may prevail over a rule of international law. Conversely, a court operating under a dualist system may rely on unincorporated international law rule in order to fulfil the international obligation of the state. Clearly, the status and role of international law in municipal law depends, by and large, on the legal system and practice of each State especially the approach of its courts towards international law. Thus municipal courts in particular have a significant role to play in adapting international law to the national legal system.

This study aims at applying these concepts and ideas to the particular experience of the three countries under consideration especially with regard to the domestic application of international human rights law. It examines the extent to which the place and role of international law (including international human rights law) in national laws of these countries can adequately be discussed with the aid of the traditional theories of monism and dualism. It demonstrates that the treatment of international law in these countries is increasingly becoming autochthonous. In particular, there is an emerging judicial trend of relying on and drawing inspiration from international law especially international human rights law in interpreting ambiguous, uncertain and unreasonable national human rights law even in the

---

[28] Shearer, *Starke's International Law*, at 66; Butler, "Comparative Approaches," at 49; Schreuer, *Decisions*, at 161.

absence of express constitutional or legislative mandate or without relying on monism or dualism.

Part II:
Colonial Period

2 Legal Legacy of Colonialism

This chapter examines the status of international human rights law in Botswana, Namibia and Zimbabwe before independence. Although the three countries emerged from different colonial Administrations and circumstances, they have a common unifying factor. They all received the same legal system: the Roman-Dutch law. This law provides the basis and context within which the reception and place of international human rights law in the municipal law of these countries should be analysed. The chapter examines the process of colonial legal imposition, the actual reception of international human rights law, customary and conventional, in these countries, the extent to which the legal position was informed by classical monist and dualist theories, and the influence of the legal position in the former colonial Powers. The aim is to determine whether international law was accorded a categorical place and role in municipal law of the countries under consideration.

Colonial Legacy

A legal legacy common to the Developing World has been the introduction of changes in the institutions and norms governing the local people. Colonialism brought fundamental change and the application of norms that were external to society or alien in origins.[1] It resulted, for example, in the creation of surrogate native governments, the domination and weakening of traditional authorities through the systems of treaties, courts and civil service.[2] It led to the resocialisation

---

[1]   Takirambudde, "External Law," at 209. See also Okoth-Ogendo, "The Imposition of Property Law," in Burman and Harrell-Bond, *The Imposition of Law*, at 147-66; Radipati, "Legal Semiotics," in Kevelson, *Crossroads in Law*, at 262-3; Forer, "American Indian Tribes," in Burman and Harrell-Bond, *The Imposition of Law*, at 91.

[2]   For a general discussion of the effects of the imposition of external law on indigenous law and institutions, see Takirambudde, "External Law," at 208; Burman and Harrell-Bond, *The Imposition of Law*, at 92; Yadin, "English Law in Israeli," at 59.

of the entire native population to the acceptance of the authority of these institutions as well as the authority of the colonial and native bureaucrats. It aimed at eliminating traditional and local group identities in deference to individualistic identification with the goals and life-styles of the colonial State. Most importantly, the colonial legal legacy weakened indigenous authority and radically altered the normative content of key legal areas of the local communities.[3]

Generally, the process that led to the imposition of law in Namibia and Zimbabwe was not very different. It involved armed struggles against the former colonial Powers. By contrast, the process in Botswana involved a relatively peaceful transition.[4] As a result, Namibia and Zimbabwe have been more involved with international law issues than Botswana. The struggle for independence of both countries attracted the attention of the international community especially the United Nations. In particular, principles such as the right of colonised peoples to self-determination, recognition and non-discrimination were partly developed and clearly articulated within the context of the struggle for independence of both countries. It is not the aim here to recount the historical evolution of these countries. Rather, the objective is to trace the legal developments with a view to providing the legal basis and background for analysing the treatment of international law in general and international human rights law in particular in the municipal law of these countries.[5]

---

[3] Normative imposition cannot be attributed solely and wholly to foreign Euro-centric intrusion. It can exist in all societies including non-European ones where these societies are divided between dominant and subordinate groups, and the former imposes its norms and authority on the former resulting in internal normative imposition. See Radipati, "Legal Semiotics," in Kevelson, *Crossroads in Law*, at 262-3; Okoth-Ogendo, "The Imposition of Property Law," in Burman and Harrell-Bond, *The Imposition of Law*, at 147-9.

[4] Commenting on the legal development in Botswana, Aguda has noted that, "One significant point to bear in mind is that the offer of a protectorate by the British Government and the acceptance of the same by Bechuanaland was not as a result of a conquest of the territory by Britain but arose purely by reason of a desire of all concerned for peace, order and good government." See Aguda, "Legal Development," at 54.

[5] The discussion will start with the legal situation in Namibia because of the three countries, it is the only   country where the domestic status of international law, conventional and customary, has attracted attention mainly of the courts.

Reception clause

Before the Republic of Namibia, formerly South West Africa,[6] attained independence on 21 March, 1990,[7] it first went through German colonial rule[8] which lasted only from 1884 to 1915 when the territory was occupied by the Union of South Africa at the beginning of World War One. Consequently, Germany's contribution to the development of South West African legal system was very insignificant, if at all.

In 1919, the Allied powers decided at the Paris Peace Conference that since the Namibian peoples were not sufficiently advanced to govern themselves,[9] they had to be placed under an international mandate through the mandate system.[10] South West

---

[6] Literature on the historical evolution of Namibia is extensive. For instance, see Imishue, *An International Problem*, 1965; Bruwer, *The Disputed Land*, 1966; Wellington, *South West Africa*, 1967; Cockram, *South West Africa*, 1976; Serfontein, *Namibia?*, 1976; Mbuende, *Namibia*, 1986.

[7] For a discussion of the events leading immediately to the independence of the Republic of Namibia, see Cottrell, "The Constitution of Namibia," at 56-74; Cleary, "South West Africa/Namibia," at 290-355; Naldi, *Constitutional Rights*, at 1-9.

[8] For a discussion of the Germany's administration of Namibia, see Imishue, *An International Problem*, at 1; Wellington, *South West Africa*, at 167; Mbuende, *Namibia*, at 47-8; Bruwer, *The Disputed Land*, at 567; Wiechers, "Constitutional Principles," in Wyk, *Namibia*, at 1-21; Cliffe, *Transition to Independence*, at 1-23.

[9] The principal objectives in the settlement of all colonies were the paramount protection of the interests of the indigenous peoples and the establishment of the system of tutelage to ensure this protection, non-annexation of ex-enemy colonies and the expression of the settlement reached in formal legal terms. See Imishue, *An International Problem*, at 2.

[10] The central idea of the mandate or trusteeship system was embodied in the first paragraph of Article 22 of the Covenant of the League of Nations. This clause provided that "To those colonies and territories which as a consequence of the late war have ceased to be under the sovereignty of states which formerly governed them and which are inhabited by people not yet able to stand by themselves under the strenuous conditions of the modern world, should be applied the principle that

19

Africa was placed under "C" mandate. This meant that it had to be administered under the laws of the mandatory as an integral part of its territory.[11] The mandate for South West Africa was conferred on His Britannic Majesty but to be exercised on his behalf by the government of the Union of South Africa, as a mandatory. A Mandate agreement was concluded between the Union of South Africa and the Council of the League of Nations. Article 2 thereof empowered the mandatory to, inter alia, apply its laws to South West Africa, subject to the mandate and such local modifications as the circumstances may require.

The Union of South Africa then issued the 1919 Proclamation which introduced a formal legal order into South West Africa.[12] This marked an important watershed in the legal system of South West Africa by explicitly and clearly transposing the Roman-Dutch law of the Cape Colony of Good Hope into South West Africa.[13] The proclamation also made provision for the establishment of courts to administer the imposed Cape colonial law.[14]

---

the well being and development of such peoples form a sacred trust of civilisation." See Imishue, *An International Problem,* at 2-3; Kaela, *Namibia,* at 1-12.

[11] The League of Nations made a distinction between three types of mandates distributed on the basis of the stage of development of the inhabitants and other circumstances such as economic conditions and geographical location. For "A" mandates independence was in sight. These were communities formerly belonging to the Turkish Empire. "B" mandates were former German colonies especially those of Central Africa, to be administered as separate entities from the mandatory power. "C" mandates were to be administered under the laws of the mandatory as integral parts of its territory. South West Africa fell into this category. See Imishue, *An International Problem,* at 2-3.

[12] Administration of Justice Proclamation No. 21 of 1919 (South West Africa).

[13] Ibid., Section 1(1). According to this clause, "The Roman-Dutch law as existing and applied in the province of the Cape of Good Hope at the date of the coming into effect of this proclamation shall, from and after the said date, be the common law of the Protectorate, and all laws within the Protectorate in conflict therewith shall, to the extent of such conflict and subject to the provisions of this section, be repealed." For an analysis of this clause, see Tittel v. R 1921 (2) S.A. (SWA) 58; R v. Goseb 1956 (1) S.A. (SWA) 666 at 671-2.

[14] Ibid., Section 3 (4). This section provides that the seat of the High Court shall be at Windhoek, and subject to the provision of this Proclamation, it shall exercise within the territory all such jurisdiction as may lawfully be exercised within the

It is generally acknowledged that the Roman-Dutch law reception instrument also introduced, albeit implicitly, the English common law into South West Africa. In *R v. Goseb*, Claassen, J. P., as he then was, authoritatively confirmed:

> If the Learned Judge by his remark intended to convey that the common law of the Cape of Good Hope was by this section excluded, then I must respectfully differ, for in my opinion it was the intention of the legislature to introduce also the common law of that Province into the territory, otherwise the state of the law would be uncertain. [The] law has been continuously developed and improved by the courts as well as by legislation. Other systems of law have had a marked influence, particularly English law. Much of our practice, procedure and mercantile law comes from English law.[15]

The English common law was introduced into the Cape of Good Hope following Britain's occupation of the territory in 1795. Dutch rule was restored in 1803, but only briefly, for in 1806 the Cape passed again to the British. The British, through legislation, introduced English common law into the Cape colony particularly with a view to bringing the general law in line with the English public in areas such as commercial law, administrative law and the law of procedure.[16] This law greatly influenced the Roman-Dutch law until the Dutch regained the territory. The influence resulted in the "Roman-Dutch common law" which became the basic law of South West Africa. Consequently, an examination of the transmutation of international law into the pre-existing Namibian legal order on the basis of the Roman-Dutch law should also take cognisance of the relationship between international law and the English common law. The English common law also influenced, albeit indirectly, the treatment of international law in the pre-independence Namibian municipal law.

Province of the Cape of Good Hope by the judges of the Cape Provincial Division of the Supreme Court.

[15] 1956 (2) S.A. (SWA) 667 at 672.

[16] Otlhogile, *Higher Courts in Botswana*, at 2-3; Sanders, Sanders, "Legal Dualism," at 52.

Status of international law

Customary international law The reception instrument embodied in the 1919 Proclamation which superimposed external Roman-Dutch law, with its English common law influence, on South West Africa did not make any specific reference to general international law. It merely referred to Roman-Dutch law in a general sense. Thus there was no legislation in the form of a Proclamation explicitly and specifically assigning customary international law (including customary international human rights law) a place and role in South West African municipal law.[17] Consequently, the domestic status of customary international law in South West Africa had to be examined on the basis of the superimposed external Roman-Dutch common law. Put differently, in determining the position of customary international law in municipal law, the South West African judiciary had to look to the practice of its South African counterpart.

Judicial practice in South Africa, at least, before the adoption of the new Constitution of South Africa in 1996[18] was that customary international law formed part of South African municipal law.[19] Rules

---

[17] Legislative enactments constitute the best evidence of reception of international law in municipal law. It provides certainty and clarity concerning the extent of the reception of rules of international law in national law. See Fawcett, *The British Commonwealth*, at 33; Crawford, "International Standards in Statutes," at 628-46; Nobel, "Model Legislation," in Melander and Nobel, *African Refugees*, at 58-76.

[18] The status of customary international law in South African law is now regulated by the new South African Constitution. Section 232 thereof makes customary international law part of South African law provided it is not inconsistent with the Constitution or an Act of Parliament. The Constitution is reprinted in Blaustein, P. Albert and Gisbert H. Flanz, eds, *Constitutions of the Countries of the World* (Dobbs Ferry. New York: Oceana, 1997).

[19] Parkin v. Government of the Republique Democratique du Congo and Another 1971 (1) S.A. 259 (W) at 261; South Atlantic Islands Development Ltd v. Buchan 1971 (1) S.A. (C) at 238; Inter-science Research and Development Corporation Services (Pty) Ltd v. Republica Popular de Mozambique 1980 (2) S.A. 111 (T) at 124; S v. Petane 1988 (3) S.A. 51 (C) at 56-7. See also Dugard, "International Law," at 15; Id, *International law*, at 42-56; Bridge, "International Law," at 746; Erasmus, "The Namibian Constitution," at 81; Schaffer, "The Law of South Africa," at 283; Maluwa, "International Human Rights Norms," 31; Devine, "International Law in South Africa," at 13.

of customary international law were directly and automatically applicable in the municipal law of South Africa. The *locus classicus* of this legal position was *Nduli and Another v. Minister of Justice and Another* in which Rumpff, C.J., observed:

> It is too obvious that international law is to be regarded as part of our law, though the *fons et origo* of this proposition must be found in Roman-Dutch law. [Only] such rules of customary international law are to be regarded as part of South Africa law as are either universally recognised or have received the assent of this country.[20]

According to Rumpff, C.J., once a particular rule crystallised into a rule of customary international law and South Africa consented to be bound by it, such a rule automatically became part of South African municipal law binding upon its municipal institutions. It conferred direct rights and obligations on individuals in municipal law. Moreover, the domestic courts could directly invoke and rely on such a rule in municipal court proceedings.

Significantly, the South African legal position derived from, and was largely based upon, the English common law. As Erasmus has poignantly remarked:

> The South African Constitutions have never contained any provisions on the application of international law. The matter is determined by common law principles and the rulings of English courts are often referred to and followed.[21]

In essence, according to Erasmus, before the adoption of the new 1996 South African Constitution, South Africa did not have clearly defined legal rules regarding the treatment of international law in municipal law. Its legal position was, for a variety of reasons, largely based on English common law rather than Roman-Dutch law. First, both countries share a common law tradition. Secondly, the South African governmental structure is derived from the English

---

[20] 1978 (1) S.A. 893 (A).

[21] Erasmus, "The Namibian Constitution," at 86. See also Dugard, "International Human Rights Norms," in Kahn, *Essays*, at 221; Schaffer, "The Law of South Africa," at 283.

model and is accordingly characterised by a balance of power between the three branches of government similar to the English one. Thirdly and most significantly, a close scrutiny of the legal systems of both countries displays a common approach to the relationship between municipal law and international law especially customary international law.[22]

Similarly, under English common law, customary international law is, as a general rule, treated as part of municipal law of the United kingdom. This rule was authoritatively confirmed in *Trendtex Trading Corporation Ltd v. Central Bank of Nigeria.*[23] The question for determination by the Court was whether or not the Central Bank of Nigeria, as a department of the State of Nigeria, could successfully claim sovereign immunity on a suit by the plaintiffs before the English courts on the letters of credit. The plaintiffs argued that the transaction was of a commercial nature to which sovereign immunity does not apply. The Court accepted the plaintiffs' argument. It held that sovereign immunity, as a rule of international law, does not apply to commercial transactions. According to the Court, this rule forms part and parcel of English common law. It is directly and automatically integrated into English common law.

This principle received judicial *imprimatur* from the House of Lords in *Alcom Limited v. Republic of Colombia and Others.*[24] The Court held that the accounts of the Colombian Embassy enjoyed restrictive immunity, which principle has been absorbed into the United Kingdom law. Additionally, the Court noted that a rule of customary international law in question must be the "existing law, English common law and public international law alike." This added

---

[22] Dugard, "Human Rights Norms in Domestic Courts," in Kahn,*Essays* , at 222. See also Schaffer, "The Law of South Africa," at 283; Sanders, "Customary International Law," at 150.

[23] [1977] 1 All E.R. 881. The earlier cases include Buvot v. Barbuit [1737] Talbot 281; R v. Keyn (Franconia) [1876] 2 Ex. D 63; Mortensen v. Peters [1906] S.L.R 227; Chung Chi Cheung v. R [1939] A.C. 160. See also Westlake "Law of England," at 14; Lauterpacht, "International Law," at 51; Watson, "British Courts," at 61; Duffy, "English Law," at 585; Collier, "Law of England," at 924; Cunningham, "European Convention," at 537; Drzemczewski, *European Convention, at* 170-84; Beyleveld, "Human Right," in Oliver and Marshall, *Public Law*, at 577.

[24] [1984] 2 W.L.R. 770.

dimension enjoins the courts to give effect to the changes and developments that take place in international law.

The approach of South African and United Kingdom courts towards customary international law was adopted by the Namibian courts. The issue arose mainly in cases where the administration of South West Africa by the Union of South Africa was being challenged. It was one of the sticking points in *Binga v. Administrator-General, South West Africa and Others.*[25] Erick Binga, a South West African citizen, lodged an application with the South West Africa Supreme Court challenging an order made by the Administrator-General of the territory requiring him, Erick Binga, to render national service at Walvis Bay in South Africa. The order was made pursuant to Proclamation 198 of 1980 which required "non-white" inhabitants of South West Africa to render military service in South West Africa. In exercise of the powers transferred to him by the South African State President under Proclamation 131 of 1980 to administer the Defence Act No. 44 of 1957, the Administrator-General registered and enrolled Erick Binga to undertake national service at Walvis Bay.

In his founding affidavit, Erick Binga averred that the South African Parliament had no power to make laws for South West Africa. As a corollary, the South African State President had no power to issue a proclamation over the territory authorising the Administrator-General to conscript citizens of South West Africa to serve in national service. Moreover, Walvis Bay, where he was ordered to render national service, was not part of the mandated territory. Erick Binga based his argument on the fact that the League of Nations Mandate, being part of the "grundnorm" by which the South African government derives its authority and hence the power to legislate for the territory, had been revoked by the General Assembly Resolution 2145 of 1966 as confirmed by Security Council Resolution 276 of 1970. Alternatively, if the Mandate was still in existence, it was part of the municipal law of the land and all legislation applicable to the territory had to be subject to its provisions particularly Article 4. This clause prohibited any military training of the natives, otherwise than for purposes of internal

---

[25] 1984 (3) S.A. 949. For an analysis of this case in relation to the absorption of customary international law into the pre-independence Namibian law, see Erasmus, "Namibian Constitution," at 81; Dugard, "International Law," at 15.

police and the local defence of the territory. It also prohibited any establishment or erection of fortifications of military or naval bases in Namibia.

The applicant contended that the military conscription for national service in Walvis Bay, an area then outside and beyond the territorial limit of South West Africa, violated the South African undertaking under the Mandate, as a treaty, not to enlist natives for military training outside the territory.

The Court did not dispute the fact that the Mandate was a treaty binding on the Union of South Africa. It also did not contest its place in South West African municipal law. In making a determination regarding the latter point, the Court made the following remark respecting the place and effect of customary international law in South West African municipal law:

> Although it was accepted by Rumpff CJ in Nduli and Another v Minister of Justice and Another (supra at 906) *that the rules of customary international law are to be regarded as part of our law* "*as are either universally recognised or have received the assent of this country,*" it follows that decisions of the United Nations, of the nature here under discussion, are not part of customary international law.[26]

This *dictum* marked a first judicial proclamation that rules of customary international law that are either universally recognised or have received the assent of South West Africa were automatically applicable in South West African legal order. They were governed by the monist theory. It is clear that Justice Strydom's approach was partly based on the Roman-Dutch law reception formula which bequeathed, implicitly, to South West Africa the manner in which the South African judiciary treated customary international law in South African municipal law.

The Namibian courts were furthermore inclined to look at the South African position because South Africa and Namibia applied the same legal system and common law, organisationally the legal profession of Namibia formed part of the South African legal profession, South African judges were appointed to the Supreme Court

---

[26] 1984 (3) S.A. 949 at 968-9 (emphasis supplied).

in Windhoek, Namibia's final court of appeal was the South African Appellate Division in Bloemfontein. Essentially, there was no separate Namibian legal order. Namibian law formed part of the South African system.[27] Thus, because of the exceptional position in which Namibian courts found themselves, it meant that they closely followed the practice of courts in South Africa in the way they treated rules of customary international law in South African municipal legal order.

The question that arises is whether this approach also applied to customary international human rights law such as the principle of non discrimination or equality before the law? This issue has never been specifically decided by the Namibian courts. But, it can be argued, at least analogically, that the position of customary international human rights law in pre-independence Namibian law was not different from general rules of customary international law. Customary international human rights law was also, in the absence of any express position to the contrary, governed by the incorporation, or rather the monist theory. This law was part of the pre-independence Namibian law notwithstanding its non-observance in practice. As in the Union of South Africa, it could only be excluded from operating directly in municipal law by clear and unambiguous legislation, the act of state doctrine and *the stare decisis* rule.[28]

Treaties: The Mandate Agreement As with customary international law, the Roman-Dutch law reception clause was silent on the legal position and role of treaties in general in the pre-independence Namibian municipal law. Consequently, it meant that the domestic status of treaties in South West Africa had to be examined on the basis of the superimposed external Roman-Dutch common law. In other words, the South West African judiciary had to look to the practice of its South African counterpart dealing with the status of treaties in South African municipal law.

---

[27] Erasmus, "The Namibian Constitution," at 86. See also Schaffer, "The Law of South Africa," at 283; Dugard, "International Human Rights Norms," in Kahn, *Essays*, at 232.

[28] Binga v. Administrator-General, South West Africa, and Others 1984 (3) S.A. 949 at 968-9; S v. Tuhadeleni and Others 1967 (4) S.A. 511. See also Trendtex Trading Corporation Ltd v. Central Bank of Nigeria [1977] 1 All E.R. 881.

The legal position in South Africa before the adoption of the present South African Constitution[29] was that provisions of international conventions to which South Africa was a party were not automatically part of the South African municipal law unless explicitly translated into municipal law.[30] To become part of municipal law, treaties in general required legislative incorporation. They could not in themselves create subjective rights and duties for individuals in the absence of legislation. According to Dugard, the South African legal position was influenced by the English common law practice. Both countries share a common law tradition.[31] Under British law, according to the *Parlement Belge* case,[32] although the Crown retains the prerogative to negotiate and sign treaties externally, for treaties to have internal effect especially those requiring changes in municipal law they require parliamentary approval.[33]

Adopting the South African and British approach, the South West African courts articulated the legal position of treaties especially in relation to the status of the Mandate Agreement in South West

---

[29]   Section 231(4) of the post-Apartheid Constitution of South Africa states that, "any international agreement becomes law in the Republic when it is enacted into law by national legislation; but a self-executing provision of an agreement that has been approved by Parliament is law in the Republic unless   it is inconsistent with the Constitution or an Act of Parliament." See generally, Shaw, *International law*, at 124-6.

[30]   The landmark case on the status of treaties in the pre-1996 South African order was Pan American World Airways Inc. v. South African Wire and Accident Insurance Company Ltd 1965 (3) S.A. 150 (A). See also Devine, "International Law in South Africa," at 5-6; Schaffer, "The Law of South Africa," 283; Dugard, *International Law*, 51-6; Sanders, "Transformation of Treaties," at 356; Erasmus, "The Namibian Constitution," at 91-2; Maluwa, "International Human Rights Norms," at 32; Botha, "Incorporation of Treaties," at 196.

[31]   Dugard, " International Human Rights Norms," in Kahn, *Essays*, at 221. See also Schaffer, "The Law of South Africa," 283.

[32]   [1879] 4 P.D. 129.

[33]   McNair, *Law of Treaties*, at 81; Id, "Treaties," at 59-68; Fawcett, *British Commonwealth*, 45-51; Brownlie, *Principles*, at 47; Shearer, *Starke's International Law*, at 72; Jennings and Watts, *Oppenheim's International Law*, at 58-9; Duffy, "English Law," at 585-91; Drzemczwski, *European Convention*, at 177-80; Beyleveld, "Human Right," in Oliver and Marshall, *Public Law*, at 721-6.

African municipal law. In the fore-discussed *Binga v. Administrator-General, South West Africa and Others* Justice Strydom, as he then was, observed:

> Obligations incurred by international treaty and resolutions by international organisations such as the United Nations stand on a different footing from customary international law and generally speaking a court in South Africa, and for that matter a court in this country, will only give effect thereto if such a treaty or resolution was incorporated by legislative act into the laws of the land.[34]

This legal position was further confirmed in *S v. Tuhadeleni* in which Justice Ludorf, as he then was, remarked:

> In Act 49 of 1919 the Union Parliament enshrined the terms of the Mandate in our legislation. The courts must enforce the mandate and are not bound by the terms of any treaty which has not been embodied in our municipal law.[35]

Thus international conventions were not automatically part of the pre-existing Namibian municipal law. For these conventions to have internal effect, they required legislative approval. Rights and obligations in these conventions were not of themselves part of the Namibian municipal law. It is clear that Namibia observed the classical dualist or transformation theory as far as the position of international conventions in municipal law were concerned whose tenet is that, for treaty rules to have domestic application and thus confer rights and obligations on individuals, they should be transformed by legislation into municipal law. This approach was authorised by the imposed Roman-Dutch common law.

The question that recommends itself is whether this practice also applied to human rights treaties? This question is particularly pertinent with respect to the Mandate agreement because, strictly, it was not *per se* a human rights treaty. Nevertheless, its primary aim was the realisation of the right to self-determination, a right securely

---

[34] 1984 (3) S.A. 949 (SWA) at 968-9. See also Binga v. Cabinet of South West Africa 1988(3) S.A. 154 (SWA).

[35] 1967 (4) S.A. 511 (SWA) at 520.

established in international law, for the Namibian people. Moreover, it provided for basic minimum standards of treatment of the inhabitants of South West Africa. In particular, the mandatory undertook to promote to the utmost the material and moral well-being and the social progress of the inhabitants of the territory.[36] Needless to say that the Mandate expressly outlawed slavery, slave trade and forced labour.[37] But, these standards were not protected in the municipal sphere of South West Africa. Therefore, while the Mandate did not relate specifically and exclusively to human rights norms, but to the extent that it contained some internationally recognised human rights norms, in a broader sense, it can appropriately be treated under human rights instruments within the context of Namibia and thus required legislation to make it part of municipal law.

From the fore-going, it is clear that Namibia inherited a monist approach from the Union of South Africa in its treatment of customary international law in municipal law and dualism with respect to treaties. Customary international human rights law was directly applicable in Namibian law and human rights treaties required legislation to become part of municipal law. The legal position was essentially the same as under the South African legal system. This legacy was also inspired by the United Kingdom approach.

Self-governing Colony: Southern Rhodesia

Reception instruments

The present day Zimbabwe, formerly Southern Rhodesia, was brought under British colonial rule in 1889.[38] Pursuant to the Royal Charter (hereinafter the Charter) of 1889,[39] Her Majesty Queen Victoria

---

[36]   The Mandate of South West Africa, Article 2.

[37]   Ibid., Article 3.

[38]   Nkala, *Rhodesia Independence Crisis* at 1; Palley, *The Law of Southern Rhodesia* , at 494; Devine, "Rhodesia in International Law," at 1; Zimmerli, "Southern Rhodesia," at 239; In re Southern Rhodesia [1919] A.C. 211.

[39]   The Royal Charter of 29 October, 1889. For a detailed discussion of the Charter, see Devine, "Rhodesia in International Law," at 1-12; Palley, *The Law of Southern Rhodesia* , at 494-7.

authorised the British South Africa Company (hereinafter the BSA Company),[40] under Cecil John Rhodes, to administer the territory. The Charter empowered the BSA Company to preserve peace and order in the territory and establish a judiciary for the administration of justice.[41] It, however, did not prescribe the law which the company was to utilise for the administration of justice.[42]

In May 1891 Britain issued an Order in Council declaring Southern Rhodesia a protectorate.[43] The protectorate status enabled Britain to assume control of important external affairs of the territory. It also necessitated the establishment of an administration and legal system for Southern Rhodesia. In terms of this Order in Council, the British High Commissioner in South Africa was appointed the High Commissioner for Southern Rhodesia.[44] He was empowered to legislate for the territory subject to the proviso that he had to respect native laws and customs, the so-called repugnancy clause.[45]

---

[40] The BSA Company was formed by European Settlers who first arrived in the territory on 12 September, 1890 led by Cecil John Rhodes. See Nkala, *Rhodesia Independence Crisis*, at 1; Palley, *The Law of Southern Rhodesia*, at 493; Zacklin, *Rhodesia*, at 1-15.

[41] The Royal Charter, Article 10.

[42] In terms of the Administrator's Proclamation No. 1, 28 September, 1890, the BSA Company issued a Proclamation in 1890 which declared that the laws of the Cape Colony were to be applicable to the territory. Although the Proclamation marked the first step in the introduction of a rudimentary legal system in Zimbabwe, the precise nature of the laws operating at the Cape Colony was not made explicitly clear. See Palley, *The Law of Southern Rhodesia*, at 493.

[43] South African Order in Council, 9 May, 1891. A protectorate was declared over Southern Rhodesia because Britain realised that its rights in, and authority over, the territory were not sufficiently secured under the sphere of influence arrangement. The government also realised that a proposed Boer trek from the South African Republic into the Banyai territory north of Limpopo river, with a view to forming a Republic as far as Zambesi meant that it would be difficult to support the BSA Company in repelling the advance of the trekkers. See Palley, *The Law of Southern Rhodesia*, at 87-9; Zacklin, *Rhodesia*, at 9-12.

[44] Section 2.

[45] Section 4.

31

In pursuance of the powers conferred upon him by Proclamation of 9 May, 1891, the High Commissioner issued the Order in Council of 10 June 1891 which introduced the law in force in the Cape Colony of Good Hope into Southern Rhodesia.[46] However, this Order in Council, as with the BSA Company Proclamation, did not indicate precisely the nature of the law operating in the Cape Colony of Good Hope that was transmuted into Southern Rhodesia. Furthermore, the Order in Council of 18 July 1894[47] which extended the Crown's full and unfettered powers of administration over the territory did not, as with earlier reception instruments, clearly and precisely indicate the nature of Cape law that was transposed into Southern Rhodesia. It continued to employ the phraseology "the law in force in the Colony of the Cape of Good Hope."[48]

The imposition of the external Cape law continued to be effected through the various constitutional instruments issued by the High Commissioner for the territory. The first Constitution was adopted following the annexation of the territory by an Order in Council in 1923 and the creation of a Colony.[49] By Letters Patent of 1 September 1923, Southern Rhodesia was provided with a responsible government Constitution, which came into force on 1 October 1923. The 1923 Constitution established an elected Legislative Assembly and the Governor as the executive authority.[50] This Constitution left unaffected the judiciary that existed before 1923 and most

---

[46] Section 19. This clause stated that, "In any proceedings in such courts the law to be administered shall be as nearly as the circumstances of the country will permit, be the same as the law for the time being in force in the Colony of the Cape of Good Hope; provided that no Act passed after this time by the Colony of the Cape of Good Hope shall be deemed to apply to the said territory."

[47] Matebeleland Order in Council 18 July 1894. This order commenced on 5 October, 1894.

[48] Section 26.

[49] Southern Rhodesia (Annexation) Order in Council, 30 July, 1923.

[50] The Letters Patent provided for a Legislature that was initially to comprise thirty elected members representing electoral districts to be increased progressively. For a detailed discussion of the composition of the Legislative Assembly, its powers and their limitations, See Palley, *The Law of Southern Rhodesia*, at 217-26; Nkala, *Rhodesian Independence Crisis*, at 10-13.

significantly, reinstated the original provisions for the application of the Cape law. The reception provision in the 1923 Constitution was re-enacted as section 13 of the High Court Act, 1939.[51]

In 1953 the constitutional structure of the Colony was changed by the creation of the Federation of Rhodesia and Nyasaland.[52] Before its dissolution in 1963, Southern Rhodesia was given a new constitution in 1961.[53] The 1961 Southern Rhodesia Constitution first, introduced the concept of British parliamentary democracy into the territory.[54] Secondly, in terms of section 56(d) of this Constitution, the applicability of Cape law was now accorded constitutional status.[55] This reception provision was re-enacted in subsequent Southern Rhodesian Constitutions: in Section 57 of the 1965 Constitution which was adopted following the Unilateral Declaration of Independence (the UDI) by Prime Minister Ian Smith;[56] in Section 87 of the Constitution

---

[51]   This clause provided that subject to the provisions with regard to native law and custom contained in the Native Law and Courts Act, the law to be administered by the High Court and by the Magistrates' Courts shall be the same as the law in force in the colony of the Cape of Good Hope on the tenth day of June, 1891, as modified by subsequent legislation having in this colony the force of law.

[52]   Rhodesia and Nyasaland (Federation) Act 1953; Rhodesia and Nyasaland Order in Council 1953, Section 1, 1953 No 1200. Generally, see Zacklin, *Rhodesia*, at 31-7.

[53]   Southern Rhodesia (Constitution) Order in Council 1961, No 2314.

[54]   Palley, *The Law of Southern Rhodesia*, at 413; Zimmerli, "Southern Rhodesia," at 240-45.

[55]   This clause stipulated that subject to the provisions of any law for the time being in force in Southern Rhodesia relating to the application of customary law, the law to be administered by the High Court and by any courts in Southern Rhodesia subordinate to the High Court shall be the law in force in the Colony of the Cape of Good Hope on the 10th day of June, 1891, as modified by subsequent legislation having in Southern Rhodesia the force of law. Generally, see Palley, *The Law of Southern Rhodesia*, at 414-17.

[56]   Southern Rhodesia declared a UDI on 11 November 1965. For a general and detailed discussion of the effect of the UDI in Southern Rhodesia, see Madzimbamuto v. Lardner-Burke and Another [1968] 3 All E.R. 561.

of Zimbabwe Rhodesia of 1979[57] and Section 89 of the Zimbabwe Constitution Order, 1979.[58]

A common feature of these reception instruments is that, unlike in Namibia, they did not clarify the exact nature of the law operating at the Cape of Good Hope that was being transmuted into Southern Rhodesia. The question is, did Britain bequeath to Southern Rhodesia its own common law or the Cape law commonly called the Roman-Dutch law? The predominant view, however, is that the various reception instruments imposed the Roman-Dutch law on Southern Rhodesia subject to changes introduced by statute and the preservation in certain spheres of African customary law.[59] As in Namibia, this law was influenced by English common law concepts and principles.[60] Consequently, an examination of the place of international human rights law in the old Zimbabwean legal order should take account of not only the South African legal position and practice, but also of practice in the United Kingdom.

Status of International Law

Customary international law As in Namibia, the reception instrument that imposed the Roman-Dutch law on Zimbabwe did not make any express and specific reference to the place of customary international law in pre-independence Zimbabwean municipal law. However, unlike in Namibia, the courts have never been seized with the question whether or not customary international law was part of Zimbabwean

---

[57]   The Constitution of Zimbabwe Rhodesia was issued in October 1979.

[58]   The Zimbabwe Constitution Order, 1979 No. 1600. Issued on April 1980.

[59]   Allot, *Legal Systems in Africa*, at 161; Palley, *The Law of Southern Rhodesia*, at 495. This view has been augmented by Christie who retorted that, "the effect of section 89 is that the Roman-Dutch law of the Cape became and is still the common law of this country. The Zimbabwean law combines two very different legal traditions." See Christie, R.H, *Business Law*, (Cape Town: Juta, 1985), at 25.

[60]   Significantly, appeals from the High Court of Southern Rhodesia lay first to the Cape Supreme Court and later to the Appellate Division in Bloemfontein. Judges in these courts were trained in English common law. Thus Southern Rhodesia received direct benefit of the work of these judges across the whole spectrum of the legal and judicial establishment.

municipal law. This means that the status of customary international law in pre-independence Zimbabwean municipal law was not altogether clear and certain.

It is important to note that pre-independence Zimbabwe had a constitutional schema for the protection of human rights and fundamental freedoms. The various Constitutions adopted for the territory contained entrenched Declarations of Rights.[61] These Declarations of Rights recognised and protected human rights norms found in major human rights treaties and instruments such as the Universal Declaration of Human Rights (hereafter UDHR), International Covenant on Civil and Political Rights (hereafter ICCPR) and the ECHR. They recognised rights such as the right to life, personal liberty, fair trial, freedom of association and non-discrimination. The question that arises is, did the constitutional recognition of human rights norms amount to an assignment, explicitly or implicitly, of international human rights law a place in pre-independence Zimbabwean municipal law?

It is submitted that, according to the monist-dualist debate, the constitutional recognition of human rights norms in pre-independence Zimbabwean law fell short of assigning customary international human rights law a specific and categorical place in municipal law in the sense that they could be disregarded without breaching a rule in national law. Their non-observance did not, in a legal sense, amount to a breach of national law. The intention to accord customary international law (including customary international human rights law) a place in municipal law could have been made more clearer, categorical and unequivocal by an insertion of a clause in these Constitutions or similar national law to that effect.

Consequently, it meant that, in ascertaining the place of customary international human rights law in municipal law Zimbabwean courts were obliged to fall back to the South African Roman-Dutch law position, with its English common law influence, in terms of which, unless excluded by legislation, the act of state doctrine or judicial decisions, customary international law was, as a general

---

[61] See the 1961, 1965, 1969, 1979 Southern Rhodesian Constitutions.

rule, treated as part of municipal law.[62] Thus Zimbabwe inherited the South African monist approach through the Roman-Dutch law reception instrument.

Treaties The pre-independence Zimbabwean law did not have express constitutional or legislative stipulations on the status of treaties in municipal law. Moreover, as in Namibia, the Roman-Dutch law reception instrument was silent on the matter. The only provision concerning conventional international law was contained in the 1953 Constitution of the Federation of Rhodesia and Nyasaland. The Constitution assigned the Federal Parliament the exclusive right to legislate, inter alia, on the implementation of treaties and agreements with, and other obligations towards, countries or organisations outside the Federation affecting the federation as a whole or any of the territories whether entered into by Her Majesty's Government in the United Kingdom on behalf of the Federation or any of the territories; by the federation with the authority of Her Majesty's Government in the United Kingdom; or by any of the territories with the said territory.[63]

Clearly, the Federation did not enjoy any international personality. Its international affairs were conducted by the United Kingdom. Moreover, although the federal Constitution made reference to international conventions, it nevertheless did not assign them any place and role in the Federation municipal law. It merely dealt with the power of the federal parliament to honour or implement obligations assumed under these treaties towards other countries and organisations outside the Federation, that is, externally. In any case, the dissolution of the Federation in 1963 resulted in each territory adopting its national constitution providing an opportunity for each country to clarify the domestic status of treaties.

The position of treaties in pre-independence Zimbabwean municipal law was to a limited extent determined by the judiciary. It

---

[62] For a detailed discussion of the exceptions to the automatic incorporation of customary international law in Zimbabwean municipal law, see *chapter three* below.

[63] Fawcett, *The British Commonwealth*, at 31.

was discussed in *R v. Muirhead*.[64] The accused, Muirhead, was indicted on several counts of contravening certain provisions of the Customs and Excise Management Act and the regulations thereunder concerning the import and export of goods manufactured from the Union of South Africa into Southern Rhodesia. He was alleged to have made a false representation to an officer of the Customs and Excise Department that certain goods, plastic toys, were produced in Southern Rhodesia while, as a matter of fact, they were not for purposes of importing them into the Union. In terms of the Customs and Excise Management Act, the goods had to conform to the definition provided in Article 21 of the Customs Union Agreement between the Union of South Africa and the Colony of Southern Rhodesia. The relevant Article 21 of the Agreement provided:

> An article shall not be deemed to have been manufactured in the territory of either of the parties to this agreement unless it was wholly manufactured in such territory, or, if partially manufactured therein, unless at least 25 per cent of the factory cost of such article in its finished condition is represented by the products and labour of such territory or unless 50 per cent of such factory cost is represented by the combined products and labour of that territory and of any other part of the British Commonwealth.

Counsel for the accused objected to the invocation and use by the Court of the Customs Union Agreement particularly Article 21 and regulations thereunder on the basis that its terms had not been incorporated into the municipal law of Southern Rhodesia. This meant that it could not impose any rights and obligations on the subjects of the territory. In upholding the objection, Justice Hathorn, as he then was, observed:

> the terms of a Customs Union Agreement do not bind the subject unless they are made binding by virtue of some statutory provision. That such is the case appears to me upon general principle to be beyond question.[65]

---

[64]   1954 (3) S.A. (SR) 558.

[65]   Ibid., at 665.

Justice Hathorn's *dictum* invites several comments. First, for the Customs Union Agreement to bind individual subjects of Southern Rhodesia it required legislative approval. It is not by its very nature internally applicable until parliament has enacted it into law. Secondly, by requiring parliament approval of the terms of the Customs Union Agreement, as a treaty, the court was endorsing an established principle of international law that treaties, as a general rule, require statutory enactment for them to create rights and obligations for individuals in municipal law. It was a judicial affirmation of the classical dualist theory which requires legislation to accord treaties internal force. Thirdly, the judge's intimation that for him the theory that treaties require domestic legislation to bind subjects was a "general principle to be beyond question," merely amounted to a judicial recognition of the common law principle observed in Zimbabwe and South Africa, and judicial practice in Britain and other Commonwealth countries on the relationship of treaties to municipal law.

Thus, during the pre-independence Zimbabwean era, at least on the authority of *Muirhead* case, treaties including those dealing with human rights were not, generally speaking, automatically applicable in municipal law. Clearly, *Muirhead's* case confirmed Zimbabwe's adherence to the dualistic theory according to which treaties were not in themselves capable of creating rights and obligations for individuals without the necessary assent of the legislature. However, this principle was not acted upon by the Southern Rhodesian judiciary so as to secure it firmly in domestic law and jurisprudence.

As in Namibia, the pre-existing Zimbabwean national law inherited the monist and dualistic approach towards the treatment of custom and treaties in municipal law respectively. The status and function of international law in municipal law was a direct legacy of the South African practice with the English common law influence.

Protectorate: Bechuanaland

The imposition clauses

The present day Botswana was declared a Bechuanaland Protectorate[66] by Great Britain in 1885.[67] The declaration of a protectorate meant that Britain assumed full and complete control over external affairs of Bechuanaland Protectorate, while internal matters were left to the government of the territory.[68] However, the absence of a government with effective control over Bechuanaland Protectorate at the material time and the desire to incorporate the territory into the Union of South Africa prevailed over the United Kingdom Government to assume complete control of both external and internal affairs of Bechuanaland Protectorate. This policy was largely followed in British protected territories.[69] It was amply illustrated by *R v. Earl Crewe, Ex parte*

---

[66] The Tswana territories were divided into two parts, namely, British Bechuanaland and Bechuanaland Protectorate. A decade later the former, which formed the southern part of the territory, was incorporated into the Cape Colony and later became part of the Union of South Africa. It was the territory designated Bechuanaland Protectorate which later became the independent state of Botswana. See Sillery, *Founding a Protectorate*, at 39-41. Generally, see Picard, *Evolution*, at 5-45; Hailley, *Native Administration*, at 202-15.

[67] Proclamation No. 1 of 30 September, 1885. For an analysis of the legal perspective of the historical developments leading to independence of Botswana, see generally Pain, "English and Roman-Dutch Law in Africa," at 163-4; Aguda, "Legal Development," at 52-63; Sanders, "Sekgoma Letsholathebe," at 348-60; Otlhogile, *Higher Courts in Botswana*, at 1-9; Brewer, "Sources of Criminal Law," at 24-25; Molokomme, "Roman-Dutch Law," at 123.

[68] Okoye, *International Law*, at 8. See also Sillery, "Comments on Two Articles," at 294. For a general discussion of the concept of a protectorate in international law and its legal consequences, see Oppenheim, *International Law*, at 192-6; Palley, *The Law of Southern Rhodesia*, at 9-15; Sanders, "Sekgoma Lesholathebe's Detention," 356-60; Okoth-Ogendo, "Property Law in Kenya," in Burman and Harrell-Bond, *The Imposition of Law*, at 149; Forster, "The Administration of Justice," at 90; Nationality Decrees in Tunisia and Morocco Case, 1923 P.C.I.J, Series B, No. 4, 27; In R v. Earl Crewe, Ex parte Sekgome [1910] 2 K.B. 576 (CA) at 620.

[69] It was applied to British protectorates of Basutoland and Swaziland. See for instance Sobhuza 11 v. Miller [1926] A.C. 518.

Sekgome.[70] The case concerned the validity of the High Commissioners' Proclamation authorising the detention and ultimate deportation of Sekgome, a chief of Batawana tribe in Bechuanaland Protectorate, who was considered to be a threat to peace in the Protectorate following a dispute over chieftainship which he lost. The Court of Appeal upheld the validity of the Proclamation holding that the Crown had unfettered jurisdiction over the Protectorate and could expect obedience to a practically unlimited extent. According to the Court, the Crown exercised complete unrestricted authority over Bechuanaland Protectorate.

Consequently, by an Order in Council of 9 May, 1891,[71] the British government established a High Commissioner for the territory and enjoined him to, inter alia, legislate for Bechuanaland Protectorate from time to time by proclamations provided the High Commissioner respected any native law and customs.[72] The High Commissioner issued a Proclamation on 10 June, 1891[73] section 19 of which provided that, the law to be administered was, as nearly as circumstances of the country will permit, to be the same as the law for the time being in force in the Colony of the Cape of Good Hope.[74] As in Zimbabwe, this clause radically departed from the English practice in the sense that in other colonial territories in which British rule was imposed, it was normal to provide for the reception of English common law and the

---

[70] [1910] 2 K.B. 576 (Court of Appeal). For an analysis of this case, see Sanders, "Sekgoma Letsholathebe's Detention," at 348-60.

[71] Bechuanaland Protectorate General Administration Order in Council, 9 May, 1891.

[72] Ibid., Article 2.

[73] Bechuanaland Protectorate General Administration Order in Council, 10 June, 1891. This proclamation also gave the territory a complete new system of administration and legal system. Section 2 thereof established courts of law, provided for the appointment of officials such as judges, magistrates and other officers, and defined the districts within which such officers should discharge their functions. See Hailley, *Native Administration*, at 202-30.

[74] For an analysis of this clause, see Molokomme, "Roman-Dutch Law in Botswana," at 121-22; Sanders, "Legal Dualism," at 51; Aguda, "Legal Development in Botswana," at 52-63. See further Otlhogile, *A History of the Higher Courts*, at 1-9.

doctrines of equity, and statutes of general application.[75] But the proximity of Bechuanaland to the Cape Colony and Britain's vision that the whole of Southern African including Bechuanaland would be a white dominion administered from the Cape Colony led instead to the introduction of the Cape colonial law.[76]

There is divergence of opinion regarding the exact nature of law that Section 19 transposed into Bechuanaland Protectorate.[77] However, the dominant view is that this clause introduced the Roman-Dutch Law instead of the English common law into the territory.[78] But, at the same time, as in Namibia and Zimbabwe, the said Roman-Dutch law was greatly influenced by English common law principles and concepts. By the 1909 Proclamation, the High Commissioner was empowered to continue legislating for the territory.[79] As a result, the High Commissioner issued a series of proclamations which, directly or indirectly, introduced some English common law principles into the territory.[80] Moreover, the Protectorate courts were staffed by judges

---

[75] For instance, see The Supreme Court of Ghana Ordinance, Section 14. This clause provided that "The common law, the doctrines of equity, and the statutes of general application which were in force in England at the date when the colony obtained a local legislature, that is to say, on the 24th day of July 1874, shall be in force within the jurisdiction of the court."

[76] Sanders, "Legal Dualism," at 54; Molokomme, "Roman -Dutch Law in Botswana," at 123.

[77] Some scholars have argued that the law that the proclamation introduced into the Protectorate was the Roman-Dutch Law because the United Kingdom envisaged the day when the entire Southern African sub-region would become white territories administered from the Cape. See Pain, "English and Roman Dutch Law in Africa," at 163. Other scholars have argued, on the other hand, that the proclamation introduced the "Cape Colonial law". See Takirambudde, "External Law," at 209-28. Still other scholars have adopted a neutral approach and argued that the law that was transposed into Bechuanaland was simply the South African common law, that is, the general law of South Africa found in legislation and judicial pronouncements. See Otlhogile, *History of the Higher Courts*, at 5-9.

[78] Aguda, "Legal Development in Botswana," at 57; Forster, "The Administration of Justice," at 89.

[79] Section 2.

[80] For instance, the High Commissioner issued the General Law (Cape Statutes) Revision Proclamation of 1959 which was designed to clarify the question of the

having an English common law background. In applying Roman-Dutch law which they were enjoined to enforce, English common law doctrines and precedent filtered in their decisions. These doctrines and principles profoundly impacted upon the legal system of Bechuanaland Protectorate.[81] The influence resulted in the "Roman-Dutch common law."[82] This law became the basic law of the Bechuanaland Protectorate. It was administered and applied by the courts as the common law of the Protectorate until independence in 1966 and beyond.

Thus, as in Namibia and Zimbabwe, in tracing the reception of rules of international law (including international human rights law) into Bechuanaland Protectorate through the Roman-Dutch law reception formula and background regard should be had to the impact of the English common law principles, rules and concepts on the Roman-Dutch law.

Status of International Law

Customary international law The legal position of customary international law in the pre-independence Botswana domestic law was

---

authority for the application of both the common law and the Roman Dutch law. Further, the Roman Dutch Criminal law received and applied in the Protectorate was supplemented by proclamations issued from the office of the High Commissioner. This led to the adoption of the Penal Code in 1964 which was founded largely, though not exclusively, on English law rather than Cape colonial law. See Molokomme, "Roman Dutch Law" at 125; Forster, "Administration of Justice," at 89.

[81] Sanders, "Legal Dualism," at 53. See also Otlhogile, *History of the Higher Courts*, at 4-5. Molokomme observes that, "At a meeting of the Law Reform Committee held in Francistown on 18 and 19 December 1961, the then Assistant Attorney-General explained the advantages of introducing a Penal Code, one of which was consistency, which the other members agreed with enthusiasm. The idea was not to codify the existing criminal law as this would be difficult, but rather to adopt a code from another territory. A Penal Code Bill was later drafted and discussed. *When the Botswana Penal Code finally came out, [it] was founded largely, though not conclusively, on English law rather than the Cape Colonial Law.* (emphasis supplied). See Molokomme, "Roman-Dutch Law in Botswana," at 125.

[82] This phrase was employed in subsequent proclamations. See for instance General Law (Cape Statutes) Rev. Proclamation, No. 2 of 1959, Section 3(d).

never clarified. As in Namibia and Zimbabwe, the Roman-Dutch law reception instrument did not contain any express provision on the position of customary international law in domestic law. Moreover, the subject has never attracted any judicial or legislative articulation. There were no clear rules guiding national institutions particularly the courts on how to handle questions involving international law.

The position could, however, be examined from two possible approaches. First, the common law approach. As a British protectorate, Botswana did not exist as an independent entity and was not a subject of international law. It lacked international personality. It means that, legally speaking, the question of the relationship between international law and the "municipal law" of Bechuanaland Protectorate did not arise. At the same time, according to British constitutional law, the colonial territories, at least, in terms of the 1931 Statute of Westminster, were regarded as part of the United Kingdom. Consequently, it meant that rules and principles which governed the status of customary international law in these territories, including Bechuanaland Protectorate, were the same as those governing the relationship between customary international law and the municipal law of the United Kingdom.[83]

Secondly, the Roman-Dutch law approach. As indicated above, instead of introducing its own legal system in the territory the United Kingdom opted for the Roman-Dutch law operating in the Union of South Africa. This legal system became the common law of Bechuanaland Protectorate. It, among other things, constituted the background and legal basis for examining the position of customary international law in pre-independence period of Botswana. Significantly, as it has been amply demonstrated above in relation to South West Africa and Southern Rhodesia, the Roman-Dutch legal system did not treat customary international law differently from the English common law. The latter had a tremendous influence on the former. In both legal systems, customary international law is deemed to be automatically applicable in municipal law.

Thus, whether the position of customary international law in pre-independence Botswana is examined on the basis of the Roman-Dutch law reception formula or the English common law, the position

---

[83] Fawcett, *The British Commonwealth*, at 19-20; Duffy, "English Law," 585-6. Cf Alexander, "International Law in India," at 289.

is the same. The status of customary international law in Botswana was regulated by the monist theory. According to this theory, customary international law (including customary international human rights law) formed part of the legal system of Bechuanaland Protectorate unless excluded by legislation, the act of state doctrine or *stare decisis* rule.[84] This position was a legacy of the erstwhile colonial Powers. However, the legal position was never clearly articulated and largely remained blurred and uncertain.

Treaties The legal position of treaties (including human rights treaties) in pre-independence Botswana, unlike in Namibia and Zimbabwe, was also never clarified. There was no express reference to the place and role of treaties in the Roman-Dutch law reception instrument in local law. Moreover, the position did not receive any express judicial or legislative affirmation.

However, as with customary international law, the legal position could be tackled from two perspectives. First, the common law perspective. As a British protected territory, Botswana's rules concerning the treatment of treaties were, in principle, the same as those governing the place of treaties in the United Kingdom common law. Botswana constitutional principle including the attendant division of powers and functions between the various organs of government derived from the English constitutional model. Thus treaties such as the ECHR, which were extended to the Protectorate, did not become part of the local law until legislated according to the constitutional structure of the Protectorate.[85]

The question regarding which body exercised legislative powers during the Protectorate period would be answered by the constitutional structure in existence in the territory at the time. This was a period where the separation and distribution of power among the three branches of government: the executive, legislature and judiciary were not clear cut. However, the High Commissioner, in terms of the

---

[84] For a detailed discussion of the exceptions to direct application of customary international law in Botswana municipal law, see *chapter three* below.

[85] In terms of Article 63 of the ECHR, contracting parties are supposed to extend the Convention to territories for whose international affairs they were responsible. The Convention was extended to the High Commission territories of Bechuanaland Protectorate, Basutoland and the Kingdom of Swaziland in January 1969. See Maope, *Human Rights*, at 14; Vasak, "European Convention," at 1206-31.

9th May, 1891, Proclamation exercised the overall jurisdiction over the territory, although he was empowered to, and did, establish the judiciary for the administration of justice. The proclamation also assigned the High Commissioner the power to legislate for the territory by proclamations. This meant that treaties duly entered into by the United Kingdom and extended to the Protectorate in view of its incapacity to conduct external relations especially those relating to entering into treaties under the protectorate regime had, theoretically speaking, to be legislated into municipal law by the High Commissioner.

Secondly, the legal position of conventional international law during the pre-independence era could be determined by the principles and concepts of the Roman-Dutch law imposed on the territory during colonial rule. This law formed the foundation of the South African legal system. The practice under this legal system was that, as a general rule, treaties needed legislative action to be internally applicable. But the crucial fact is that the South African courts borrowed from, and depended heavily upon, the English common law on their domestic treatment of treaties.

Viewed from either the English common law or Roman-Dutch law perspective, treaties (including human rights treaties) did not have automatic application in Bechuanaland Protectorate. They required legislation to be part of the local law. Thus the status of treaties in the pre-existing Botswana municipal law was regulated by dualism inherited from Britain.

Conclusion

It is abundantly clear that despite differences in historical experiences and circumstances, Botswana, Namibia and Zimbabwe inherited the same legal system from the former colonial Powers; Britain with respect to Botswana and Zimbabwe, and the Union of South Africa in relation to Namibia. They all received the Roman-Dutch law. This law became the basic and common law of the three countries.

It is also clear that the Roman-Dutch law was influenced by the English common law due to the interaction between both legal systems at the Cape Colony in the Union of South Africa at the height of colonialism. The influence was reflected, among other things, in the way South Africa, at least before the adoption of the new Constitution in 1996, and United Kingdom treat international law in municipal law. Thus both legal systems provide a background to the absorption of international human rights law in the local law of the three countries. In both countries, customary international law is automatically applicable in municipal law. It does not require legislative transformation. But treaties require legislation to be part of municipal law. Both countries adhere to monist theory with respect to the domestic status of customary international law and dualism in relation to treaties.

These theories were bequeathed to Botswana, Namibia and Zimbabwe through the Roman-Dutch law reception formulae notwithstanding the fact that the reception instruments were silent on the subject and that no constitutional or legislative provisions, that is, the various proclamations and Orders in Council issued for these territories, provided any guidance on how international law ought to have been treated in domestic law. In all the three countries, customary international law (including customary international human rights law) was automatically applicable in pre-independence municipal law and treaties were not. Treaties required legislation to be interacted into municipal law. Thus the three countries inherited from the former colonial Powers the classical monist theory in the way they treated international customary rules in domestic law and the dualist theory with respect to treaties. The domestic absorption and treatment of international law was greatly influenced by the external legal systems. It was not autochthonous. Rather, it was a legacy of colonial rule.

In Namibia, but not Botswana, the legal position of both treaties and customary rules was articulated and confirmed by the courts. In Zimbabwe, only the legal position of treaties was confirmed by the courts. In Namibia, the subject attracted most attention mainly where the mandate of the Union of South Africa to administer South West Africa was being challenged. In the process, Namibian courts declared that the Mandate, as a treaty, required legislation to be part of pre-independence Namibian national law. They also declared that customary international law had direct domestic application. It effectively means that in Botswana, the legal position remained very unclear and uncertain. However, in all the three countries the place of international law in municipal law was not acted upon in a consistent, uniform and categorical way in order to firmly secure it in municipal law.

Part III:
Independence - New Departures

3 Colonial Heritage Retained: Zimbabwe and Botswana

The preceding chapter has analysed the status of international law (including international human rights law), conventional and customary, in the pre-existing municipal legal orders of the countries under consideration. This chapter analyses the extant status of that law in the municipal laws of independent Botswana and Zimbabwe in order to find out whether its legal position in both countries underwent any changes at independence and whether and how the judiciary has handled the subject.

Zimbabwe

The Legal Framework: an Overview

The Zimbabwean post-colonial Constitution did not clarify the legal position and role of international law, customary and conventional, in municipal law. The 1980 Independence Constitution of Zimbabwe[1] has an entrenched Bill of Rights protecting human rights norms similar to those recognised under major international human rights treaties and instruments.[2] However, the Constitution does not have an express provision categorically and unambiguously according international law (including international human rights law) a place and role in Zimbabwean municipal law. The entrenchment of a Bill of Rights does not in itself *ipso facto* make international human rights law part of

---

[1] The Zimbabwean Constitution is reprinted in Blaustein, P. Albert and Flanz, H. Gisbert., eds. *Constitutions of Countries of the World*. Vol. 32 (Dobbs Ferry. New York: Oceana Publications, 1980). For a general discussion of the developments leading to the adoption of the Zimbabwean Constitution, see Tshuma, "Lancaster House Constitution," at 195; Ncube, "Human Rights," at 54.

[2] Hatchard, *Individual Freedoms*, at 1-11; Eze, *Human Rights*, at 119-20; De Smith, *The New Commonwealth*, at 199; Heyns, "Human Rights Law," at 252-63.

municipal law. Significantly, Section 89 of the Constitution retains the Roman-Dutch common law. This law provides the basis for assessing the inter-relation between international law and Zimbabwean municipal law.

Customary International Law

Judicial practice under both the Roman-Dutch law and English common law is that rules of customary international law are deemed to be self-operative in municipal law.[3] These rules are automatically applicable in national law. They confer rights and obligations directly on individuals at the national level. Thus viewed either from the common law position or the Roman-Dutch law customary international law is part of Zimbabwean municipal law. The inherited monist theory continues to regulate the inter-relationship between customary international law (including customary international human rights law) and Zimbabwean municipal law.

The uncertainty and lack of clarity inherited from the colonial era concerning the place of customary international law in the municipal legal dispensation of Zimbabwe has to some extent been addressed by the judiciary since independence. This has, however, occurred in relatively few and isolated cases.

The subject was discussed in *Barker McCormac (Pvt) Ltd v. The Government of Kenya.*[4] A detailed analysis of this case is in order, for it is one of the first few judicial pronouncements that laid down quite unambiguously the principle concerning the place and function of customary international law in Zimbabwean municipal law although it deals with state immunity rather than international human rights law. The appellant company, Barker McCormac (Pvt) Ltd, had been lessee of certain premises in Harare, Zimbabwe, under a lease agreement containing an option to renew the lease in respect of which the

---

[3] For an analysis of the practice under the South African Roman-Dutch law, see Dugard, "International Law," at 13; Id, *International Law*, at 41-51; Sanders, "South Africa's Monist Tradition," at 147; Maluwa, "International Human Rights Norms," at 14; Devine, "International Law in South Africa," at 1-18. As regards English common law, see Brownlie, *Principles*, at 43-7; Collier, " Law of England," at 924.

[4] 1983 (4) S.A. 803 (ZSC).

respondent, the Government of Kenya, had acquired the lessor's interest, with a view to using the premises as its High Commission. The respondent refused to renew the lease arguing, inter alia, that the appellant's occupation of part of the premises created unacceptable security concerns. The upshot of the case was that the appellant claimed that it was forced to move to other premises at a higher rental and decided to commence legal proceedings against the respondent Government of Kenya to recover damages arising from the alleged wrongful repudiation of the lease. The respondent having refused service of the summons, the appellant applied to the High Court of Zimbabwe for a substituted service under Order 6, Rule 4(6) of the High Court Rules. The High Court, per Justice Waddington, dismissed the application on the ground that the lease of the premises by the respondent was an act *jure imperii* and it could not therefore against its will be made party to legal proceedings in municipal courts of Zimbabwe.

On appeal to the Supreme Court against the ruling of the High Court, the respondent raised a special plea in bar, arguing, inter alia, that according to the doctrine of absolute sovereign immunity which applies in Zimbabwe legal proceedings could not be instituted against it. The respondent also argued that the earlier decision was given *per incuriam* and that even if the restrictive theory of sovereign immunity was adopted the defendant's plea of jurisdictional immunity was still valid as its actions in the matter at issue were *acta jure imperii*.

After examining the issues and points raised by the parties, the Court held that the doctrine of sovereign immunity generally applied in international law is restrictive immunity. Significantly, the Court also held that there being no judicial pronouncements in Zimbabwe on the matter the restrictive sovereign immunity doctrine should be incorporated as part of the law of Zimbabwe. In particular, Justice Georges aptly noted that:

> The major issue as to the nature of the doctrine of sovereign immunity is a question of international law. Although there appears to be no pronouncements on the matter in our courts until now, there is no doubt that international law is part of the law of this country. In so far as the common law of Zimbabwe is Roman-Dutch law there is

support for the proposition in Nduli and Another v Minister of Justice and Others 1978 (1) S.A 893 (a).[5]

The Judge continued to emphasise that he was:

> completely satisfied therefore that the doctrine of sovereign immunity generally applied in international law is that of restrictive immunity. There are no decisions of courts of this country and no legislation inconsistent with that doctrine and it should be incorporated as part of our law.[6]

The legal battle in the case continued. After the Supreme Court's ruling allowing an appeal on the procedural point, the case was referred back to the High Court for arguments on the merits.[7] The High Court endorsed the Supreme Court ruling that the nature of the doctrine of sovereign immunity was a question of international law to be applied as part and parcel of the municipal law of Zimbabwe. Justice Samatta traced the development of the concept of sovereign immunity and on the question of its status and role in Zimbabwean municipal law specifically observed:

> I have held that it is the restrictive doctrine of sovereign immunity which *forms part of the law of this country*.[8]

This case unequivocally endorses the principle that international law forms part of the domestic law of Zimbabwe. As Justice Georges acknowledged in his judgment, the case is a first judicial recognition and affirmation of the principle that international law forms part of the domestic law of Zimbabwe.[9] Until this decision

---

[5] Ibid., at 819.

[6] Ibid., at 821 (JJ Baron and Beck concurring).

[7] Barker McCormac (Pvt) Ltd v. Government of Kenya [1986] L.R.C. (Const) 215 (ZHC).

[8] Ibid., at 222 (emphasis supplied).

[9] Barker McCormac (Pvt) Ltd v. Government of Kenya 1983 (4) S.A. 803 (ZSC) at 819.

the matter has never entertained the Zimbabwean courts and has as a result remained blurred, unclear and uncertain.

The decision raises two important issues. First, in arriving at the conclusion that international law is part of the law of Zimbabwe the Court relied partly on Roman-Dutch law superimposed on Zimbabwe prior to independence. As indicated above, this law continues to apply in Zimbabwe and constitutes a significant component of the common law of the country. Moreover, the Court reinforced its conclusion by relying on the South African decisions dealing with the status and function of international law in South African municipal law.[10] This evidences the influence and inspiration of the South African Roman-Dutch law on the Zimbabwean courts.

Secondly, the Zimbabwean courts (the High Court and the Supreme Court), also relied on the English decisions on the subject. They proceeded to examine how English courts have applied the common law principles on the relationship of customary international law with British law. By relying on authorities from both jurisdictions, the Zimbabwean courts underscored the impact of the trend in both countries on the way the Zimbabwean courts treat and ought to treat international law in municipal law.

It is, however, significant to note that the judges in *Barker McCormac's case* referred generally to the fact that international law is part of the law of Zimbabwe and did not specifically mention customary international law or use the language to that effect or even any applicable treaty. They consistently used the phrases 'international law is part of our law,' 'international law should be incorporated as part of our law' and 'the doctrine of sovereign immunity forms part of the law of this country.' The use of these phrases has been construed to refer to customary international law but not treaty law.[11] They refer to general rules of international law recognised by a vast majority of states.

---

[10] Ibid., at 819. In particular, the Court relied on Nduli and Another v. Minister of Justice and Others 1978 (1) S.A. 893 (A); Inter-science Research and Development Services (Pty) Ltd v. Republic Popular de Mozambique 1980 (2) S.A. 112 (T); Kaffraria Property Co. (Pty) Ltd v. Government of Zambia 1980 (2) S.A. 709.

[11] Sanders, "Customary International Law," at 147; Lauterpacht, "The Law of England," at 51; Vitanyi, "Article 25," at 578-88.

Another case in which the place of customary international law in Zimbabwean municipal law was discussed is *Mharapara v. The State*.[12] Also, this case did not deal with human rights law. Rather, it concerned exterritorial jurisdiction of Zimbabwean courts. The appellant, an Executive Officer in the Ministry of Foreign Affairs, appeared before the Zimbabwean High Court charged with stealing money, the property of the Government of Zimbabwe, at the Zimbabwean Embassy in Brussels, Belgium while working as Zimbabwean consul. He raised an exception to the indictment that the court had no jurisdiction to try him as the crime had been committed in Belgium. The Court, per Justice Mfalila, dismissed the exception holding that the Court had jurisdiction in accordance with the nationality or active personality principle of international law. An appeal to the Supreme Court was also dismissed on almost the same grounds.

In determining whether the Court could exercise jurisdiction over cases governed by international law, Justice Gubbay noted that:

> As I perceive the position, there is no rule of international law directing or obliging states to exercise criminal jurisdiction over their nationals for offences committed abroad...*Thus the fact that customary international law is part of the municipal law of a state does not assist*, because there is only a permissive principle involved and not a mandatory rule.[13]

This *dictum* firmly endorses the decision in *Barker McCormac's case* that customary international law is part of Zimbabwean municipal law. It is an affirmation of the automatic incorporation principle. Although the two cases did not deal with international human rights law *per se*, their *ratio* applies with equal force to that regime. International human rights law is subsumed under general international law.

It is, however, significant to note that the courts in Zimbabwe have not consistently and systematically acted upon the automatic incorporation principle as enunciated in *Barker McCormac's case*.

---

[12]   [1986] L.R.C. (Const) 234.

[13]   Ibid., at 239 (emphasis supplied).

They have not internalised this principle. They seem to be doubtful or even oblivious of the fact that rules of customary international law form part of the domestic law of the country and should be enforced as such.[14]

Exceptions to the Automatic Incorporation of Customary Rules

Legislation   The post independence Zimbabwean municipal law continues to recognise that the automatic incorporation of customary international law is subject to the will of parliament. The legislature can exclude direct operation of customary international law in Zimbabwe municipal law by statute. The operation of this exception in the extant Zimbabwean municipal law was expressly confirmed in *Barker McCormac (Pvt) Ltd v. Government of Kenya.* Justice Georges of the Supreme Court of Zimbabwe observed:

> I am completely satisfied therefore that the doctrine of sovereign immunity generally applied in international law is that of restrictive immunity. *There is..no legislation inconsistent with that doctrine* and it should be incorporated as part of our law.[15]

An inconsistency occurs between legislation and a rule of customary international law where Zimbabwean national law is in conflict, for instance, with obligations assumed by Zimbabwe under international law or a general rule of international law. Under these circumstances, national law prevails and the Zimbabwean courts are bound to apply a rule of municipal law and not a customary international law rule. This exception does not relate to legislation enacted prior to the emergence of a rule of customary international law. It applies to later, or rather posterior legislation. The intention of the

---

[14]   S v. A Juvenile 1990 (4) S.A. 151. The lack of judicial certainty has been expressed by Dumbutshena, formerly Chief Justice of Zimbabwe, in these words "An added advantage is that the courts of this country are free to import into the interpretation of section 15(1) interpretations of similar provisions in international and regional human rights instrument. *In the end international human rights norms will become part of our domestic human rights law. In this way our domestic human rights jurisprudence is enriched.*" Ibid., at 155 (emphasis supplied).

[15]   1983 (4) S.A. 817 at 821 (ZSC) (emphasis supplied).

legislature to disregard a rule of customary international law should be very clear and unambiguous. Where the intention of parliament is clear and unequivocal, a posterior legislation will exclude the domestic operation of customary international law. This limitation operates mainly to forestall the unsupervised application of customary international law in Zimbabwean municipal law. However, the Zimbabwean courts will seek to ensure that municipal law conforms to the international law obligations of Zimbabwe. They will construe any legislation to ensure that Zimbabwe complies with, rather than contravenes, its international legal obligations.

Judicial precedent Judicial precedent or *stare decisis* rule can also exclude the automatic application of customary international law in the present Zimbabwean municipal law, as was confirmed in the fore-cited *Barker McCormac (Pvt) Ltd v. Government of Kenya.*[16] According to this rule, lower courts are bound by decisions of higher courts even if those decisions were made in disregard of customary international law. Its effect is to limit the automatic application of customary international law in municipal law. However, in the United Kingdom, this rule is overridden by the *Trendtex case.*

The rationale for the *stare decisis* rule is generally to ensure uniformity and consistency in the application of rules of law. It also ensures predictability in their growth. It has never been intended to mean stagnation in the rules.[17] It is submitted, however, that in cases dealing especially with international human rights law the courts should not be impeded by the doctrine of *stare decisis* in applying such law. They should endeavour to limit its application. Thus where the utilisation of international human rights law in a particular case affords the individual maximum protection in fundamental justice, a divergent *stare decisis* rule should be disregarded. This has the advantage of making international human rights standards more effective in municipal law. It enhances the role of international law in municipal law.

---

[16] [1986] L.R.C. (Const) 214 at 220.

[17] Sanders, "Customary International law," at 149.

Justiciability In certain circumstances, the direct applicability of customary international human rights law in municipal law may be excluded on the basis that it is not justiciable in domestic courts.[18] This may occur mainly where domestic courts are compelled to effectuate executive decisions even if such decisions would be in conflict with a rule or rules of customary international human rights law. These decisions would not be justiciable or reviewable in courts.[19] The principle precludes the courts from judging in accordance with what they believe to be the rules of international law. It is mainly a judicial policy of restraints or abstention in matters within the domain of the executive. It signifies judicial deference to the executive branch imposed by the doctrine of separation of powers.

The principle of justiciability has been judicially recognised in Zimbabwean municipal law. It arose in *Patriotic Front-ZAPU v. Minister of Justice, Legal and Parliamentary Affairs.*[20] The appellant, a political party, sought an order from the High Court of Zimbabwe declaring that Proclamation No. 2 of 1985 by which the President fixed the nomination date for the general election was *ultra vires* Section 12 of the Electoral Act, 1979 as modified by Section 4 of the Electoral Act (Modification) Notice 1985 or else void for unreasonableness. The basis of the claim was that the nomination date fixed, 10 June 1985, did not allow the appellant's prospective candidates enough time to comply with the requirements for submission of nominations papers. In essence, the appellants were asking the Court to order that the declaration made by the President was void. The respondent, for their part, argued that the nomination date fixed by the President was an

---

[18] The principle of justiciability should be distinguished from the act of state doctrine. An act of state concerns the activities of the executive in relations with other states. Thus the act of state doctrine asserts that no state can exercise jurisdiction over another states. This doctrine is based on the principles of sovereignty and equality of states. Generally, see Shaw, *International Law*, at 128-33; Zander, "The Act of State Doctrine," at 826-52.

[19] Shaw, *International law*, 120; Sanders, "Customary International law," at 149-50; Lauterpacht, "The Law of England," at 76-77; Zander, "The Act of State," at 826; Oppenheim, *International Law*, at 329-30; Brownlie, *Principles*, at 52-3; Maluwa, "International Human Rights Norms," at 32; Luther v. Sagor [1921] 3 K.B. 532; West Rand Central Mining Company Co. v. R [1905] 2 K.B. 391.

[20] [1986] L.R.C. (Const) 672.

executive act which could not be questioned in a court of law even if it curtailed the constitutional right of the members of the appellant party to participate in the elections.

The Court examined the powers of the President under the Constitution of Zimbabwe and held, per Dumbutshena, C.J., that there are prerogatives exercisable by the President, and which are conferred on the President by the Constitution, which the courts, all things being equal, cannot inquire into because the President, acting on the advice of the Government, is the best judge in those circumstances of matters of policy in those areas covered by the prerogatives. These matters are not justiciable. Although the case does not deal *per se* with the domestic status of customary international law but with constitutional rights, analogically, it is submitted that it also applies with equal force to that regime. Matters falling within executive domain can operate to exclude the application of rules of customary international human rights law in Zimbabwe.

The rationale for the principle of justiciability is to ensure that the courts do not hinder the executive in the performance of its function. In fact, the executive has the responsibility of ensuring that the court's decisions conform to international law. But at the same time, the rule seeks to maintain a desirable harmony between the courts and the executive branch of government.[21]

It is submitted that, while the courts should respect executive decisions under certain circumstances, they should also not take a rigid and inflexible view in the application of the justiciability principle. Cognisance should be taken not only of the executive's role of handling issues relating to matters such as national security but also of the courts' own function to uphold the law and, most significantly, to protect the fundamental rights and freedoms of the individual. As Chief Justice Dumbutshena correctly observed in the fore-cited *Patriotic Front-ZAPU v Minister of Justice, Legal and Parliamentary Affairs*:

> such matters of executive prerogatives are now very few and far between because whenever the exercise of executive prerogative

---

[21] Zander, "The Act of State Doctrine," at 834; Sanders, " Customary International Law," at 149.

affects the private rights, interests and legitimate expectation of the subjects or citizens, the jurisdiction of the courts is not ousted.[22]

The private rights, interests and legitimate expectations of the citizens subject to judicial review acts of the executive which would otherwise oust the jurisdiction of the courts. Because of the concerns of the private rights and legitimate expectation of the citizens of Zimbabwe, the High Court was asked to look into and to find out whether by fixing 10th June 1985 as nomination day there would be sufficient time for interested parties to participate in the general elections without any obstacles being placed in their way through the lack of enough time to go through the procedures leading to nomination day.

Treaties

At independence, the status and role of treaties in Zimbabwean municipal law was regulated by the 1980 Lancaster House Constitution. Section 111B(1)(b) thereof provided that "except as otherwise provided by this Constitution or by an Act of Parliament, any convention, treaty or agreement acceded to, concluded or executed by or under the authority of the President with one or more foreign states or governments or international organisations shall not form part of the law of Zimbabwe unless it has been incorporated into the law by or under an Act of Parliament." According to this clause, subject to the Constitution or an Act of Parliament, international agreements became part of the Zimbabwean municipal law only when they have been specifically enacted into law.

Section 111B(1) has been amended by the Constitution of Zimbabwe Amendment (No. 7) Act, 1987 and substituted with a new clause. Section 17 thereof briefly provides that "any international convention, treaty or agreement which (a) has been entered into or executed by or under the authority of the President; and (b) imposes fiscal obligations upon Zimbabwe; shall be subject to ratification by the House of Assembly." This clause requires any international treaties which impose fiscal responsibility on Zimbabwe to be approved by parliament if they are to be binding on Zimbabwe.

---

[22] [1986] L.R.C. (Const) 672 at 680-1. See also Johnstone v. Peddlar [1921] 2 A.C. 262.

Germane to this discussion is paragraph 17(b). This clause raises several issues. First, not all treaties that have been executed by the president are subject to parliamentary ratification. Only those treaties which impose fiscal obligation need parliamentary approval. The question is, what about other treaties which do not impose fiscal obligation on Zimbabwe such as human rights treaties? Do these treaties require parliamentary approval? Secondly, what does ratification by the House of Assembly really mean? Does it mean ratification, or rather expression of consent to be bound at the international level as envisaged by the Vienna Convention of Law on Treaties of 1969[23] whereby for a treaty that is signed by the competent State official to be binding externally as against Zimbabwe and other States it needs parliamentary approval? Or does it mean ratification at municipal level in the sense that a duly executed treaty by the competent State official has to be approved by parliament for it to be part of the Zimbabwean municipal law? Last but not least, does clause 7(b) encompass both stages or processes?

Concerning the first issue, a reasonable and plausible interpretation of paragraph 17(b) is that it does not cover treaties which do not impose fiscal obligations on Zimbabwe. Treaties falling under this category do not require parliamentary approval to be binding upon Zimbabwe. The initial position in Section 111B(1)(a) of the Lancaster Constitution requiring *any* convention, treaty or agreement binding on Zimbabwe to be approved by parliament has been altered to relate narrowly and only to treaties imposing fiscal obligation. Paragraph (b) thereof confines parliamentary ratification only to treaties imposing fiscal responsibility upon Zimbabwe.[24] It leaves the status of other treaties such as human rights treaties in Zimbabwe unclear and uncertain.

With respect to the issue of whether paragraph (b) relates to either expression of consent to be bound at the international level or

---

[23] Article 11. This clause provides that "The consent of a State to be bound by a treaty may be expressed by signature, exchange of instruments constituting a treaty, ratification, acceptance, approval or accession, by any other means if so agreed." See generally Brownlie, *Principles*, at 606-8.

[24] Patel, "Treaties," at 28. Patel has noted that "Accordingly, a treaty - unless it falls into the narrow class of treaties which, as above, indicated, do not require transformation." *Id.*, at 28.

ratification at municipal level, that is, parliamentary approval, or both, it is submitted that it relates only to consent to be bound at the international level. This is apparent from the phrase "entered into or executed by or under the authority of the President." A treaty that is "entered into or executed" already becomes binding externally and does not require parliamentary approval. Thus it is redundant to require that subsequent parliament approval is necessary for such a treaty to be binding on Zimbabwe vis-à-vis other States.

Most importantly, even those international agreements covered by Section 17 are not part of the municipal law of Zimbabwe. Section 17 is silent on the position and role of these treaties in Zimbabwe. It does not incorporate these treaties into municipal law. This means that their status in municipal law is not entirely clear. Clearly, the new legal position embodied in Section 17(b) is a complete reversal of the initial Section 111B(1)(b) of the Zimbabwean Constitution which provided that treaties shall not form part of the law of Zimbabwe unless they have been incorporated into the law by or under an Act of Parliament.

This effectively means that the present status of treaties in Zimbabwean municipal law should be examined on the basis of the inherited Roman-Dutch common law model which, in terms of Section 89 of the Independence Constitution of Zimbabwe, continues to operate in the country. According to the Roman-Dutch common law, treaties or international agreements are not self-executing. They require legislation to be operative in Zimbabwean municipal law. The classical dualist theory has been endorsed by the fore-cited *R v. Muirhead*.[25]

Moreover, as a commonwealth country, Zimbabwe, adheres to the practice observed by other common law and commonwealth countries whereby treaties are referred to the legislature to translate them into municipal law and make them internally effective.[26] This is posited on the notion that within the general principle of state sovereignty, a State must, through its legislature, agree, expressly or impliedly, to international law particularly conventional international law in order for it to have force of municipal law. Thus on the basis of

---

[25] In fact, the Court categorically stated that it was following its counterparts in South Africa and indeed made references to decisions of South African Courts. For instance, the Court referred to cases such as Policansky v. Minister of Agriculture 1946 C.P.D. 860 at 865.

[26] Patel, "Treaties," at 28; Umozurike, *The African Charter*, at 109.

the Roman-Dutch common law human rights treaties do not enjoy automatic application in the extant Zimbabwean municipal law. They need legislative translation if they are to be effective in domestic law and confer rights and duties on individuals. Thus Zimbabwe has retained the imposed classical dualist theory in the way it treats international conventions in municipal law.

It is significant to observe in this regard that upon attaining independence in 1980, the newly elected Government of Zimbabwe acceded to and ratified several treaties dealing with a wide ranging universal or general, regional and specific human rights issues. As regards universal or general treaties, Zimbabwe has acceded to the Convention on the Prevention and Punishment of the Crime of Genocide of 1948, the Convention on the Suppression and Punishment of the Crime of Apartheid of 1973, the Convention on the Elimination of All Forms of Discrimination Against Women of 1979 and the Convention on the Elimination of All Forms of Racial Discrimination of 1966.[27] Zimbabwe has similarly acceded to the Convention on the Rights of the Child of 1989.[28]

Regional treaties that Zimbabwe is party to are the African Charter on Human and People's Rights (hereafter the ACHPR), the Southern African Development Community Treaty (hereafter the SADC Treaty) and the Charter of the Organisation of the African Unity (hereafter the OAU Charter). These treaties deal with a wide variety of subjects and do not specifically deal with human rights norms. But they have provisions that enjoin the contracting parties to respect and protect human rights.[29] Zimbabwe has also acceded to conventions on the rights of refugees and people in like situations such as the 1951

---

[27] These conventions were signed on 13 May 1991. See United Nations, *Multilateral Treaties Deposited with the Secretary General of the United Nations: Status as at 1 December 1996*.

[28] Zimbabwe acceded to the Convention on the Rights of the Child on 2 September 1992. See United Nations, *Multilateral Treaties Deposited with the Secretary General of the United Nations: Status as at 1 December 1996*.

[29] For instance, Article 2(e) of the OAU Charter provides, inter alia, that one of the purposes of the Charter is to promote international co-operation, having due regard to the Charter of the United Nations and the Universal Declaration of Human Rights. The SADC Treaty provides in Article 4(c) that Member States shall act in accordance with the principles of human rights, democracy, and the rule of law.

Convention relating to the Status of Refugees and its 1967 Protocol, and the 1969 OAU Convention Governing the Specific Aspects of Refugee Problems in Africa.[30]

There are, however, other international human rights conventions which Zimbabwe is yet to ratify. For instance, Zimbabwe is yet to be party to the Convention against Torture and Other Cruel, Inhuman, or Degrading Punishment and Treatment of 10 December 1984, the Optional Protocol to the International Covenant on Civil and Political Rights of 1966[31] and the Second Optional Protocol to the International Covenant on Civil and Political Rights Aiming at the Abolition of the Death Penalty of 15 December 1989 which entered into force on 11 July 1991.[32] According to the inherited dualist theory, these treaties are not part of Zimbabwean municipal law. In order for them to be integrated into municipal law, they require parliamentary approval in addition to ratification at the international level.

Botswana

The Legal Framework: a General Comment

The 1966 Independence Constitution of Botswana does not have a clear and express provision categorically and unambiguously according international law (including international human rights law) a place and role in Botswana municipal law.[33] Although the Bill of Rights embodied in the Constitution recognises and protects human rights norms fashioned along the internationally recognised rights found in various human rights treaties this in itself does not mean that international human rights norms are automatically part of municipal law of Botswana. According to the monist-dualist controversy, there is

---

[30] See United Nations, *Multilateral Treaties Deposited with the Secretary General of the United Nations: Status as at 1 December 1996.*

[31] (1967) 6 ILM 383.

[32] (1990) 29 ILM 1464.

[33] Botswana attained independence on 30 September, 1966 pursuant to the Botswana Independence Order (1966), Statutory Instrument No. 1171, 1966.

need for an express provision according international human rights law a specific place in municipal law. Thus, as in Zimbabwe, Botswana post-colonial constitutional and municipal legal order has not clarified the legal position of both conventional and customary international law in municipal law.

Consequently, the legal position of international law in Botswana municipal law should be analysed on the basis of the inherited Roman-Dutch common law approach. This law should provide the basis for analysing the place of both customary and conventional international human rights law in the existing municipal law of Botswana. The received Roman-Dutch law was not abrogated at independence. It continues to operate alongside the general law of Botswana found in statutes, subordinate legislation and judicial decisions.[34]

Rules of Customary International Law

As amply demonstrated in relation to Zimbabwe, judicial practice under the Roman-Dutch common law is that rules of customary international law are considered to be part of the law of the land. Likewise, under the municipal law of Botswana customary international law is deemed to be automatically applicable in national law. The inter-relationship between customary international law (including customary international human rights law) and municipal law of Botswana continues to be regulated by the classical monist theory.

The inherited monist theory has been confirmed by Botswana courts.[35] It was given express judicial endorsement in *Agnes Bojang v.*

---

[34] Aguda, "Legal Development," at 54; Sanders, "Legal Dualism," at 54-5; Molokomme, "Roman-Dutch Law in Botswana," at 133; Forster, "Administration of Justice," at 90. Forster notes that although the association with the Cape Colony came to an end in 1909 it has left a profound and what Aguda calls an " unfortunate" effect on the legal system of Botswana even till today.

[35] The theory has been implicitly endorsed in Attorney-General v. Moagi, Criminal Appeal No. 73/1978 (unreported) but discussed in Sanders, "Constitutionalism in Botswana," at 50-2; Clover Petrus and Another v. The State [1985] L.R.C (Const) 699; Unity Dow v. Attorney General of Botswana [1991] L.R.C (Const) 574. In these cases, both the High Court and Court of Appeal of Botswana emphasised that universally recognised human rights norms are directly applicable in Botswana.

The State.[36] The Applicant was charged with and convicted by a Magistrate Court on a plea of guilty of stealing by persons employed in the public service contrary to Section 271 as read with Section 276 of the Penal Code of Botswana. She was sentenced to a term of imprisonment. In an application to the High Court for a judicial review, she argued, first and foremost, that the Magistrate Court had denied her the right to legal representation by failing to ask her whether or not she wished to be represented by a lawyer, a right to which she was entitled under municipal law of Botswana.

The approach adopted by the High Court to the question of the right to legal representation went far beyond the usual practice of the courts in the country when dealing with issues involving human or constitutional rights. The Court noted that due to the paucity of case law in the country to guide it in resolving the question before it, it had to seek assistance not only from comparative judicial pronouncements but also from human rights treaties protecting the right to legal representation.[37] In the process, the Court found itself having to deal with the status and role of human rights treaties in the municipal law of Botswana. Justice Gyeke-Dako, the presiding Judge, recognised that the embodiment of laudable human rights principles in various human rights instruments reflects a universal acceptance of the right to legal representation as an important factor in the concept of a fair trial. In particular, Justice Gyeke-Dako's reference to the domestic status of customary international law took this form:

> But, even assuming that the right to legal representation is part of customary international law, can it be seriously contended that such right to legal representation as embodied in international instruments, automatically forms part of the municipal laws of Botswana without any act of legislative incorporation. I doubt it.[38]

Two points emerge from this *dictum*. First, the Court can only assume that the right to legal representation forms part of customary international law. It is not an express judicial affirmation that this right

---

[36] Miscellaneous Case No. 6/1993 (HC) (unreported).

[37] Ibid., at 7.

[38] Ibid., at 14-15.

has matured into customary international law. Secondly, the Court pointed out that it doubted whether the right to legal representation forms part of municipal law without having been incorporated by legislation. This demonstrates the uncertainty and lack of clarity on the part of the judiciary concerning the rules governing the application and function of international law in municipal law. In particular, the observation signifies that the status of customary international law in general in the municipal law of Botswana is not yet firmly anchored.

However, Justice Gyeke-Dako proceeded to say:

> I find nothing in the laws of this country to the effect that international law or for that matter provisions of international conventions can dispense with the theory of incorporation to operate directly on individuals.[39]

This observation reveals two issues. In the first instance it clearly demonstrates the fact that the Court assumed that the theory of automatic incorporation applies to both international treaties and customary international law. This assumption and failure to clearly distinguish the circumstances under which the theory applies further makes the legal position more blurred and uncertain.

The second issue is that the observation, despite its apparent imprecision, raises a double-pronged inquiry. The first relates to the phrase "international law." The second concerns the phrase "can dispense with the theory of incorporation to operate directly on individuals." As regards the former, it is submitted that international law here refers to customary international law. It is well settled that phrases such as "international is part of the law of the land" or general reference to international law in this context does not include or relate to international treaties since international treaties, generally speaking, require legislation to make them part of municipal law. They need legislative transformation in order to be integrated into municipal legal sphere.

The statement is an immediate reminder of the well known observation made by Sir William Blackstone that "the law of nations, whenever any question arises which is properly the object of its jurisdiction, is here adopted in its full extent by the common law, and

---

[39] Ibid., at 15.

is held to be part of the law of land." It is generally acknowledged that this observation relates to customary international law but not treaties.[40]

The second point raised by Justice Gyeke-Dako's observation is that nothing in the municipal law of Botswana can dispense with the "theory of incorporation to operate directly on individuals." This remark is a judicial recognition and confirmation of a well settled doctrine in international law regarding the receivability and absorption of customary international law in domestic law. According to this doctrine, customary international law (including customary international human rights law) is, as a general rule, considered or deemed to be part of municipal law.[41] Thus, despite the imperfection in the language, the case establishes that Botswana municipal law adheres to the automatic incorporation theory in its treatment of customary international law (including international human rights law). It represents the first judicial proclamation of the incorporation theory in the municipal normative order of Botswana.

The above analysis leads to several conclusions. First, cases in which the place and role of customary international law in municipal law has arisen are comparatively few and isolated. In fact, *Agnes Bojang v. The State*, a very low key case indeed, is the only case in which the issue was expressly raised. But even in this case, the subject was raised just incidentally. This explains why the judge expressed his avowed doubts as to its status in Botswana domestic law. It also explains why the court gave the issue a brief and cursory treatment. Moreover, the case shows lack of consistency and uniformity in handling the subject.

Secondly, in most of the cases where the subject was discussed, either directly or indirectly, the courts were primarily examining decisions on constitutional law especially constitutional rights at points where it touches upon international interests. This does

---

[40] Lauterpacht, " The Law of England," at 52. See also Westlake, "International Law," at 14; West Rand Central Gold Mining Co. Ltd v. R [1905] 2 K.B. 391 (per Lord Alverstone C.J.); Chung Chi Cheung v. R [1939] A.C. 160 (per Lord Atkin).

[41] Brownlie, *Principles*, at 43; Collier, "The Law of England," at 935; Cunningham, "The European Convention," at 547; Trendtex Trading Corporation v. Central Bank of Nigeria [1977] 1 Q.B. 529 (CA); International Tin Council Appeals v. R [1989] 3 W.L.R. 969 (HL).

not demonstrate the position the courts take on any question of international law. It clearly shows that Botswana courts have not exhibited a positive approach towards international law in general. Thus a firm and solid judicial internalisation of the automatic incorporation principle in Botswana has not yet been established.

Limitations of the Monist Theory

Legislation As under the pre-existing inherited municipal law of Botswana, the present legal order of Botswana recognises that an act of parliament, or rather legislative sovereignty may operate to exclude the direct application of customary international law (including customary international human rights law) in municipal law. This exception was confirmed by Justice Gyeke-Dako in the fore-discussed *Agnes Bojang v. The State* where he noted that even assuming that the right to legal representation is part of customary international law, it does not automatically form part of the municipal law of Botswana because it may be excluded by legislation. Thus although Botswana courts are enjoined to directly apply customary international human rights law as part of municipal law, they are nevertheless bound to respect acts of parliament which derogate from such norms. Although the Court was not explicit, the exception applies to legislation that is enacted subsequent, but not earlier in date, to the customary rule in question.

The question that arises in the light of the authority of parliament to exclude the automatic operation of customary international human rights law in municipal law is, does it mean that national law is supreme to international law, at least in Botswana national law? This question is indeed important because by qualifying the incorporation principle with the will of parliament, it implies a cautious approach and a moderate submission to the will of the international normative regime. This may also connote an implied opposition to international law. Moreover, this ranking may have the negative effects of lessening the effectiveness of international law in national law. On the other hand, an unqualified domestic application of customary international law is not a preferable option. Rules of customary international law need not be left to operate unregulated in domestic law.

Significantly, however, despite the limitation on the internal operation of customary international human rights law by the will of the legislature, in practice parliament respects and observes Botswana's international obligations. Domestic courts try as much as is practicably possible to reconcile domestic legislation with a particular rule in question in order to ensure that the international obligation of Botswana is fulfilled. This was emphasised in *Attorney General of Botswana v. Unity Dow*. Justice Aguda noted that he was:

> bound to accept the position that this country will not deliberately enact laws in contravention of its international undertakings... The courts must interpret domestic statutory laws in a way as is compatible with the State's international responsibility.[42]

It effectively means that if legislation is explicitly clear and unambiguous that the legislature wanted to disregard customary international law Botswana courts have no choice but to apply the legislation. They would not want to substitute legislative act with their own will.

Stare decisis rule As in Zimbabwe, the independence municipal law of Botswana recognises that the *stare decisis* rule, or rather the doctrine of judicial precedent can exclude the direct domestic application of customary international human rights law. In applying customary international law as part of municipal law Botswana courts are obliged to have regard to the doctrine of *stare decisis*. Although this doctrine has not as yet received any express judicial endorsement, at least in relation to the automatic incorporation principle, there is no doubt that on the basis of the inherited Roman-Dutch common law approach, Botswana courts will be more readily inclined to follow decisions of other higher courts. This notwithstanding the fact that in so doing they will be limiting the direct application of international human rights law in municipal law.

It is, however, submitted that Botswana courts should not rigidly apply the *stare decisis* limitation in such a way that the effectiveness and role of international human rights law in municipal law of Botswana is lessened. They should limit its application especially in human rights related cases in order to afford individuals maximum protection in fundamental justice.

---

[42]   (1992) L.R.C. (Const) 623 at 647.

Justiciability The principle of justiciability has also not been judicially confirmed in municipal law of Botswana. However, as in Zimbabwe, the automatic applicability of customary international human rights law in municipal law may be excluded by the principle of justiciability. As a common law country, Botswana courts are bound by statements from the executive even where such statements are in conflict with an established rule of customary international human rights law. Where, for instance, there is a matter which falls within the prerogatives of the executive such as whether a particular conduct concerns national security, the courts would have to follow the executive statement. The courts would be excluded from making a determination with respect to such matter.

The rationale for this principle is to ensure that courts do not hinder the executive in the performance of its function. In this regard the executive has the responsibility of ensuring that judicial decisions conform to international law. But at the same time, the rule seeks to maintain a desirable harmony between the courts and the executive branch of government.[43] However, as argued above in relation to Zimbabwe, it is contended that the exception should not be applied rigidly as to limit the protection of the fundamental human rights and interests of individuals. Botswana courts should strictly construe the executive discretion especially where they impinge upon individual human rights and liberties.

Treaties

The legal framework

An attempt, albeit inconclusively, to assign international agreements a place and role in municipal law of Botswana has been made in the General Provisions and Interpretation Act of 1984 (hereafter the Interpretation Act).[44] The Act provides:

---

[43] Zander, "The Act of State Doctrine," at 834; Sanders, "Customary International Law," at 149.

[44] Laws of Botswana, vol. 1, Cap. 01:01, 1984.

For the purposes of ensuring that which an enactment was made to correct and as an aid to the construction of an enactment a court may have regard to any *relevant international treaty, agreement or convention* and to any papers laid before the National Assembly in reference to the enactment or to its subject matter, but not to the debates in the Assembly.[45]

The Interpretation Act authorises courts in Botswana to construe domestic legislation and law in general by reference to relevant international treaties, agreements or conventions. This Act serves as a basis for invoking international conventions in any sphere of international law to interpret and ascertain the meaning of ordinary domestic legislation. Moreover, the Interpretation Act can also be used to interpret constitutional provisions including those clauses dealing with fundamental human rights norms.[46] Thus the domestic law of Botswana empowers the judiciary to have regard to rules of international law embodied in treaties (including human rights treaties) in discharging their role of interpreting ordinary domestic law and the Constitution.

It is worth stressing that, although Section 24(1) of the Interpretation Act authorises Botswana courts to construe national law by reference to international agreements, it clearly does not of itself make international agreements part of municipal law. It only means that, under certain circumstances, international conventions may be used to construe and ascertain the meaning of municipal law where that law is uncertain, unreasonable and vague or unclear in order to fill in the gaps. Thus according to the monist-dualist debate, the Act does not make international agreements part of Botswana municipal law.

It essentially means that the legal position of treaties in Botswana continues to be governed by the dualist theory which Botswana inherited from the United Kingdom through the Roman-

---

[45] Ibid., Section 24(1) [emphasis supplied].

[46] The Constitution of Botswana, Laws of Botswana, Chapter 01, Section 127(3). This clause provides that the General Provisions and Interpretation Act shall apply, with the necessary adaptations, for the purpose of interpreting the Constitution. For a discussion of the General Provisions and Interpretation Act, see Attorney General of Botswana v. Unity Dow [1992] L.R.C. (Const) 623 at 634-5 (per Justice Amissah).

Dutch common law reception instrument. According to classical dualist theory, treaties, as a general, require legislation to have a role in, and be part of, domestic law.[47] They require a specific act of legislative translation in order to benefit individuals and be invoked and relied upon by national institutions particularly the courts in municipal law.

Botswana Courts and the Dualist Theory

There have been very few cases in post-colonial Botswana where international conventions have been a subject of discussion before domestic courts. This has occurred mainly in relation to the human rights provisions of the Constitution. One of the first cases in which human rights conventions were actively invoked is *Unity Dow v. Attorney General of Botswana.*[48] This case deserves a detailed consideration since it is one of the few cases in Botswana municipal and constitutional legal order in which human rights treaties were invoked and referred to at some considerable length. It is also in this case that for the first time in the functioning of the judiciary of Botswana the question of the status and role of human rights treaties, and indeed treaties in general in the municipal law of Botswana, was specifically posed.

Unity Dow, a female citizen of Botswana, was married to Peter Nathan Dow on 7 March 1984, a citizen of the United States who had lived in Botswana for a period of fourteen years. By that time, Unity Dow had already had a child born out of wedlock in 1979. Subsequently, two children were born of the marriage, in 1985 and

---

[47] Cf *R v. Mngomezulu and Others* [1978] Swaz. L. R. 159. In this case Nathan C.J., as he then was, observed that OAU Resolutions recommending to member states, including Swaziland, to assist liberation organisations to prosecute liberation wars could not be invoked in courts in Swaziland because they had not been made part of the law of Swaziland by legislation.

[48] For a discussion of this case from the point of view of international human rights law, see Maluwa, T. "Changing Power Relations Between Men and Women in Southern Africa: Some Recent Legal Developments," a paper presented at a Workshop on the Transformation of Power and Culture, CAAS, University of Michigan, Ann Arbor, November 11-20, 1996. See further Coldham, "Human Rights in Botswana," at 91; Beyani, "Women's Rights," in Cook, *Human Rights of Women*, at 289-92.

1987 respectively. By virtue of Section 21 of the Constitution every person born in Botswana on or after 30 September 1966 shall become a citizen of Botswana at the date of his birth. The first child became a citizen of Botswana. Meanwhile, earlier in 1984, a new Citizenship Act had been enacted, which repealed Section 21 of the Constitution and Section 4(1) thereof provided, inter alia, that "A person born in Botswana shall be a citizen of Botswana by birth and descent if, at the time of his birth - (a) his father was a citizen of Botswana; or (b) in the case of a person born out of wedlock, his mother was a citizen of Botswana." The last two children were therefore not citizens of Botswana because their father was not a citizen of Botswana. Unity Dow applied to the High Court of Botswana for an order declaring that Section 4 of the Citizenship Act was *ultra vires* the Constitution of Botswana since it violated her fundamental rights to pass her citizenship to her children. In a wider sense, the applicant was arguing that the Citizenship Act was discriminatory against female citizens of Botswana married to foreigners.

The Court examined the Citizenship Act against the constitutional clauses on non-discrimination, Sections 3 and 15, and came to the conclusion that by preventing female citizens of Botswana married to foreigners from bequeathing their citizenship to their children, the Citizenship Act was discriminatory. It held that the Act was indeed *ultra vires* the Constitution of Botswana. The presiding judge, Horwitz, A.J., cited in support of his judgment the United Nations Declaration on the Elimination of All Forms of Discrimination Against Women of 1967, Convention on the Rights of the Child of 1989 and what he called the "OAU Convention on non-discrimination" presumably referring to the ACHPR and proceeded to observe that:

> I bear in mind that *signing a convention does not give it the power of law in Botswana.*[49]

In the Court's view, the mere fact of signing an international treaty does not give it the force of law in Botswana. In other words, signature does not *per se* make treaties part of Botswana municipal law.

---

[49] [1991] L.R.C. (Const) 574 at 586 (emphasis supplied).

On appeal to the Court of Appeal, the State argued, among other things, that the trial Court had no authority to invoke and rely upon the ACHPR and other human rights treaties and instruments because although Botswana was a party to these conventions and instruments, domestic courts could not use them because "none of them had been incorporated into domestic law by legislation."[50]

On this question, the Judge President of the Court of Appeal, Austin Amissah, accepted without hesitation that "treaties and conventions do not confer enforceable rights on individuals within the State until Parliament has legislated their provisions into the law of the land."[51] According to Justice Amissah, treaties require legislation to transform them into Botswana municipal law.

The view of Justice Amissah was shared by other members of the Court. Akinola Aguda, J. A., opined that "if an international convention, agreement, treaty, protocol or obligation has been incorporated into domestic law, there seems to me to be no problem since such convention, agreement and so on will be treated as part of the domestic law for purposes of adjudication in a domestic court."[52]

In sum, according to the Court of Appeal, international agreements do not have automatic application within Botswana municipal law. They require legislation to assign them a place and role in municipal law. This decision is significant for two major reasons. Firstly, the decision confirms a well established principle observed in the Anglo-American common law tradition and practice that international conventions are not automatically part of, and cannot affect the liberties and behaviour of private citizens unless and until they have been transmuted into municipal law.[53] It also marks a firm

---

[50]   Attorney General (Botswana) v. Unity Dow [1992] L.R.C. (Const) 623 at 654.

[51]   Ibid., at 656.

[52]   Ibid., at 673. Also, see *Agnes Bojang v. The State* Miscellaneous Criminal Case No. 6/1993 (HC) [unreported] at 14-15 (per Justice Gyeko-Dako).

[53]   For the practice under English common law, see for instance Shaw, *International Law*, at 113-17; Brownlie, *Principles*, at 47-50; Duffy, "English Law," at 585-86; Parlement Belge Case [1879] 4 PD 129. As regards practice in the United States, see Scott, "The Nature of International Law," at 852-66; Paust, "Self-executing Treaties," at 760-81; Pitman, "International Law and National Law," at 314-26; Lillich, "Domestic Courts," in Takirambudde, *Individual under African Law*, at 160-79; Id, "Role of Domestic Courts," in Hannum, *Guide*, at 228-46.

judicial affirmation that Botswana continues to adhere to the dualist approach inherited from the erstwhile colonial Power: the United Kingdom.

Second, the *Unity Dow case* is the first decision of its kind to categorically and explicitly declare that the status and role of treaties in Botswana municipal law is governed by the classical dualist theory. Subsequent judicial pronouncements have not, however, actively and vigorously acted on this theory in order to securely confirm its place in Botswana municipal law. Also, Botswana courts have not clarified the precise parameters of the dualist theory.

It is significant to note in this regard that, unlike Zimbabwe, Botswana has ratified only a few international human rights conventions. It has acceded to the International Convention on the Elimination of All Forms of Racial Discrimination of 1966, International Convention on the Elimination of All Forms of Discrimination against Women, 1979, Convention Relating to the Status of Refugees of 1951 and its 1967 Protocol, and the OAU 1969 Convention Governing Specific Aspects of Refugee Problems in Africa. It has just recently acceded to the Convention on the Rights of the Child of 1989.[54] Further, Botswana has succeeded to the Convention Relating to the Status of Stateless Persons of 1954.[55] It has also signed the ACHPR adopted at Banjul in Gambia in 1981.[56] Significantly, most of these treaties have not been enacted into law. This means that in terms of the inherited classical dualist theory, they are not part of Botswana municipal law. They can only form part of municipal law and thus confer rights and impose obligations on individuals after they have been specifically translated into national law by a statutory enactment.

---

[54] United Nations, *Multilateral Treaties Deposited with the Secretary General of the United Nations: Status at 1 December 1996*, at 95. Botswana acceded to the Convention on the Rights of the Child on 14 March 1995. For a general discussion of the implication of Botswana being a party to the Convention on the Rights of the Child on the rights of children, see Dow and Mogwe, *Children in Botswana*, at 36-53.

[55] United Nations, *Multilateral Treaties Deposited with the Secretary General of the United Nations: Status at 1 December 1996*.

[56] Reproduced in Brownlie, *Human Rights*, at 551.

Conclusion

It is evidently clear from the fore-going discussion that the status of international human rights law, conventional and customary, in the municipal legal orders of Botswana and Zimbabwe has not undergone any fundamental changes at independence. The national Constitutions of both countries do not accord international law (including international human rights law) an express and categorical position and role in municipal law. Moreover, there is no legislation specifically making international law part of municipal law of both countries.

Clearly, both countries do not lay down a firm foundation for the operation of international human rights law. Their legal systems do not stand out in law for compliance with international law. They adopt a 'closed up' approach. It is submitted that Botswana and Zimbabwe should adopt an approach that makes their municipal law international law friendly. They should have provisions in their national Constitutions directly and expressly incorporating international law in general in municipal law. Alternatively, the same objective can be achieved by ordinary legislation. A reform of this nature will not only fill in the gaps in the law but has the beneficial effect of ensuring certainty, uniformity and predictability regarding the status and function of international law in municipal law. This mechanism also ensures harmony between both legal regimes.

Attempts at clarifying the legal situation in both countries have mainly been made by Courts. Judicial practice in both countries is that, subject to acceptable exceptions of *stare decisis*, parliamentary supremacy and justiciability, existing customary international human rights law has automatic application in the national law. Court decisions have also revealed that treaties are not *per se* part of municipal law of the two countries. They require explicit legislative translation into municipal law.

Thus judicial practice reveals that the legal position of the inter-relationship between international law (including international human rights law) continues to be governed by the inherited Roman-Dutch common law approach. The pre-existing legal position has been left unaffected. Both countries still adhere to the monist theory with respect to customary international law and dualist conception in relation to treaties.

However, these theories have not been vigorously and positively, not in a positivist sense, acted upon by the national institutions especially the judiciary so as to accord them a definite place in municipal law and also to delimit their precise parameters. Both theories have been discussed, albeit implicitly, in comparatively few and isolated cases mainly dealing with human rights clauses of the constitution. National courts have not internalised these theories. Thus until and unless judicial attitude sways in favour of international law, its position in the national laws of both countries will continue to be blurred, unclear and uncertain for sometime in the future.

4 A Monist Experiment: Namibia

It has been demonstrated in chapter two that the inter-relationship between international law (including international human rights law) and pre-independence Namibian municipal law was based on the inherited Roman-Dutch common law. This position underwent fundamental changes after independence. The legal position of international law in general and international human rights law in particular in the Namibian municipal legal order is now regulated by the independence Constitution. This chapter analyses the extant position of international human rights law, customary and conventional, in Namibian municipal law. It also examines how and the extent to which the judiciary has dealt with the subject.

Automatic Incorporation

The Legal Framework: Constitutional Strategy

The extant status and role of both customary and conventional international law in municipal law of Namibia is now regulated by the 1990 Constitution. The Constitution explicitly recognises international law and its role and function in Namibian municipal law. The relevant Article 144 of the Constitution of the Republic of Namibia explicitly and unequivocally declares that:

> Unless otherwise provided by this Constitution or an Act of Parliament, the general rules of public international law and international agreements binding upon Namibia under this Constitution shall form part of the law of Namibia.

The effect of this provision is to accord both the general rules of public international law and international agreements or treaties direct and automatic application in Namibian municipal law subject to two main qualifications. First, the general rules of international law and treaties may be excluded from applying directly in municipal law by the Namibian Constitution itself. Secondly, they may be excluded by an Act of Parliament.[1] But for these two qualifications, the general rules of international law and treaties are directly incorporated into Namibian municipal law. These rules are directly enforceable by municipal institutions particularly by the courts. Likewise, individuals can directly invoke and rely on these rules in municipal legal proceedings.

The Namibian international law clause is a clear *indicia* of the proactiveness or friendliness of the Constitution to international law.[2] This approach is predicated on a variety of factors. In the first instance, the experience of a long period of apartheid colonial rule in total disregard of international law and defiance of the international community reminded the architects of the Constitution that they had to ensure that the legal system of Namibia is anchored on firm principles of international law. Moreover, the founding fathers of the Constitution felt that the intent to introduce the minimum democratic values in the territory long denied by the South African apartheid regime to the great majority of Namibian people does not stop at the national boundaries, but should also be extended to Namibia's international conduct; hence, the proclaimed adherence of the newly constituted Namibian State to the general standards of behaviour agreed upon by the vast majority of members of the international community.[3]

It is also worth-noting that in terms of Article 66(1) of the Constitution of Namibia, the common law of Namibia in force on the date of independence shall remain valid to the extent to which such

---

[1] For a detailed analysis of these exceptions, see *infra*.

[2] According to Devine, the Constitution of the Republic of Namibia of 1990 can be described as "international-law-friendly" because it incorporates a number of the provisions which create this effect. For example, see Article 143 of the Constitution concerning Namibia's succession to international agreements. See Devine, "International Law in South Africa," at 17. See also Erasmus, "The Namibian Constitution," at 93.

[3] For instance, see Preamble to the Namibian Constitution which provides that 'these rights have for so long been denied to the people of Namibia by colonialism, racism and apartheid.' See Erasmus, "The Namibian Constitution," at 81-2; Richardson, "Negotiations for Namibian Independence," at 76-120. Cf Cassese, "Modern Constitutions," at 370-71.

common law does not conflict with the Namibian Constitution or any other statutory enactment. This clause ensures continuity of legal rules from the period of South African rule to the independence period and beyond. It introduces a possibility, it is submitted, of considering the status and role of international law in Namibian municipal law on the same basis as it is under the South African Roman-Dutch common law.[4] Thus Article 66(1) complements Article 144 of the Constitution. It also reinforces the status of international law in Namibian municipal law.

Since general rules of public international law and international agreements are part of municipal law, that is, they have direct and automatic application in Namibian national law, the Namibian courts are obliged to take judicial notice of them. The Namibian courts are enjoined to have recourse to these rules as a source of national law. In essence, the Namibian Constitution has adopted a monist approach regarding the relationship between international law and Namibian national law. It is thus important to distinguish between general rules of international law and treaty rules.

General Rules of International Law

The Namibian international clause: Article 144 directly incorporates "general rules of public international law" into Namibian municipal law. It is significant to emphasise that this provision is a constitutional confirmation of the previous Roman-Dutch common law position that general rules of public international law binding upon the Republic of Namibia law have always been part of Namibian municipal law.[5]

However, the phrase "general rules of public international law" raises several fundamental questions. First, what do these general rules of public international law really entail? The reference in Article 144 to general rules of public international law should obviously refer to customary international law. The term "general" in this context means

---

[4] For a detailed discussion of Article 66(1) of the Constitution of Namibia, see Erasmus, "Namibia Constitution," at 94; Cottrell, " The Constitution of Namibia," at 56-74.

[5] Binga v. Administrator-General, South West Africa and Others 1984 (3) S.A. 949. Cf Maluwa, "Malawian Constitution of 1995," at 69.

rules widely supported and accepted by the representatively large number of States. It denotes clear and certain rules that have attracted widespread support from the international society. It effectively makes all kinds of rules of customary international law part of municipal law except those specifically and expressly excluded by the Constitution or an Act of Parliament.[6]

This interpretation has been placed on similar provisions found in other national Constitutions. The Basic Law of the German Federal Republic which provides at Article 25 that "the general rules of Public International Law are an integral part of the Federal law" is widely understood to refer only to the rules of customary international law, not the rules embodied in international treaties or agreements.[7] Similarly, Article 10, paragraph 1, of the Italian Constitution enacted in 1947 and brought into force on 1 January 1948 which provides that "The Italian legal order shall conform with the generally recognised rules of international law" has been interpreted to refer to customary international law.[8]

The second inquiry that emerges from Article 144 is whether reference to general rules of public international law implies an automatic exclusion of regional or particular rules of customary international law. This is because the rights and obligations of States in the international plane may be of a general or particular character.[9] In

---

[6] Erasmus, "The Constitution of Namibia," at 98.

[7] Rupp, "The Law of the Land," at 541; Id, "International Agreements," at 286. Vitanyi, "The German Federal Republic," at 578.

[8] Cassese, "Modern Constitutions," at 370. A similar construction has been given to the French Constitutional provision to the effect that general rules of international law are part of the French municipal law. See Preuss, "The French Constitution," at 641-69; Id, "Constitutions of the Lander," 888-99.

[9] The Asylum Case I.C.J. Reports, 1950, 266. The case, Peru and Colombia, involved a local custom among the Latin American States relating to diplomatic asylum which Colombia wanted to invoke against Peru to justify its refusal to allow a safe conduct of the rebel leader out of Peru. The Court held that such a custom was not proven because the alleged practice between the States involved was inconsistent and uncertain. The case, nonetheless, establishes that customary international law may emerge from a local custom. See generally Brownlie, *Principles*, at 4-11; Shaw, *International Law*, at 60-79; Kopelmanas, "Custom," at 127-51; Kunz, "Customary International Law," at 662-69.

this regard, this provision may be contrasted with Section 211(3) of the Constitution of Malawi which declares that, "Customary international law, unless inconsistent with this Constitution or an Act of Parliament, shall have continued application in Malawi." This clause ensures the incorporation of customary international law in Malawian municipal law in its entirety.[10]

It is submitted that, in line with the general positive attitude of the extant Namibian normative regime to international law, the local or regional customary rules, that is, rules developed in a particular region should necessarily be included in the general rules of international law. This means that local or particular custom based on a proven constant and uniform practice should be captured under Article 144.[11] Commenting on the new South African Constitution which has similarly adopted rules of customary international law binding upon the Republic of South Africa as part of the South African municipal law, Devine has argued that:

> It does not matter what kind of international customary law is under consideration, whether it be universal, general, local or particular. All kinds are in principle incorporated. There is no distinction as to the types of international law. This is a satisfactory provision.[12]

The necessity for the inclusion of regional (local) rules of international law in Article 144 serves the significant purpose of broadening the scope of this provision. It ensures that in discharging their interpretative role, courts should be free to invoke and apply customary international law in its totality. It avoids the adoption of a

---

[10] See Maluwa, "Malawian Constitution of 1995," at 70-1. The Constitution of Malawi is reprinted in Gisbert H. Flanz, ed. *Constitutions of the Countries of the World.* (Dobbs Ferry. New York: Oceana, 1995).

[11] Erasmus, "The Namibian Constitution," at 98-9. For example, it is important to note that within the Southern African regional context there is in existence the Southern African Development Community (SADC), an organisation established in 1980 by the Southern African States to regulate and co-ordinate their economic, social and other affairs in the region. Namibia acceded to this organisation on 17 August 1992 and is thus bound by the normative regional rules that are created by the organisation.

[12] Devine, "International Law in South Africa," at 12.

narrow construction of Article 144. The basic objective of this clause is to incorporate customary international law in general except that which is expressly excluded for being incompatible with the Constitution or an Act of Parliament.

The Constitution of Namibia does not, however, make all general rules of international law part of the national law. Only those rules which are "binding upon Namibia" are deemed to be part of Namibian national law. It is submitted that any determination of whether or not general rules of international law bind Namibia should meet the criteria set by international law itself. Certain rules of customary international law may not bind Namibia in international law where, for example, there is evidence that it has opted out of the rule during its formation due to its persistent objection.[13]

The Namibian Courts and Customary Rules

One of the first cases that came before the Namibian courts after the Independence Constitution was adopted in which international human rights law and implicitly the monist theory, or rather the incorporation principle emerged is *Ex parte Attorney General, Namibia: In re Corporal Punishment by Organs of State.*[14] The case involved a petition by the Attorney General to the Chief Justice of Namibia in terms of Section 15(2) of the Supreme Court Act 15 of 1990 in which he sought the consent of the Chief Justice, or such other Judge designated for the purpose by the Chief Justice, for the Supreme Court to exercise its jurisdiction to act as a Court of first instance in hearing and determining a constitutional question which the Attorney-General sought to refer to the Supreme Court under the powers vested in him by Article 87(c) read with Article 79(2) of the Namibian Constitution. The relevant question was whether corporal punishment by or on the authority of the organ of State contemplated in legislation is *per se*; or in respect of certain categories of persons; or in respect of certain

---

[13]   Brownlie, *Principles*, at 10; Kunz, "Customary International Law," at 662-69; Anglo-Norwegian Fisheries Case I.C.J. Reports, 1969, 3; Asylum Case I.C.J. Reports, 1950, 266.

[14]   1991 (3) S.A. 76 (Nm SC). Generally, see Naldi, "The Namibian Bill of Rights," at 54-6.

offences or misbehaviours; or in respect of the procedure employed during the infliction thereof in conflict with any provisions of Chapter 3 entitled "Fundamental Human Rights and Freedoms" of the Constitution of the Republic of Namibia particularly Article 8 thereof and, if so, to deal with such laws as contemplated in Article 25(1) of the Constitution. The latter clause deals with the enforcement of fundamental rights and freedoms. The material Article 8(2)(b) of the Namibian Constitution provides that "No persons shall be subject to torture or to cruel, inhuman or degrading treatment or punishment." Corporal punishment in question fell into two categories. First, legislation permitting judicial and administrative corporal punishment. Secondly, corporal punishment in schools.

In examining whether or not the institution of corporal punishment as embedded in Namibian law was repugnant to the type of treatment or punishment outlawed by the Constitution, the Court, per Mahomed, A. J. A, began by analysing Article 8(2)(b). The Court interpreted this provision disjunctively in relation to seven distinct conditions: torture, cruel treatment, cruel punishment, inhuman treatment, inhuman punishment, degrading treatment and degrading punishment, and held that the imposition of any corporal punishment by any judicial or quasi-judicial authority, or directing any corporal punishment upon any person is unlawful and in conflict with Article 8 of the Constitution of Namibia. In the process, the Court had recourse to, and relied upon, international human rights norms embodied in treaties such as the ECHR.[15] Finally, the Court held that whipping whether by organs of State or in respect of certain offences or persons is a degrading and inhuman treatment.

However, the Court did not expressly affirm that the prohibition of whipping has matured into customary international human rights law which forms part of Namibian municipal law. It also did not make any specific and express reference to Article 144 of the Namibian Constitution. It is submitted that this case presented the Court with an opportunity to positively and expressly confirm the status of customary international law in Namibian municipal law and give effect to, and define the exact parameters of, Article 144.

---

[15] 1991 (3) S.A. 75 (Nm SC) at 87 (judgment).

By contrast, specific and express reference to the Namibian international law clause and international human rights norms in general as well as the importance of these norms in Namibian municipal law was made in *Government of the Republic of Namibia and Another v. Cultura 2000 and Another.*[16] The Namibian High Court had to determine the constitutionality of domestic legislation in relation to Article 16 of the Namibian Constitution protecting the right to culture. Cultura 2000, the first respondent, and the chairman of its board of directors, the second respondent, brought an application against the appellants, the Government of the Republic of Namibia and others for an order, inter alia, declaring the State Repudiation (Cultura 2000) Act 32 of 1991 which authorised the repudiation of the loans granted to them, the respondents, by the association called the "Administration for Whites," a body established for the cultural activities of the "whites," and divesting them to the State to be unconstitutional.

The first respondent was an association incorporated under the Companies Act No. 61 of 1973 (Republic of South Africa) the main object of which was the preservation of the culture of the Afrikaans, German, Portuguese, English and other communities of European descent. In his founding affidavit, the second respondent, alleged that the main object in forming the first respondent was the maintenance, development and promotion of the culture of the west European cultural groups. In furtherance of its proclaimed objective the first respondent solicited and obtained funds from the "Administration for Whites." In March, 1989, just one year before the independence of Namibia and during the transitional period leading to such independence, the first respondent received valuable assets from the "Administration for Whites." On 28 March, 1989 it also received a donation of four million South African rands from the same authority. On the same date, a further sum of four million South African rands was paid by the same authority to the first respondent as a loan carrying interest of 1% per annum repayable in seventy six instalments half yearly. On 28 February, 1990 approximately three weeks prior to the formal independence of Namibia the four million rands donated on

---

[16]   1994 (1) S.A. 407 (Nm SC).

28 March, 1989 was converted into a loan by the then Administrator-General appointed by the South African Government.

In court the appellants argued that the payments made to the first respondent were made as a deliberate stratagem to support the operation of Cultura 2000 in order to frustrate the anticipated results of the election and "because of the apprehension of a new democratic society in which privilege on a racial basis would not be permitted." They further argued that the funds were allocated in pursuance of a policy of compulsory, pseudo-ethnic and racial classification. They argued, therefore, that it was perfectly in order for the Namibian Parliament to pass legislation (the State Repudiation (Cultura 2000) Act 32 of 1991) repudiating the loans and divesting them to the government.

In holding that the State Repudiation (Cultura 2000) Act 32 of 1991 violated the respondents cultural rights and was as such unconstitutional, the Namibian High Court made the following remark concerning Article 144 and particularly general rules of international human rights law:

> It is manifest that the constitutional jurisprudence of a free and independent Namibia is premised on the values of a broad and universalist human rights culture which has began to emerge in substantial areas of the world in recent times. Article 144 of the Constitution sought to give expression to the intention of the Constitution to make Namibia part of the international community.[17]

This remark confirms the significance of universal human rights norms in Namibian municipal law. The pronouncement represents a firm judicial recognition that universal human rights norms and values are part of Namibia national law. This means that, as a member of the international community, Namibia should abide by these norms. Most importantly, the pronouncement underlines the fact that the effect of the Namibian international law clause is to make these norms part of the national law. It creates unity between these norms and Namibian legal order. The pronouncement clearly demonstrates that, in line with the classical monist theory, the Namibian courts have begun to explicitly act upon the international law clause of the

---

[17] Ibid., at 412.

Namibian Constitution. This provision provides a platform for the courts to give life, value and substance to the automatic incorporation of customary international law.

It is submitted, however, that a more and regular judicial activity is necessary if these norms are to be firmly secured and Article 144 given substantial effect to in Namibian municipal law in so far as it domestically incorporates customary international law.

International Agreements

According to Article 144 of the Constitution of Namibia "international agreements binding upon Namibia.. shall form part of the law of Namibia." This provision assigns all international treaties that are binding upon Namibia automatic operation in Namibian domestic law. It effectively means that national institutions and courts in particular can directly apply and enforce international treaties that are binding on Namibia if they establish subjective rights and duties for the individual without having been translated into municipal law by legislative and other mechanisms to the same effect. It similarly means that such treaties can be directly relied upon by individuals before national courts and other related institutions.

The provision, however, raises two main questions. First, when do treaties become binding on Namibia? Secondly, assuming a treaty becomes binding on Namibia, at what stage does it become part of Namibian municipal law? These questions require Article 144 to be reconciled with other provisions of the Constitution especially those concerning Namibia's participation in international agreements.

As regards the first question, for a treaty to become binding on Namibia, that is, at international level between Namibia and other states, it would have to comply with the requirements laid down in the Namibian law particularly the Constitution. Article 32(3)(e) of the Constitution empowers the President of Namibia to "negotiate and sign international agreements, and to delegate such power." The meaning of this provision is not entirely clear. Read in isolation, it conveys the impression that the president can, following negotiation, sign treaties that enter into force upon signature and bind Namibia without the approval of parliament. This, however, is not the case because according to Article 63(2)e) of the Constitution, the National Assembly of Namibia "shall agree to the ratification of or accession to international agreements which have been negotiated and signed in terms of Article 32(3)(e) hereof." Thus for treaties that have been negotiated by the president or his delegate or representative in terms of Article 32(3)(e) to be binding on Namibia externally they require parliamentary approval.[18] These treaties can only be binding on Namibia internationally once they have been ratified or acceded to by the Namibian parliament. It is the Namibian parliament that expresses consent to be bound by treaties on the international plane.[19] In other words, signature of the president or his delegate alone is not sufficient for a treaty to bind Namibia externally. Additional parliamentary approval is necessary for such a treaty to bind Namibia in relation to other states which are parties to the treaty.

The second question, that is, regarding when international treaties really become part of Namibian municipal law depends upon whether a treaty enters into force upon mere signature or ratification. A treaty that enters into force upon ratification becomes part of Namibian municipal law as soon as the legislature ratifies it or expresses its consent to be bound thereby by a resolution in parliament. However, a treaty that enters into force on mere signature is not automatically part of Namibian law unless an enabling legislation is passed to enable it to become part and parcel of Namibian municipal law.[20] The signature of the president or his delegate is not enough to translate it into Namibian law. For it to be part of Namibian municipal law in terms of Article 144 it requires legislative approval in the form of an enabling legislation.

It essentially means that although the Namibian international law clause, that is, Article 144, purports to make all international treaties automatically effective in Namibian municipal law, it does not

---

[18] Mtopa, "Namibian Constitution," at 109-10; Erasmus, "Namibian Constitution," at 103.

[19] Cf the Constitution of South Africa, Section 82(1(i) which grants the South African President the power to 'negotiate and sign' international agreements. This power is however, subject to approval by parliament both in the international and constitutional senses. See the Constitution of South Africa, Section 231(2) and (3). For a detailed discussion of this provision, see Maluwa, "Malawian Constitution of 1995," at 72-3.

[20] Mtopa, "Namibian Constitution," at 111-2.

completely erode the sovereign power of the Namibian legislative authority to transform treaties. In fact, provisions similar to the one found in the Constitution of Namibia appear in constitutions of other countries. The interpretation that has been posited to these provisions is that they do not take away the sovereign power of parliament to enact treaties into municipal law.[21]

Moreover, it is submitted that the automatic application of treaties in Namibian municipal law does not apply to all sorts of treaties irrespective of the nature and purposes of the treaty(ies) involved. The role of the Namibian parliament to transform treaties, at least in relation to some categories of treaties, has not been completely withered away. The argument advanced here is not that Namibia should fall back to the pre-existing legal position in terms of which all treaties required parliamentary approval. Quite the contrary. The argument is mainly that a distinction could be made between those treaties requiring legislative incorporation and those which do not. The obvious example of the treaties requiring parliamentary approval would be those treaties affecting the liberties and duties of private citizens. Treaties of this kind would in most cases require legislation to implement them given that international treaties are largely drafted in vague and general terms. The specific details on the modes of implementation would require special legislation.[22]

Thus, although the Namibian international law clause may attract laudable commendation for making treaties a source of municipal law problems abound as to whether all treaties of a wide ranging variety should be treated as part of the law of the land. It is entirely possible that Namibia will continue to ratify and incorporate treaties notwithstanding Article 144 of the Constitution in order, for instance, to ensure democratic control of the nation's conduct of its foreign relations and also make possible the implementation of treaties. It is necessary to distinguish between those treaties which require parliamentary approval and those which do not.

In this regard, it is worth noting that even after the Namibian Constitution was adopted in 1990, Article 144 has been reinforced by

---

[21]   See Cassese, "Modern Constitutions," at 370; Preuss, "The French Constitution," at 641-69; Id, "Constitutions of the Lander," 888-99.

[22]   Maluwa, "International Human Rights Norms," at 36-7.

Namibia's participation in international conventions. Despite its relatively few years of over half a decade as an independent State, Namibia has ratified and acceded to a number of international conventions including human rights treaties both universal or general and regional. As regards universal or general human rights treaties, Namibia ratified the United Nations Charter on 23 April 1990. It has also acceded to the International Covenants of 1966.[23] The regional conventions which Namibia has ratified are the OAU Charter and the SADC Treaty.[24]

Namibia is also party to several treaties which deal with specific human rights such as the Convention on the Prevention and Punishment of the Crime of Genocide of 1948, the International Convention on the Elimination of All Forms of Racial Discrimination of 1966, the Convention on the Suppression and Punishment of the Crime of Apartheid of 1973, the Convention on the Elimination of All Forms of Discrimination against Women of 1979, the Convention against Torture and Other Cruel, Inhuman or Degrading Treatment or Punishment of 1984, the Convention on the Rights of the Child of 1989, the Optional Protocol to the International Covenant on Civil and Political Rights of 1966 and the Second Protocol to the International Covenant on Civil and Political Rights, aiming at the Abolition of the Death Penalty of 1989.[25] Moreover, Namibia has acceded to the 1951 Convention relating to the Status of Refugees.[26] Namibia has, however, not acceded to the 1967 Protocol relating to the Status of Refugees or to the 1969 OAU Convention Governing the Specific Aspects of Refugee Problems in Africa.

---

[23] Namibia acceded to both Covenants on 29 November 1991. See United Nations, *Multilateral Treaties Deposited with the Secretary General of the United Nations: Status as at 1 December 1996,* at 111.

[24] Namibia was admitted to SADC on 17 August 1990 the same date it acceded to the SADC Treaty.

[25] Generally, see United Nations, *Multilateral Treaties Deposited with the Secretary General of the United Nations: Status as at 1 December 1996.*

[26] United Nations, *Multilateral Treaties Deposited with the Secretary General of the United Nations: Status as at 1 December 1996,* at 218.

The significance of Article 144 of the Constitution of Namibia in so far as it makes international agreements (including human rights treaties) part of Namibian municipal law has received positive confirmation and reinforcement from Namibian courts. It was reinforced in *Kauesa v. Minister of Home* Affairs *and Others.*[27] Commenting on the domestic status of the ACHPR, the Supreme Court of Namibia noted that, "The Namibian Government has, as far as can be formally established recognised the African Charter in accordance with art 143 read with art 63(2)(d) of the Namibian Constitution. The provisions of the Charter have therefore become binding on Namibia and form part of the law of Namibia in accordance with art 143, as read with art 144 of the Namibian Constitution."[28] In other words, according to the Court, Namibia's ratification of the ACHPR meant that it, the ACHPR, was directly applicable in Namibian national law. It directly created rights and duties for individuals in municipal law. It could, therefore, be given domestic effect by Namibian courts.[29] Similarly, in *Government of the Republic of Namibia v. Cultura 2000 and Another*, the Namibian Supreme Court emphasised that, "Article 144 of the Constitution sought to give expression to the intention of the Constitution to make Namibia part of the international community by providing that... international agreements binding upon Namibia ... shall be part of the law of Namibia."[30]

As with customary international law, it is clear that the Namibian judiciary has started to give domestic effect to the international law clause of the Namibian Constitution in relation to international agreements. In so doing, the judiciary has affirmed its significance and role in Namibian national law. Importantly, however, this has only occurred in relatively few cases. Moreover, no judicial

---

[27] 1995 [1] S.A. 51 (Nm SC). This case is discussed below in detail in Chapter Five.

[28] Ibid., at 86.

[29] Although the Court opined that the ACHPR formed part of the Namibian municipal law, it is significant to emphasise that the Namibian parliament has yet to enact it into law.

[30] 1994 (1) S.A. 407 (Nm SC) at 412.

decision has so far attempted to critically analyse Article 144 of the Namibian Constitution in so far as it makes treaties self-operative in municipal law in order to define its scope and precise parameters.

It is submitted that the Namibian courts should play a pivotal role in domestically effectuating Article 144 of the Constitution of Namibia. This clause enables the courts and similar tribunals to enrich national law especially human rights law and jurisprudence with international standards. It provides an opportunity for the judiciary to take international normative standards into account in developing national human rights law.

Exceptions to Automatic Incorporation

According to Article 144 of the Constitution of Namibia, general rules of public international law and international agreements form part of the law of Namibia unless otherwise provided by the Constitution or Act of Parliament. Article 144 creates two main exceptions to direct and automatic application of customary and treaty rules in Namibian municipal law: constitutional supremacy and legislative sovereignty.

Constitutional Supremacy

Article 144 recognises that automatic and direct application of international law (including international human rights law), customary and conventional, in Namibian municipal law may be excluded by the Namibian Constitution itself. A clear and unambiguous clause in the Constitution of Namibia overrides, or rather limits the direct operation of international law in municipal law.[31] In *Kauesa v. Minister of Home Affairs and Others,* Justice O'linn, commenting on this exception, has aptly observed:

---

[31] This exception is almost similar to the one found in the 1996 South African Constitution, article 213(4). For the discussion of the South African provision, see Devine, "International Law in South Africa," at 11.

The specific provisions of the Constitution of Namibia, where specific and unequivocal, override provisions of international agreements which have become part of Namibian law.[32]

The conditioning of the automatic application of international law (including customary international human rights law) by the doctrine of constitutional supremacy underscores the predominant nature of the Constitution of Namibia. It further underlines the significance attached by the Namibian people to the Constitution as a compact that enshrines their goals and aspirations.

However, the Constitution does not provide guidelines on how it or a provision therein may exclude the operation of customary and treaty rules in Namibian municipal law. This means that all sorts of possible situations may be invoked to exclude the operation of customary international law and treaties in Namibian municipal law on the basis that the Constitution provides otherwise. For instance, if an international agreement were in conflict with the Constitution itself or a clause in the Constitution, then the treaty in question will not form part of municipal law. Thus if a treaty duly entered into or executed by the relevant executive authority and confirmed by the Namibian parliament conflicts with the substantive provisions of the Constitution it will be possible to challenge it in municipal courts. In other words, an argument would be advanced that since the treaty in question conflicts with some substantive clause(s) of the Constitution, it is overridden by the Constitution. This notwithstanding the fact that under international law the treaty is binding on Namibia.[33] There is an example of this situation arising from Ireland. In *Christopher McGimpsy and Michael Mcgimpsey v. Ireland and Others*[34] it was held that the treaty which was fully binding at international law could be challenged on the grounds of conflict with a substantive constitutional provision. But the Court proceeded to warn that such a challenge would not be lightly entertained by the courts since there is a

---

[32] 1995 (1) S.A. 51 (Nm HC) at 86.

[33] Devine, "International Law in South Africa, at 10.

[34] [1988] 1. R. 567.

presumption in favour of the constitutionality of treaties in particular and international law in general.

Whether or not the Constitution or provision thereof is in conflict with an international law rule will depend on each case and the issue will have to be decided by the Namibian courts.[35] Significantly, in effectuating this exception, Namibian courts will have to bear in mind the responsibility incumbent upon Namibia not to violate its international obligations especially the protection of individual human rights norms. They will have to construe Namibian law particularly a constitutional rule so as not to be in conflict with Namibia's international obligations to protect human rights and fundamental freedoms of its citizens undertaken under various human rights treaties.

Legislative Sovereignty

The new municipal legal order of Namibia also recognises that an act of parliament may operate to exclude the application of international human rights law in municipal law. According to Article 144 of the Namibian Constitution, if an Act of Parliament provides otherwise, the general rules of public international law and international agreements binding upon Namibia under this Constitution shall not form part of the law of Namibia. This provision conditions the automatic municipal application of international law (including international human rights law) on the doctrine of legislative sovereignty.

This exception existed in the pre-existing Namibian legal dispensation and was endorsed by the Namibian judiciary.[36] However, unlike in the previous Namibian law where legislative sovereignty only excluded the domestic operation of rules of customary international law, the present Namibian law has extended it also to treaty rules. Article 144 empowers Namibian parliament to pass legislation overriding the direct automatic operation of international law both

---

[35] Naldi, *Constitutional Law*, at 29; Erasmus, "Namibian Constitution," at 103; Kauesa v. Minister of Home Affairs 1994 [3] S.A. 76.

[36] It was affirmed in Binga v. Administrator- General, South West Africa, and Others 1984 (3) S.A. 949. In determining whether the League of Nations Mandate, as a treaty, formed part of the Namibia municipal law Justice Strydom noted that rules of customary international law are subject to the will of Namibian parliament. See further S v. Acheson 1991 (2) S.A. 805 (Nm HC).

customary and conventional in Namibian municipal law. Significantly, the provision does not only make the new legal position clearer but it also elevates Namibian legislative supremacy in this regard to a constitutional status.

The exclusion of automatic application of international law in municipal law by legislative sovereignty may arise where, for instance, an international law rule embodied either in a treaty or custom is inconsistent with an Act of Parliament. Under these circumstances, an Act of Parliament predominates and the operation of an international law rule in Namibian municipal law is excluded. The legislative sovereignty qualification serves to underscore the sovereignty of parliament. It signifies the supremacy of the will of the legislature within Namibian municipal legal sphere.[37]

As in Botswana and Zimbabwe, by qualifying the incorporation principle with the will of parliament, it means that the adoption of international law in Namibian municipal law is not radical but rather cautious. It is a manifestation of a moderate submission to the will of the international community. The enactment of a statute to exclude a rule of international law from operating in municipal law may in certain instances amount to an implied opposition to a rule of international law. Thus, if it is obvious that legislation may operate to exclude a rule of international law from operating in municipal law, it means that national legislation is higher in rank. The effect of this ranking would be to lessen the effectiveness of international law in national law. On the other hand, an unqualified domestic application of international law seems not to be a preferable option since that would undermine state sovereignty by allowing rules of international law to operate unsupervised in municipal law of Namibia.

It is not, however, abundantly clear whether the limitation applies to earlier or later statutes, or both. It is submitted that as regards earlier statutes which are inconsistent with a rule of international law binding on Namibia, the effect of Article 144 is to accord international law a predominant position. Statutes falling under this category are superseded by a rule of both customary and conventional international law.

---

[37] Lauterpacht, " The Law of England," at 73.

But certainly, a later unambiguous and clear statute duly passed by the Namibian parliament would override a rule of both customary and conventional international law which has become part of the law of Namibia. This is in accordance with the *lex posterior derogat priori* principle.[38] Parliament's intention to violate a rule of international law in question should be manifestly clear and unequivocal. However, the presumption that the legislature will not violate the State's obligation in international law will continue to apply. Courts will have to construe a municipal law provision in order to give domestic effect to Namibia's international legal obligations.

The rationale for this presumption is that Namibia will in any case remain bound by its international obligations irrespective of whether or not a treaty provision fails to be given effect to because of its inconsistency with municipal legislation. A State can not invoke its municipal law as a defence for inability to perform its international obligations.[39] This was specifically enunciated in the *Greco-Bulgarian "Communities"* Case in which the Permanent Court of International Justice noted that "it is a generally accepted principle of international law that in the relations between Powers who are Contracting Parties to a treaty, the provisions of municipal law cannot prevail over those of the treaty."[40]

The important point to note, however, is that the effectiveness of this exception will depend on the approach of the judiciary. In practice, domestic courts endeavour as much as is practicably possible to reconcile domestic legislation with a treaty or customary rule in question with a view to ensuring that the international obligation of the State is fulfilled.[41] The intention to repudiate a treaty must be clear and unequivocal although the courts would have to try and harmonise the

---

[38] Cunningham, "European Convention," at 537-67.

[39] Brownlie, *Principles*, at 35; Advisory Opinion on Treatment of Polish Nationals in Danzig 1932 P.C.I.J. Reports Ser A/B No 44 at 22; Vitanyi, "Article 25 of the Constitution," at 580; Erasmus, "The Namibian Constitution," at 95.

[40] (1930) P.C.I.J. Series B, No 17 at 32. See also Free Zones of Upper Savoy and the District of Gex 1932 P.C.I.J. Series A/B, No 46.

[41] Erasmus, "The Namibian Constitution, " at 95.

treaty with municipal law.[42] It is only where it is explicitly clear that parliament wanted to disregard international law that the courts have no choice but to apply legislation. They would not allow their own predilections to supersede legislative will.

It is submitted that, although these exceptions ensure that international law should not have an absolute and unregulated operation in Namibian national law, their net effect is to limit the role of international law (including international human rights law) both customary and conventional in municipal law. They weaken the effectiveness of Namibia's newly adopted monist approach to the inter-relation between international law and national law. Also, they demonstrate Namibia's cautious approach of according international law a firm place and function in its municipal law.

Conclusion

The extant Namibian legal order has fundamentally improved and enhanced the domestic status and role of international law (including international human rights law). A constitutional strategy has been adopted to directly incorporate customary and treaty rules into municipal law of Namibia. These rules do not only enjoy statute-like effect in Namibian municipal law, they have also been accorded a constitutional status. This device makes Namibian municipal law international law friendly. It enhances unity and interaction between the two legal regimes. It also makes international law more effective in municipal law. Individuals can invoke and rely directly on international norms before national institutions: national courts and other bodies with similar trappings, under acceptable limitations. There is a recognition of individuals not only as objects but also as subjects of international law capable of claiming human rights norms independently of the State of Namibia.

Thus Namibia has embraced a monist approach in its domestic treatment of both customary and treaty rules. As regards customary international law, Namibia has not altered the previous legal position. Customary international law is directly applicable in municipal law. The domestic position of treaties on the other hand has been

---

[42] Id.

fundamentally changed. Unlike in the pre-existing law where treaties were governed by traditional dualist theory, under the new 1990 legal dispensation, they are regulated by monism. This theory implies that it is not necessary to legislatively incorporate treaties into municipal law of Namibia. They are self-executing. It seeks to erode the power of parliament to transform treaties. However, if the Namibian international law clause is reconciled with other constitutional provisions especially those on the powers of the president and parliament of Namibia in relation to treaties, it is clear that treaties especially those which come into force on signature require parliamentary ratification in order to be part of the Namibian law. Moreover, Namibia will continue to ratify and incorporate certain kinds of treaties notwithstanding Article 144. Some treaties particularly human rights treaties require legislation that is sufficiently clear in order to implement them in national law. Therefore, Article 144 does not completely displace the transformation theory requiring treaties, or certain category of treaties to be internally legislated.

It also emerges from Article 144 that the automatic application of international law in Namibian law is not absolute. It can be excluded by the Constitution or statute. These are the only recognised exceptions to, and limitations upon, automatic incorporation of international law into Namibian law. They have displaced the act of state doctrine and *stare decisis* rule which, under the pre-existing law were also recognised as capable of excluding the domestic operation of customary international law. The abandonment of these exceptions raises problems especially for the judiciary and executive. First, the *stare decisis* rule is a significant aspect of any legal system especially the one with common law attributes such as Namibia. Namibian lower courts would have to follow precedent of higher courts even where their decisions are in conflict with a rule of international law especially customary international law. Similarly, there are certain matters with respect to which the executive arm of government should have a final say. A typical example is national security. However, given the proactiveness of Namibian national law to international law the courts would reasonably be expected to reconcile the international obligations of Namibia with these two rules and ensure that they effectuate the former.

It is submitted that the Namibian constitutional strategy is an attractive and most preferable mode of incorporating international law (including international human rights law) into domestic law. It ensures clarity, certainty and predictability. Most significantly, as supreme law of the land, the Constitution commands universal national respect. Moreover, as a social compact, it would not be easily disregarded and whimsically tampered with in order to reduce the effectiveness of international law in municipal law.

It is, however, important to note that Namibian courts have yet to reinforce the significance of Article 144 in Namibian law. This clause in particular and international law, customary and conventional, in general have been discussed in comparatively few and isolated cases. They have only been referred to incidentally in cases dealing with the interpretation of the human rights provisions of the constitution. Thus Namibian courts have not internalised the Namibian monist theory. It is submitted that municipal courts should adopt a positive and proactive attitude towards international law generally so as to accord it a firm ground in municipal law. This approach further gives additional impetus and force to the newly adopted Namibia's monist theory.

Part IV:
Post-Independence Practice

5 Namibia: Monism Compromised

It has been demonstrated in chapter four that Namibia's post independence legal order has embraced a monist theory on the relationship between international law and national law. This chapter examines the extent to which this theory has been observed in the post-independence legal dispensation in the enforcement of human rights norms. The human rights norms embodied in a constitutionally entrenched Bill of Rights are juxtaposed with similar norms in major international human rights instruments in order to examine whether, in line with the monist theory, the national human rights norms reflect international standards for the protection of such norms.

In the process, the study examines the extent, if any, to which the Namibian judiciary has domestically effectuated the monist theory when dealing with human rights issues particularly by having recourse to international human rights law. The analysis concentrates on those human rights norms where the theory has, explicitly or implicitly, arisen and demonstrates that in actual practice the monist theory has been compromised. The emphasis is not so much on Namibia's compliance with or implementation of international human rights law. Rather, it is on the process of translating this law into municipal law of Namibia.

Limitations on the Monist Theory

The Right to Life

The right to life is fully entrenched in international law. Article 3 of the UDHR guarantees everyone the right to life. Under Article 6 of the ICCPR, every human being has the inherent right to life. These clauses are analogous to, and widened by, Article 4 of the ACHPR. According to this clause, human beings are inviolable and entitled to respect for their life. These instruments recognise the right to life as inherent in human beings. It is the supreme and inviolable human right norm. It is non-derogable and should be protected at all times. Without its effective guarantee, all other human rights are devoid of meaning.[1] Further, the right to life is not a negative right targeted solely at the State. This right calls for positive measures to ensure its protection. According to Nowak, "the right to life has been deemed *jus cogens* under international law."[2]

The right to life is similarly recognised and protected in municipal law of Namibia. Article 6 of the Constitution provides that "The right to life shall be respected and protected."[3] However, unlike the international human rights instruments, this clause does not give expression to the natural-law basis of the right to life as an inherent and inalienable right. Nevertheless, as with international human rights instruments, it protects this right in mandatory terms and more positively. Moreover, Article 6 protects the right to life absolutely. It recognises this right as a non-derogable right. This article corresponds generally to international law and particularly Article 4(2) of the ICCPR.

It is, however, worth noting that in terms of the ACHPR, the right to life may be limited. Article 4 thereof provides that "..No one may be arbitrarily deprived of this right." This clause, although phrased slightly differently, resembles, in content, Article 2(1) of the ECHR which while recognising that everyone's right to life shall be respected, proceeds to declare that no one shall be deprived of life intentionally. Both instruments do not accord the right to life absolute protection. It may be limited by law provided the limitation is not arbitrary or intentional. The ACHPR does not define what amounts to arbitrary deprivation of life. This contrasts with the ECHR, which indicates instances under which life may be intentionally taken. This may occur,

---

[1] Nowak, *U.N. Covenant*, at 104-5; Ankumah, *The African Commission*, at 112-6; Dinstein, "Life, Physical Integrity, and Liberty," in Henkin, *International Bill of Rights*, at 11-28; Jacobs and White, *European Convention*, at 41-7; Barnett, *Constitutional Law*, at 381-2; Lindholt, *Universality of Human Rights*, at 95. According to Lindholt, the right to life is absolute that it cannot be subjected to any derogation even during national emergencies. *Id.*

[2] Nowak, *U.N. Covenant*, at 105.

[3] For a detailed analysis of this clause, see Naldi, *Constitutional Rights*, at 37-40; Rukoro, "Constitution," at 36-7; Diescho, *Namibian Constitution*, at 55-67.

for instance, pursuant to a sentence of the court, in self-defence, defence of property and in lawful arrest or prevention of escape of persons lawfully detained or in action lawfully taken to quell the riot or insurrection.[4] These limitations are designed to ensure legality should the right to life be threatened. They are intended to guarantee procedural fairness.

The requirement of legality in limiting the right to life has been underscored by the Human Rights Committee. According to the Committee, the right to life includes the right not to take someone's life arbitrarily. This right imposes a duty on State authorities to regulate and limit circumstances in which life may be taken away including lawlessness and in the case of life taken by law enforcement officials to ascertain the facts and to bring the culprits to justice and if need be pay compensation.[5] The duty to respect the right to life is also imposed on private individuals and groups. Commenting on the right to life clause of the ACHPR, Article 4, Umozurike has said "The respect for life calls for obligations, not just on states but on groups and individuals as well. All other rights are contingent on the right to life; one has to be alive to benefit from them."[6] Moreover, security and similar forces have a duty to respect the right to life. Thus in *Free Legal Assistance Group et al v. Zaire*[7] the African Commission on Human and People's Rights (hereafter the African Commission) held that practices such as extra-judicial executions by members of the security forces contravene Article 4 of the ACHPR.

The basic importance of the right to life in Namibia has been underlined in *S v. Tcoeib*.[8] The accused was convicted on two counts of

---

4   ECHR, Article 2(a), (b) and (c). See generally Harris, et al, *European Convention*, at 45-54; Jacobs and White, *European Convention*, at 45-7; Soering v. UK [1989] E.H.R.R 161.

5   UN Doc HRI/GEN/1, Article 6 at 5. See also Velasquez Rodreguez v. Honduras 28 ILM 291, 328 (1989); Naldi, *Constitutional Rights*, at 36; Harris, et al, *European Convention*, at 38-44. See further Ankumah, *The African Commission*, at 113.

6   Umozurike, *The African Charter*, at 34.

7   Communication No. 25/89 reported in I.H.R.R. Vol. 4 No. 1 (1997) at 92.

8   [1992] N.R. 198. See also Naldi, "Namibian Bill of Rights," at 51-2; *Id, Constitutional Rights*, at 38.

murder and sentenced to two terms of life imprisonment. He lodged an appeal to the Supreme Court of Namibia arguing, inter alia, that the sentence of life imprisonment effectively amounted to death sentence and was therefore unconstitutional. Commenting on Article 6, the Court emphasised the fact that Article 6 incorporates the basic guarantees of the right to life. This right is immutable. Significantly, the Court invoked universal human rights standards to interpret Article 6. It observed that it "must have regard to the 'contemporary norms, aspirations, expectations, sensitivities, moral standards, relevant established beliefs, social conditions, experiences and perceptions of the Namibian people as expressed in their institutions and Constitution', as well as the consensus of values or 'emerging consensus of values' in the civilised international community."[9]

It is submitted that the reasoning of the Court is sound. By utilising international human rights norms to buttress its decision in addition to national law and comparative national jurisprudence from South Africa and the United States of America, it avoided adopting a narrow approach to the interpretation of Article 6 of the Constitution. This approach is in line with Namibia's monist theory. It is authorised by Article 144 of the Constitution of Namibia. It gives additional impetus to the Court's decision.

To underscore the significance of the right to life, Namibia has abolished the death penalty in its municipal law. Article 6 provides, in part, that ".. No law may prescribe death as a competent sentence. No Court or tribunal shall have the power to impose a sentence of death upon any person. No executions shall take place in Namibia."[10] This clause is a blanket outlawing of the death penalty in Namibian legal order. As Cottrell has observed, the outlawing of the death penalty "makes Namibia very unusual in Africa."[11] In fact, Namibia is a

---

[9]   1992 N.R. 198 (Nm HC) at 312 (emphasis supplied). See also Kauesa v. Minister of Home Affairs and Others 1995 (1) S.A. 51 (Nm HC) at 95; Naldi, *Constitutional Rights*, at 31-6.

[10] Generally, see Naldi, *Constitutional Rights*, at 38-40; *Id*, "Namibian Bill of Rights," at 52; Cottrell, "Constitution of Namibia," at 71.

[11] Cottrell, "Constitution of Namibia," at 71. It is significant to point out that while the South African Constitution does not outlaw the death penalty, the Constitutional Court has declared it unconstitutional under South African law in S v. Makwanyane and Another 1995 (1) S.A. 167.

minority country within the international community in adopting the absolutist approach with respect to the abolition of the death sentence. Importantly, Namibia fulfils its obligation under the Second Optional Protocol to the ICCPR aiming at the abolition of the Death Penalty whose Article 1(1) categorically provides, "No one within the jurisdiction of a State party to the present Protocol shall be executed."[12] However, this treaty provides for an exception to the abolition of the death penalty in relation to war crimes. The death penalty is reserved for individuals who commit war crimes. In contradistinction to this convention, the Namibian Constitution is unconditional in its abolition of the death penalty. This sentence is absolutely prohibited.

Thus, by and large, Article 6 of the Constitution of Namibia, despite variation in formulation, is in line with international human rights instruments by protecting the right to life absolutely and mandatorily. It lends support to the monist theory by merely replicating international normative standards for the protection of the inalienable right to life. The difference in its formulation emphasises that the scope of this fundamental norm varies from jurisdiction to jurisdiction.

The abolition of capital punishment in Namibia has brought the penalty of life imprisonment into the foreground, albeit, with some controversy. The question has revolved around whether life imprisonment itself amounts to a death sentence? At the inception of the abolition of the death penalty in 1990 following the adoption of the Constitution of Namibia, courts decisions on the issue were inconsistent. In the fore-cited *Tcoeib case* the appellant contended that a sentence of life imprisonment was, in effect, a sentence of death hence unconstitutional according to Article 6. The High Court of Namibia held that life imprisonment was not a sentence of death as envisaged by Article 6 of the Constitution. But in *State v. Nehemia Tjijo*, the Court held that life imprisonment effectively amounted to the death sentence.[13] Notwithstanding, the Namibian courts have in recent cases imposed life imprisonment stressing that Article 6 refers only to

---

[12] This Protocol was adopted by the United Nations General Assembly on 15 December 1989. It entered into force on 11 July 1991. Reprinted in 29 ILM 1464 (1990). See also Protocol 6 to the ECHR Concerning the Abolition of the Death Penalty of 28 April 1983, Article 1. The Protocol is reproduced in Brownlie, *Basic Documents*, at 350-2.

[13] Criminal Case No. 4 /1991 (Nm HC) (unreported).

the death sentence as understood in its ordinary meaning.[14] It is submitted that this is the correct construction of Article 6. To hold otherwise would amount to a dilution of a clear and otherwise straightforward provision.

However, it is significant to observe that in most of these cases, the Court interpreted Article 6 purely on the basis of Namibian law and jurisprudence. It did not reinforce its decision by reference to the protection of the right to life in international law in line with the adopted monist theory. It is submitted that these cases presented an opportunity for the Court to invoke and use international norms on the protection of the right to life to interpret Article 6 in order to underscore the commitment of the judiciary toward Namibia's newly adopted monist theory. The utilisation of these norms also complements the international law clause, that is, Article 144 of the Constitution of Namibia.

Personal Liberty

Personal liberty is elaborated under major human rights treaties. Under Article 3 of the UDHR everyone has the right to liberty and security of persons. This article is analogous to Article 9(1) of the ICCPR. But, additionally, the ICCPR prohibits subjection of anyone to arbitrary arrest or detention or the deprivation of liberty except in accordance with the procedure established by law. The ICCPR further improves upon the UDHR by requiring that the arrested person should be informed, at the time of his arrest, of the reasons for his arrest and of the charges against him,[15] brought promptly before court and be tried within a reasonable time[16] and if the arrest is proved to be unlawful should have an enforceable right to compensation.[17] Article 9 is similar to Article 6 of the ACHPR although the latter is broadly framed and

---

[14] For instance, see S v. Hilunaye Moses Criminal Case No. 2/1992 (unreported); S v. Shikongo Criminal Case No. 23/1991 Nm HC (unreported); S v. Alexander and Another Criminal Case No. 77/1992 (unreported).

[15] ICCPR, Article 9(2).

[16] Id., Article 9(3).

[17] Id., Article 9(5).

does not spell out in greater detail the essential elements of the right to liberty. These provisions are complemented by Article 5 of the ECHR.

Similarly, personal liberty is reflected in the Constitution of Namibia. Article 7 thereof stipulates generally that "no persons shall be deprived of personal liberty except according to procedures established by law." It is amplified by Article 11 which enshrines principles of freedom from arbitrary arrest and detention in detail. According to paragraphs 2 and 4 thereof, these principles include the detainee's entitlement to be informed of the grounds of arrest in the language that he understands and the right to be brought to court within forty-eight hours of the arrest or as is reasonably possible.

Articles 7 and 11 introduce into Namibian national law the international normative standards for the protection of personal liberty. In fact, Article 11 of the Namibian Constitution corresponds more closely to the respective Articles 9 and 5 of the ICCPR and the ECHR than other instruments by providing in detail the prerequisites of personal liberty. Thus as with international instruments, Namibian protective clauses recognise an arrested or detained person's entitlement to physical liberty.[18] The safeguard applies to arrest or detention on any ground, not just in relation to criminal proceedings. For instance, in the fore-cited *Free Legal Assistance Group et al v. Zaire* the African Commission held that the indefinite detention of individuals who protested against torture was contrary to Article 6 of the ACHPR protecting the right to personal liberty. This right constitutes the most basic protection that any person arrested or detained is entitled to know the reasons, that is, the essential legal and factual grounds for his arrest. The safeguard constitutes the most important protection in a democratic society. [19]

Personal liberty was a subject of discussion by the High Court of Namibia in *Djama v. Government of the Republic of Namibia.*[20] The applicant, who had been born in Somalia but claimed to be entitled to

---

[18] This safeguard aims basically at the prevention of the deprivation of physical liberty without legal cause and without the determination of the lawfulness of the detention by a judge or court. See Naldi, "Namibian Bill of Rights," at 52-3.

[19] Harris, et al, *European Convention*, at 128-9; Nowak, *U.N. Covenant*, at 158-82; Ankumah, *The African Commission*, at 121-23; Dinstein, "Life, Physical Integrity, and Liberty," in Henkin, *International Bill of Rights*, at 128-35.

[20] 1993 (1) S.A. 387 (Nm HC).

Namibian citizenship by virtue of his father having been born in Namibia and who had entered Namibia on 29 October 1990 under the auspices of the United Nations High Commission for Refugees as a returnee, had been arrested on 31 January 1992 under Section 5 of the Admission of Persons to the Republic of Namibia Regulation Act No. 59 of 1972. He was detained for approximately two weeks pending deportation without being brought to court. He made an urgent *habeas corpus* application to the High Court of Namibia seeking his immediate release from detention. The issue was whether the detention for two weeks without being brought to court within a reasonable time violated Article 11 of the Constitution of Namibia prohibiting arbitrary arrest and detention.

The Court was thus asked to determine whether the period of detention in question was unreasonable within Article 11. Significantly, in doing so, the Court did not only rely on Namibian jurisprudence. It also invoked and utilised both universal and regional international human rights instruments. As regards the latter, Muller, A.J., noted that "The ultimate issue to be decided was whether the applicant's detention was arbitrary and whether he should be released or not. The right of liberty is a right which features in most instruments of human rights, whether regional or international. In Namibia it is embodied in the Constitution..."[21] The Court then held that two weeks detention was unreasonably long and thus contrary to Article 11 of the Constitution of Namibia. The Court also observed that to require a person to be detained until such time as the machinery of Government to facilitate his deportation was in place could not be considered reasonable.

Clearly, the international instruments referred to by the Court constituted, in part, the basis of its decision. Reference to these instruments firmly endorsed Namibia's monist theory. It underlined the significance of the international sources in the protection of the right to personal liberty in Namibian national law. However, the Court could have been more positive and specific with respect to the regional and international instruments that it was relying on in order to make it abundantly clear which instruments influenced it to hold that two weeks detention was unreasonably long.

---

[21] Ibid., at 394.

Personal liberty was also an issue in *S v. Mbahapa*.[22] The appellant was arrested on 11 July 1990 and charged with housebreaking. He was subjected to pre-trial custody. On the 17 July 1990 he escaped from prison. He was re-arrested and brought to court on 26 July 1990 on another charge of escaping from lawful custody. The housebreaking charge was withdrawn. On a charge of escaping from lawful custody, the accused averred that he had escaped to avoid assaults by his captors. The Magistrate, however, convicted and sentenced him to twelve months imprisonment. On appeal to the High Court, the appellant argued, inter alia, that at the time of his arrest he was no longer in lawful detention and custody. Therefore, his arrest was irregular and accordingly he was entitled to escape.

The Court construed Article 11(3) in order to determine whether the appellant arrest was irregular. It held that from the time he was arrested on 11 July 1990 until his escape from prison, the accused had not been in lawful custody and his escape was justified. In arriving at this conclusion, the Court relied on comparative national decisions particularly from South Africa and Zimbabwe such as *Minister of Home Affairs v. Bickle.*

It is clear that while the Court in *Djama v. Government of the Republic of Namibia,* reinforced its decision with international human rights instruments in concluding that two weeks in custody was unreasonable and hence contrary to Article 11, in *S v. Mbahapa,* no reference was made at all to international human rights law and sources in interpreting the right to personal liberty. The Court interpreted Article 11(3) mainly on national jurisprudence and comparative national decisions. It is submitted that the Court in *S v. Mbahapa* could also have easily buttressed its decision with international human rights norms in the same way as it did with respect to comparative national jurisprudence. It has a constitutional mandate to do so. This approach gives domestic effect to Namibia's monist approach to international law. It provides an additional international human rights law dimension to the decision of the Court.

---

[22] 1991 (4) S.A. 668 (Nm HC). See also Naldi, "Namibian Bill of Rights," at 52.

The immutable guarantees of a fair trial entail all the necessary safeguards and minimum acceptable standards of justice designed to afford the individual due process of law.[23] In this regard, Article 10 of the UDHR affords everyone "full equality to a fair and public hearing by an independent and impartial tribunal." Article 11(1) thereof proclaims that "everyone charged with an offence is entitled to be presumed innocent until proved guilty according to law in a public trial at which he has all the guarantees necessary for his defence." These safeguards are replicated and amplified in a detailed and an all-embracing Article 14 of the ICCPR. But, additionally, Article 14 protects the right to legal representation, to cross-examine witnesses, to speedy trial, against self-incrimination and *autrefois acquit,* and *autrefois convict.* This clause is analogous to Article 6 of the ECHR and Article 7 of the ACHPR.

At the domestic level, fair trial guarantees have been embraced by Article 12 of the Constitution of Namibia. Paragraph (1) of this clause enshrines the right to a fair and public hearing by an independent, impartial and competent court, trial within a reasonable time, the right to a public trial, presumption of innocence, the right to legal counsel and protection against *autrefois convict* and *autrefois acquit.* This clause is in line with international instruments. As with international instruments, it reveals most of the standards terms evolved for the protection of the right to a fair hearing.

The prime aim of fair trial guarantees is the protection of the individual interest in fundamental justice, legal certainty and the interest of the accused. These protections are especially crucial in a situation where an individual is already at odds with the State and totally subjected to its powers.[24]

In examining how the laudable concept of a fair trial has been or is being effectuated in practical terms in municipal law of Namibia

---

[23] Nowak, *U.N. Covenant,* at 233-73; Ankumah, *African Commission,* at 123-32; Umozurike, *The African Charter,* at 32-3. Cf Harris, "Fair Trial," at 353-78. According to Harris, fair trial guarantees have now matured into customary international law particularly in respect of the treatment of aliens. *Id.*

[24] Naldi, *Constitutional Rights,* at 61; Diescho, *Namibian Constitution,* at 59-60; *Amkumah, The African Commission,* at 123-32.

and the extent to which the judiciary has invoked and relied upon international human rights law to interpret it, it is significant to underline that this concept encapsulates a number of safeguards.

Reasonable time   Two clauses in the Constitution of Namibia specifically protect trial within a reasonable time.[25] Article 12(1)(b) thereof requires trial to take place *within a reasonable time* failing which the accused should be released. Article 11(3) demands that an arrested person should "be brought before the nearest Magistrate or other judicial officer within a period of forty-eight hours of his arrest or, if this is not reasonably possible, as soon as possible thereafter.."[26] This clause enshrines the safeguard more clearly and positively by designating a specific number of hours, forty-eight, after which a person must be brought before a Magistrate or judicial officer.

Significantly, both clauses ensure minimum delay in the determination of the legality of the arrested person. The problematic issue concerns the guiding rule in determining whether trial should take place within a reasonable time. When does a trial fall outside reasonable time to constitute a breach of Article 12(1)(b)? Moreover, what is the effect of delay in trying the accused? The international human rights instruments do not shed any light on what this concept entails. It would seem that some element of systemic delays may be expected and are acceptable. Swift justice may equally breed injustice. What is objectionable is unreasonable or inordinate delays. Whether or not the delay is unreasonable depends on the circumstances of each particular case. These circumstances were recounted in *Barker v. Wingo* to include the nature, seriousness and complexity of the case, and prejudice to the accused.[27] Moreover, some authorities suggest that

---

[25]   At international level, speedy trial is specifically protected by the ICCPR, Article, 14(3)(c); the ACHPR, Article 7(1)(d); the ECHR, 5(3)(a). Generally, see Byre and Byfield, *Commonwealth Caribbeans*, at 63-75; Harris, et al, *European Convention*, at 128-9.

[26]   Generally, see Obadina, "The Right to Speedy Trial," at 229-38; Naldi, *Constitutional Rights*, at 66-9.

[27]   407 US 514 (1972) at 519-20. See also Bell v. Director of Public Prosecutions of Jamaica and Another [1985] 2 All E.R. 585 at 591; Obadina, "The Right to speedy Trial," at 231-2.

the attitude and conduct of the criminal justice actors is also a relevant factor.[28] Reasonableness in this context is thus a vague and amorphous concept.

The issue of a speedy trial in Namibia was raised in *S v. Amujekela*.[29] The accused was convicted of contempt of court and sentenced to a term of imprisonment. The Court record indicated that before he was convicted, the case had been postponed six times while he was in prison for six months. On review by the High Court, Justice Frank noted that to allow an accused to languish away in custody, basically at the hands of the Prosecutor-General, cannot be countenanced. It is contrary to Article 12(1)(b) of the Constitution. The Court ordered that the accused be acquitted and discharged.

While it is demonstrably clear that the High Court gave substance to the Namibian protective clause on trial within a reasonable time, it is also clear that its decision was based mainly on Namibian municipal law particularly Article 12(1)(b) of the Constitution. It is, therefore, not entirely clear whether the circumstances which constitute the basis for a determination of whether delays are inordinate or not relate to objective international standards or the local conditions prevalent in Namibia. Of course, the *S v. Amujekela* case was concerned only with local conditions and obviously to insist upon the international standards where the local circumstances do not meet the international standards required may be problematic. Yet, local standards need not be used to justify failure to accord an accused constitutionally guaranteed right to a speedy trial or trial within a reasonable time.

Trial within a reasonable time was also an issue in the fore-cited *S v. Mbahapa*. One of the appellant's grounds of appeal was that following his arrest and detention on 11 July 1990 on a charge of housebreaking, he was not brought before a judicial officer within a period of forty-eight hours or as soon as reasonably possible. The Court noted that the determination of what was possible or reasonably possible had to be judged in the light of all the prevailing circumstances in any particular case, account having to be taken of such factors as the availability of a magistrate, police power, transport,

---

[28] Musoke v. Uganda (1972) E.A. 137.

[29] 1991 N.R. 303.

but certainly not of convenience of the police. Relying on comparative national decisions particularly from South Africa and Zimbabwe, the Court found that in all the circumstances the appellant could have been brought before a judicial officer as soon as possible and ordered his immediate release. However, as in *S v. Amujekela*, the Court did not also make reference to international human rights standards and sources to buttress its decision.

Independent and impartial court or tribunal   The fundamental protection of trial by an independent and impartial court or tribunal in Namibian municipal law is found in Article 12(1)(a) of the Constitution. This clause declares that "In the determination of their civil rights and obligations or any criminal charges against them, all persons shall be entitled to a fair..hearing by an independent, impartial and competent Court or Tribunal established by law."[30] The additional requirement that a tribunal should be competent implies that a tribunal should be able to take legally binding decisions.

This fundamental protection is a basic feature of the notion of natural justice. In all proceedings whether civil or criminal or whether an ordinary court or a disciplinary or other special tribunal an individual is entitled to be heard by an independent, impartial and competent court or tribunal. The protection ensures that an individual must be afforded his day in court by a fair tribunal. Thus, Article 12(1)(a) incorporates the universal notion of a hearing by an independent and impartial tribunal or court into municipal law of Namibia.

Article 12(1)(a) enshrines two main overlapping safeguards. First, judicial independence. This concept primarily means independence of the courts or tribunals in the sense of the doctrine of separation of powers. It relates essentially to the tribunals organisation and their relationship to the executive. Tribunals especially courts must be independent from the executive, the parties to the case and outside

---

[30]   At the international level, the UDHR proclaims in Article 10 that "everyone is entitled in full equality to a fair hearing by..an independent and impartial tribunal." This clause is similar to Articles 6(1) and 7(1)(d) of the ECHR and the ACHPR respectively. Both clauses are analogous to Article 14(1) of the ICCPR except that the latter further requires the tribunal to be competent. Generally, see Nowak, *U.N. Covenant*, at 244-6; Harris, et al, *European Convention*, at 230-9.

forces, and must offer procedural guarantees. They must, in practice, be free from control, undue influence or manipulation by the executive or legislature.[31] Judicial independence is the hallmark of a fair hearing.

Judicial independence is ensured under Namibian municipal law. First, the appointment of judges. Judicial appointment is governed by Article 82 of the Constitution. Under paragraph (1) thereof, all appointments of judges to the Supreme Court and the High Court are made by the President on recommendation of an independent Judicial Service Commission. According to Article 85(1) of the Constitution, the Judicial Service Commission shall comprise the Chief Justice, a judge appointed by the President, the Attorney-General and two other additional members from the legal profession. Secondly, judges are guaranteed security of tenure of sixty-five.[32] Thirdly, should it become necessary to remove the judge from office, either for misconduct or inability to discharge his/her functions, a tribunal, one member of which must be, have held the position of, a judge is appointed to investigate him/her and makes the necessary recommendation to the President.[33] The strict procedures and mechanisms ensure the independence of judges. They make the removal of judges from office difficult thereby ensuring their independence.

Article 12(1)(a) has further been fortified by Article 78(2) of the Namibian Constitution. This clause commands that "the Courts shall be independent and subject only to this Constitution and the Law of Namibia." Paragraph (3) further states that "No member of the Cabinet or the Legislature or any other person shall interfere with Judges or judicial officers in the exercise of their judicial functions, and all organs of the State shall accord such assistance as the Courts may require to protect their independence, dignity and effectiveness, subject to the terms of this Constitution or any other law." This clause places an injunction on anybody from undermining the independence of the judiciary subject only to the Constitution and the law of Namibia. It embodies a crucial and more secure safeguard.

---

[31] Naldi, *Constitutional Rights*, at 65; Harris, et al, European Convention, at 231-4. See also Engel v. The Netherlands No. 1 (1976) 1 E.H.R.R. 647; Harris, "Fair Trial," at 354-5.

[32] The Constitution of Namibia, Article 82(4).

[33] Ibid., Article 84.

Article 78(2) and (3) in particular and judicial independence in general were points of contention in *S v. Heita and Another*.[34] The accused were charged with treason. It so happened that the trial judge, Justice O'Linn, had previously been involved in a similar case in which he convicted and sentenced three other people to a term of imprisonment. The case engendered public demonstrations. The demonstrators accused the judge of being pro-SWAPO (South West Africa People's Organisation) ruling party and calling for his dismissal, resignation and even arrest. At the commencement of the proceedings in this case, the judge adjudicated, *mero motu,* on the question whether he should recuse himself from continuing with trial because he considered the accusations relevant not only to the trial, but also to the future functioning of the judiciary. According to Justice O'Linn, the campaign for his dismissal amounted to an assault on and attack, not only to his independence, dignity and effectiveness referred to in Article 78(3) of the Constitution, but also of those of his fellow judges, including the Attorney-General and the Prosecutor-General.

Relying purely on Article 78(2), Justice O'Linn unequivocally observed that the prohibition against interference with judges and judicial officers is not restricted to members of the legislature and executive. It also extends to each and every person including pressure groups. Further, according to Justice O'Linn, it is not only the independence of the judges that must be protected, but their dignity and effectiveness. Finally, the judge found no basis to recuse himself. Moreover, both the defence and the State expressed confidence in him.

It is clear that the Court gave the concept of judicial independence a broad and liberal interpretation. It gave substance to the principle of judicial independence in Namibian national law. The rationale for this sacrosanct safeguard is to ensure that judges perform effectively their onerous functions as protectors of human rights of the individual and guarantors of a fair trial.

Secondly, is the concept of impartiality. This concept entails two main sub-rules: the rule against bias (*nemo judex in causa sua*) and the right to be heard (*audi alteram partem* rule). The latter rule requires that the accused be given the opportunity of being heard. Consequently, trial *in absentia* may constitute violation of human rights if the accused is unaware that criminal proceedings against him

---

[34] 1992 (3) S.A. 785 (Nm HC).

have been initiated or sentence handed down, or if he is excluded from the proceedings. Article 12(1)(a) of the Constitution of Namibia is, however, silent on the issue of trial in *absentia*. It does not expressly protects individuals against trials *in absentia*.

The more problematic of these rules is the rule against bias. This rule dictates that the tribunal should not have an interest in the proceedings or be biased against one of the parties thereon.[35] The significance of this rule was underlined in the Lesotho case of *Elliot Mochochoko v. Regina*.[36] The accused was charged with theft by conversion. He appeared before the Magistrate who was also a District Commissioner in the District wherein the offence was committed. He made a successful application for the Magistrate to recuse himself from the case. The Court noted that the test is not actual bias. Rather, it is whether from the point of view of a reasonable person, the appellant was afforded a fair trial. It is based on the notion that justice must not only be done, but must manifestly and undoubtedly be seen to be done.

Judicial impartiality has yet to be an issue in Namibian courts especially the rule against bias. In view of the willingness of the Namibian courts to uphold human rights norms, it can reasonably be expected that they will likewise protect the impartiality of Namibian judges. The only problem is whether in doing that, the courts will seek guidance from international human rights law and sources as mandated by the law of Namibia: Article 144 of the Constitution.

Legal counsel Article 12(1)(e) of the Namibian Constitution declares that "all persons shall be afforded adequate time and facilities for the preparation and presentation of their defence, before the commencement of and during their trial, and shall be entitled to be defended by a legal practitioner of their choice."[37] In line with

---

[35] This rule has been emphasised in several English cases. See for instance R v. Sussex Justices, Ex parte McCarthy [1924] 1 K.B. 256; R v. Cambora Justices, Ex parte Pearce [1955] 1 Q.B. 41. See also Sunday Times v. United Kingdom (1979) 2 E.H.R.R. 245.

[36] (1961-62) H.C.T.L.R. 42.

[37] This right is specifically protected at the international level in the UDHR, Article 11(1); ICCPR, Article 14(3) (d); ECHR, Article 6(3)(c); ACHPR, Article 7(1)(c). Generally, see Nowak, *U.N. Covenant*, at 258-61; Harris, "Fair Trial," at 364-7.

international instruments, this clause mandatorily entitles all persons adequate time and facilities to present their defence. It is every individuals primary and unrestricted basic right to defend themselves at a trial. If they cannot represent themselves, they should be afforded legal counsel. They should choose their own counsel. They should not be compelled to be represented by legal counsel not of their choice.[38]

Several provisions in the Constitution reinforce Article 12(1)(e). According to Article 25(2) of the Constitution, aggrieved persons who claim that a fundamental right or freedom has been infringed or threatened may apply to the Ombudsman for legal assistance or advice who at his or her discretion shall grant such request. Further, according to Article 95(h), one of the principles of State Policy is the promotion of justice on the basis of equal opportunity by providing free legal aid in defined cases with due regard to the resources of the State. However, these additional safeguards have been watered down. First, provision of legal assistance or advice under Article 25(2) is the discretion of the Ombudsman. Secondly, in Article 95(h) legal assistance depends on availability of resources. The more limited the resources, the less effective is this protection. Moreover, free legal assistance remains a State policy but not a right.

The right to legal counsel is an important safeguard in the concept of a fair trial especially in criminal proceedings in the Namibian set up. The vast majority of the population is illiterate and, most significantly, they do not understand the official language of the courts which is English. This makes it all the more necessary for them to be afforded legal counsel to ensure that they receive effective legal defence. This right guarantees effective protection of the rights of the defence. Any hindrance therewith may amount to breach of this right.[39]

In practice, however, the Government of Namibia provides free legal assistance particularly for serious cases such as murder and manslaughter. In other cases, this right is limited where the accused

---

[38] However, in the interest of administration of justice, the Strasbourg organs have taken a relatively restricted view of these rights and affirmed the right of States to assign defence counsel against the will of the accused. See Nowak, *U.N. Covenant*, at 259.

[39] S v. Mwambazi 1990 N.R. 353 (Nm HC) at 355; Golder v. United Kingdom (1975) 1 E.H.R.R. 524.

cannot afford high legal fees. However, the Legal Assistance Centre, a non-Governmental Organisation based in Windhoek, whose responsibility involves, inter alia, human rights education assists most individuals who cannot afford lawyers' fees. It too operates under severe financial constraints.

The issue that has pre-occupied Namibian judiciary is whether the courts have a general duty to inform the accused of the right to legal representation. This was the sticking point in the fore-cited *S v. Mbahapa* case where the appellant, who was arraigned before a Magistrate Court on housebreaking and escape from lawful custody charges, complained, inter alia, that he had not been afforded a fair hearing because the presiding Magistrate failed to apprise him of his right to legal counsel. He argued that the right was meaningless if he was unaware of its existence. The question, therefore, turned on whether the Magistrate was duty bound to inform the accused of his right to legal representation.

The High Court of Namibia examined the effect of Article 12(1)(e) on unrepresented accused. It noted that in every case where the accused is unrepresented the magistrate must inform him of his right to be legally represented. However, the Court further observed that failure to inform the accused of this right does not necessarily amount to failure of justice which results in nullification of the proceedings. It depends on the facts of each case and the accused's own knowledge of his right. After citing with approval a quotation from the South African decision in *S v. Mabaso and Another* on the same issue, the Court, per Hannah, A.J., said, "The logic in this passage seems to me unassailable. If an accused knows that he has a right to be legally represented but chooses not to be, what possible failure of justice can occur if the presiding Magistrate fails to tell him what he already knows..."[40] The Court found that failure to inform the accused of his right to legal counsel occasioned him no prejudice and decided not to interfere with the conviction on this ground. However, the Court did not state how the authorities are to determine the accused's knowledge of this right, the standard of such a determination and whether such a determination should take account of, inter alia, international human rights law. In fact, no reference was made at all to

---

[40]   1991 (4) S.A. 668 (Nm HC) at 672.

international human rights law notwithstanding the fact that Article 144 of the Constitution of Namibia enjoins the Court to have recourse to this law.

The duty of the presiding Magistrate to inform individuals charged with a criminal offence of their right to legal counsel was also an issue in *S v. Mwambazi*.[41] The appellant was charged with fraud. The presiding Magistrate convicted and sentenced him for twelve months imprisonment. One of the grounds of appeal was that the appellant had not been informed of the right to legal representation. The Court, per Levy, J., held that the Magistrate was duty bound to inform the accused of his right to legal representation especially where the charge against him is serious. Failure to do so amounted to an irregularity which vitiated the proceedings. The Court quashed the conviction and set aside the sentence.

It is submitted that the reasoning of the court in both cases is indeed sound. The court is under a legal obligation to inform the accused of the right to legal representation especially where he/she is unrepresented and is facing a serious charge. This facility ensures that the accused is accorded an effective legal defence. However, as in *S v. Mbahapa* case, the Court in *S v. Mwambazi* did not buttress its reasoning with international human rights norms and sources. It based its decision mainly on Article 12(1)(e) of the Constitution, national jurisprudence and comparative national judicial pronouncements.

Public trial The right to a public trial is recognised and protected by Article 12(1)(a) of the Constitution of Namibia.[42] This clause provides that "..all persons shall be entitled to a fair and public hearing.." This protection is broad enough to cover the conduct of proceedings and the announcements of decisions in public. According to the European Court of Human Rights (hereafter ECtHR) the right to a public trial also implies a right to oral hearing at the trial court level.[43]

---

[41]   1990 N.R. 353 (Nm HC).

[42]   Cf the UDHR, Article 10; ICCPR, Article 14(1); ECHR, Article 6(1); ACHPR, Article 7. See further Harris, "Fair Trial," at 357-61; Nowak, *U.N Covenant*, at 247-53.

[43]   Fredin v. Sweden (1991) 13 E.H.R.R. 784.

In line with international human rights instruments, the right to a public hearing may, however, be limited, where, for instance, it is waived by the applicant provided the waiver is done in an unequivocal manner and there is no important public interest consideration calling for the public to be present.[44] Further, under Namibian municipal law, as with international instruments, the press and public may be excluded from all or part of the trial in the interest of morals, public order or national security or where publicity would prejudice the interest of justice or if necessary in a democratic society.[45] Moreover, under Article 12(1)(c) of the Namibian Constitution the right may be excluded to protect "juvenile persons." This restriction is meant to protect the welfare of vulnerable young persons. Generally, these limitations are reasonable for the protection of the society at large. They do not diverge from international human rights standards. They serve a significant societal interest.

The concept of public trial arose in *Vaatz v. Law Society of Namibia*.[46] The applicant, a legal practitioner, was accused by the Law Society of Namibia with unprofessional conduct in that she had published an article in the Namibian newspapers soliciting for clients. The Law Society instituted disciplinary proceedings against her in terms of sections 71 and 72 of the Attorneys Act of Namibia. The proceedings were conducted *in camera*. The issue was whether the decision of the Council of the Namibian Law Society to conduct a disciplinary hearing *in camera* contravened Article 12(1)(a) of the Namibian Constitution guaranteeing a public trial.

Relying on the South African decision in *Hassim v. Incorporated Law Society of Natal,* the High Court of Namibia interpreted the right to a public hearing narrowly and restrictively, and held that this right envisages only criminal, but not disciplinary, proceedings. In the Court's view, the proceedings in question were not

---

[44] Hakansson v. Sweden (1991) 13 E.H.R.R. 1. A waiver has been criticised especially where the applicant fails to ask for public hearing before a court that by law conducted its proceedings in private because it requires the applicant to take the initiative to require the application of the exception to the rule requiring a public hearing. See Harris, et al, *European Convention*, at 220.

[45] The Constitution of Namibia, Article 12(1)(a).

[46] 1991 (3) S.A. 563 (Nm HC). See further Naldi, *Constitutional Rights*, at 66.

criminal and could appropriately be conducted *in camera*. This notwithstanding the fact that the Court referred to ECHR. It noted that "Article 12 is similar to art 6(1) of ...the European Convention for the Protection of Human Rights and Fundamental Freedoms (Rome, 4 November 1950) and was probably inspired thereby."[47] It is contended that in line with Namibia's monist approach, the Court should have seized the golden opportunity and utilised this convention to interpret Article 12 broadly and liberally to include disciplinary proceedings. This approach would also be in line with the human rights spirit of the Constitution of Namibia. It enables the court to rely on international human rights standards to reinforce the protection of the right to a public trial at the national level.

It is further submitted that the narrow approach adopted by the Court has the adverse effect of limiting the effectiveness of the right to a public trial in national law of Namibia. It is significant that proceedings including disciplinary hearings should be held in public. Public trial guarantee contributes to the maintenance of public confidence in the judiciary and indeed disciplinary tribunals. It ensures protection of litigants from secret administration of justice with no public scrutiny.

From the fore-going, it is evidently clear that except for minor differences in form, the substantive content of Namibia's fair trial clause reflects international human rights standards. It recognises the main international standards embodied in due process guarantees such as everyone's right to speedy trial, an independent and impartial tribunal or court, public trial, trial in the language understood by the accused and legal counsel. The Namibian clause incorporates these principles into Namibian municipal law and gives effect to Namibia's monist approach to the interaction between international law and municipal law. However, it is also evident that the Namibian courts have not correspondingly given effect to this theory when enforcing fair trial safeguards embodied in the Constitution. They have enforced these guarantees mainly and narrowly on the basis of Namibian municipal law. The Namibian courts have had recourse to Article 144 and human rights treaties and instruments in particular and international law in general only in few cases. This attitude has reduced

---

[47] 1991 (3) S.A. 563 at 571.

the practical usefulness of international norms in the enforcement of fair trial guarantees in Namibian municipal law. It has compromised Namibia's monist approach to international law.

Torture and Inhuman or Degrading Punishment or Treatment

The basic safeguard against torture and inhuman or degrading punishment or treatment relates to the protection of the physical and spiritual dignity of the individual. These practices occupy a prominent position in international law. The prominence of these practices in international law is underscored by the fact that not only have they been made non-derogable in the universal and regional conventions and instruments, but they also constitute customary international law.[48] Article 5 of the UDHR categorically proclaims that "no one shall be subjected to torture, or cruel and inhuman treatment or punishment." A comparable prohibition is entrenched in Article 7 of the ICCPR, which, additionally, prohibits subjection of anyone without his free consent to medical or scientific experimentation. Similar directive proscriptions appear respectively in Articles 3 and 5 of the ECHR and the ACHPR. Additionally, the latter prohibits generally all forms of exploitation and degradation of man. The realisation that these prohibitions are systematically practised globally has led to their specific outlaw by the Convention against Torture and Other Cruel, Inhuman or Degrading Treatment or Punishment of 1984 (hereafter the Torture Convention)[49] and the European Convention for the Prevention of Torture and Inhuman or Degrading Treatment or Punishment of 1987.[50]

Whether or not a particular practice falls within any of these proscribed conducts depends upon each case and certainly on the degree and intensity of the suffering inflicted. The severest of these practices is torture. As was enunciated in *Ireland v. United Kingdom*[51] torture amounts to suffering of a particularly intense and cruel nature.

---

[48] See for instance, Nowak, *U.N. Covenant*, 126-41; Harris, D. J. *Cases and Materials on International Law*. 5th ed. (London: Sweet and Maxwell, 1998), at 728; Harris, et al, *European Convention*, at 55-61; Umozurike, *The African Charter*, at 30-1.

[49] ILM 23 (1985) 1027. This Convention entered into force on 26 June 1987.

[50] This Convention entered into force on 1 February 1989.

[51] (1978) 2 E.H.R.R. 25.

Similarly, these practices are totally outlawed in municipal law of Namibia. Article 8(2)(b) of the Constitution of Namibia provides that "No persons shall be subject to torture or to cruel, inhuman or degrading treatment or punishment." In *Ex parte Attorney-General, Namibia: In re Corporal Punishment by Organs of State*[52] it was held that, read disjunctively, Article 8(2)(b) outlaws seven distinct conditions: torture; cruel treatment; cruel punishment; inhuman treatment; inhuman punishment; degrading treatment and degrading punishment. As in major international human rights instruments, the Namibian clause outlaws these practices in mandatory terms and without exceptions. They are non-derogable even in war times or state of emergencies. Namibia's obligation to protect these practices is absolute and unqualified. Thus, Article 8(2)(b) incorporates international standards on prohibition against torture and other related practices into municipal law of Namibia.

At the implementation stage, despite the fact there has not been any official confirmation of incidents of torture and none can reasonably be expected, there are cases of this form of treatment taking place in Namibia particularly by members of the police, security and defence forces.[53] Prime victims are persons opposed to, or suspected of being opposed to, the Government or the ruling SWAPO party or both. These include members and/or sympathisers of Namibian opposition political parties, human rights activists or persons suspected of being UNITA (National Union for the Total Independence of Angola) spies. These victims are blindfolded and beaten up for several days until they confess to being spies. One such case involved Petrus Nangolo Nampala, a member of the DTA (Democratic Turnhalle Alliance) party. He was accused of drink poisoning, arrested and detained at Ondangwa by a mob of ex-PLAN (People's Liberation Army of Namibia) fighters on 22 November 1992. According to eye-witnesses and affidavits presented in the High Court of Namibia, Nampala was tortured by, among other things, having his eyes gouged out with a

---

[52] 1991 (3) S.A. 75 (Nm SC) at 86. For an analysis of this case, see Naldi, *Constitutional Rights*, 48-51; Id, "Namibian Bill of Rights," at 45-58; Maluwa, "Malawian Constitution of 1995," at 77-8.

[53] Generally, see National Society for Human Rights, *Report*, at 7-9.

knife while he was still alive and then executed in the presence of the Namibian police. No one was arrested.[54]

These practices occur notwithstanding the fact that the government of Namibia has committed itself under the Torture Convention to prohibit their occurrences. Further, the Committee against Torture established under the Convention to monitor its observance by member states cannot receive and examine complaints by victims or persons on their behalf because Namibia has yet to declare under Article 22 of the Convention that it recognises its competence to do so. This factor limits the effect and significance of the Convention in domestic law of Namibia.

Issues of major concern which affect the implementation of protection against torture and related conducts in Namibia are whipping and life imprisonment. The question is, do these practices amount to cruel, degrading or inhuman punishment or treatment?

Whipping Whipping or corporal punishment, both judicial and non-judicial, has been a major concern in an attempt to implement prohibitions against inhuman or degrading punishment or treatment in Namibia and indeed in many parts of Africa. Significantly, this problem has arisen several times before the ECtHR and has thus been declared unlawful under the European Human Rights System.[55]

The institution of whipping in Namibia had been one of the prescribed methods of punishment under the customary judicial system. Its constitutionality in contemporary Namibian judicial system was at stake in the fore-discussed *Ex parte Attorney General: In re Corporal Punishment by Organs of the State.*[56] The question before the Supreme Court of Namibia was whether whipping by or on the authority of any organ of State contemplated in legislation was *per se*, or in respect of certain categories of persons or certain crimes, in

---

[54] Police Docket OND CR. 104/11/1992. See also National Society for Human Rights, *Report*, at 7-9; the Namibian Newspaper, Windhoek, 15 November 1992, at 1-2.

[55] Ireland v United Kingdom Ser A 25 (1978); Tyrer v United Kingdom (1978) 2 E.H.R.R 1. See generally Harris, et al, *European Convention*, at 55-89; Neff, "Human Rights in Africa," at 338-40; Nowak, *U.N. Covenant*, at 131-4; Umozurike, *The African Charter*, at 31.

[56] Naldi, *Constitutional Rights*, at 48-9; Id; "Namibian Bill of Rights," at 54-6.

violation of Article 8(2)(b) of the Constitution outlawing torture or cruel, inhuman or degrading punishment or treatment. The administration of whipping fell into two broad categories: legislation allowing judicial and administrative whipping, and whipping in schools. The Court, per Mohammed A.J.A., adopted a disjunctive interpretation of Article 8(2)(b) and noted that whether or not a particular practice falls under Article 8(2)(b) depends upon its severity. If the punishment contemplated was not of a sufficiently serious nature to amount to torture or cruel treatment, the fact that it constituted degrading punishment sufficed to render it unconstitutional. To establish a violation of this provision only needed an inquiry into whether the legislation or practice satisfied these criteria.

On the specific issue of judicial whipping of adults, the Court concluded that its seriousness makes it an inhuman and degrading treatment. As such, it is contrary to Article 8(2)(b) of the Constitution. It dehumanises adults and violates their inherent dignity. Significantly, the Court buttressed its decision by relying on similar Section 15 of the Constitution of Zimbabwe and Article 3 of the ECHR. As regards the latter, the Court said, per Mohammed A.J.A., that "The provisions of art 8(2) are not peculiar to Namibia; they articulate a temper throughout the civilised world which has manifested itself consciously since the Second World War. Exactly the same or similar articles are to be found in other instruments. (See for example art 3 of the European Convention for the Protection of Human Rights and Fundamental Freedoms...".[57] It proceeded to observe that, "...In Europe, art 3 of the European Convention for the Protection of Human Rights and Fundamental Freedoms, which is in the same terms as art 8(2)(b) of the Namibian Constitution was interpreted in the case of *Tyrer*(supra) to render unconstitutional an order by a juvenile court in the Isle of Man, sentencing the applicant 'to three strokes of the birch.' "[58]

The Court also relied on the ECtHR judgment in *Tyrer v United Kingdom*. It noted that adult whipping is "inconsistent with civilised values pertaining to the administration of justice...There is an impressive judicial consensus concerning most of these general

---

[57]   1991 (1) S.A. 75 (Nm SC) at 87.

[58]   Ibid., at 88.

objections...*Tyrer v United Kingdom* (1978) 2 EHRR 1 (paras 32 and 33 of the judgement)."[59]

The Court proceeded to emphasise that "The provisions of article 8(2)(b) of the Constitution are not peculiar to Namibia; they articulate a temper throughout the civilised world which has manifested itself consciously since the Second World War."[60] According to the Court, whether or not corporal punishment is inhuman or degrading requires an objective test regard being had to the emerging consensus of values in the civilised international community of which Namibia is part and which Namibians share.[61] These norms are not static but are a continually evolving dynamic. What may have been acceptable as a just form of punishment some decades ago may appear to be manifestly inhuman or degrading today. Yesterday's orthodoxy might appear to be today's heresy.[62] In the Court's view, Article 8(2)(b) of the Constitution must be read not in isolation but within the context of a fundamental humanistic philosophy introduced in the preamble to and woven into the manifold structures of the Constitution. Clearly, Article 3 of the ECHR, *Tyrer* case and the fact that corporal punishment is repugnant to universal civilised standards influenced, in part, the Court to outlaw adult judicial whipping.

As regards juvenile whipping, the Court held that the criteria, reasoning and basis which it, the Court, used for objecting to whipping of adults was also applicable to juveniles. It nonetheless made specific reference to *Tyrer* case in these words: "In the case of *Tyrer* (supra) the European Court of Human Rights also held that art 3 of the European Convention on Human Rights which corresponds with art 8(2)(b) of the Namibian Constitution rendered unlawful an order sentencing a juvenile to 'three strokes of the birch.'[63] According to the Court, juveniles too, as human beings, have an inherent dignity which is violated by whipping. It rejected the notion that whipping provides

---

[59]   Ibid., at 87.

[60]   Id., 87 (emphasis supplied).

[61]   Id., 86.

[62]   Id., 86-7. See also Maluwa, "International Human Rights Norms," at 42.

[63]   Ibid., at 90.

flexibility in sentencing and avoided unsuitable custodial sentences or that it did not adversely affect youth's character. For the Court, whipping is inherently demeaning.

On the problematic question of whipping in schools, the Court noted a divergence of judicial opinion on the matter.[64] It nevertheless invoked the same reasoning it adopted for abolishing whipping of adults and juveniles, and held that whipping in schools also violates Article 8(2)(b) of the Constitution. This approach underscored Namibia's undertaking under the 1989 Convention on the Rights of Child whose Articles 19(1) and 28(2) may be interpreted as forbidding whipping in schools notwithstanding that these clauses do not expressly outlaw this particular punishment.

The broad interpretation of Article 8(2)(b) adopted by the Court gives municipal effect to Namibia's obligation under international law in general and particularly the 1984 Torture Convention, as State party, to outlaw these practices. Furthermore, reliance on the international human rights conventions, in this case the ECHR, the judgment of the ECtHR in *Tyrer* case and universal human rights norms clearly and expressly demonstrates a preparedness by the Namibian judiciary to internally give effect to Namibia's monist theory. The approach reinforces and complements national human rights law with international standards.

Life imprisonment The last but not least issue is life imprisonment. The inquiry here is whether life imprisonment in itself amounts to an inhuman and degrading treatment. This issue arose in the *Tcoeib* case. Following a murder conviction and sentence of life imprisonment by the High Court of Namibia, the appellant case in the Supreme Court rested, inter alia, on the ground that life imprisonment was unconstitutional as it conflicted with Article 8(2)(b) of the Constitution prohibiting inhuman or degrading punishment or treatment. The Court noted that in resolving this issue it had to take into account contemporary norms and aspirations of the Namibian people. In the

---

[64] For instance, the ECtHR has opined that unreasonable corporal punishment in schools contravenes Article 3 of the ECHR. See Y v. United Kingdom (1992) 17 E.H.R.R. 238; Warwick v. United Kingdom Application No 947/81, 1986. Cf Costello-Roberts v. United Kingdom (1993) 19 E.H.R.R. 112. See also Naldi, *Constitutional Rights*, at 50.

absence of that inquiry, the Court took judicial notice of the fact that the Namibian people were in favour of life imprisonment in cases of extreme gravity in the absence of the availability of capital punishment. It accordingly, held that life imprisonment was not an inhuman and degrading punishment and was therefore not unconstitutional. This implies that in less extreme cases the courts may consider this form of penalty inhuman or degrading. Significantly, the Court's decision was based not only on domestic law and jurisprudence of Namibia but also on what it called "values or 'emerging consensus of values' in the civilised international community."[65] These values constituted, in part, the basis of the Court's decision.

It is abundantly clear that the Namibian clause prohibiting torture and related practices is in line with international human rights standards. Most significantly, in interpreting and enforcing this clause, the Namibian courts have not only relied on national law and jurisprudence, but have also invoked and drawn inspiration from international human rights norms and sources as authorised by Article 144 of the Constitution of Namibia. This approach has enabled the courts to integrate international human rights standards on prohibition of torture and similar conducts into Namibian municipal law. Obviously, the courts could have reached the same conclusion purely on the basis of the Constitution without invoking international human rights norms. But reliance on these norms ensures that Namibian jurisprudence is built firmly on international human rights law standards. It also underlines the significance of Article 144 in Namibian domestic law.

Non-discrimination

The principle of non-discrimination, as a dominant theme of the Western moral philosophy, is now an established legal concept in international law. It is *jus cogens*.[66] The principle finds expression in

---

[65] 1992 N.R. 198 (Nm HC) at 312 (emphasis supplied).

[66] McKean, *Equality*, at 283; Brownlie, *Principles*, at 598-601. See also the Commonwealth Secretariat, *Judicial Colloquium in Bloemfontein*, at 9-56. The Judicial Colloquium in Bloemfontein, South Africa, was a sixth gathering of commonwealth judges convened by the Commonwealth Secretariat from 3-5 September 1993 to discuss the domestic role of International Human Rights. The colloquium adopted the Bloemfontein Statement on the Domestic Application of

major international human rights instruments. In Article 1(3) of the United Nations Charter (hereafter the UN Charter) one of the purposes of the United Nations is the promotion of human rights for all without distinction as to race, sex, language, or religion.[67] This principle has been enshrined in subsequent universal and regional major human rights instruments.[68] These instruments are complimented by specialised treaties: the Convention on the Elimination of All Forms of Racial Discrimination, 1965 outlawing racial discrimination and the Convention on the Elimination of All Forms of Discrimination against Women, 1979 prohibiting any form of discrimination against women.[69] These instruments constitute the main sources and cornerstone of non-discrimination at universal, regional and specialised level.

The principle of non-discrimination also constitutes a significant component of the bulk of Namibian human rights law.[70] It is enshrined in several clauses of the Constitution. Article 10(1) of the Constitution begins by guaranteeing all persons equality before the law. Paragraph (2) thereof prohibits discrimination thus: "No persons may be discriminated against on the grounds of sex, race, colour, ethnic origin, religion, creed or social or economic status." This clause corresponds to Article 2 of the UDHR except that it additionally prohibits discrimination on economic status. It is reinforced by Article 23 of the Constitution which generally prohibits racial discrimination. Article 23 is singularly significant in Namibia if viewed against the backdrop of colonialism by the erstwhile apartheid South Africa whose laws were anchored on racial discrimination.

International Human Rights: Freedom of Expression and Non-Discrimination. See also Vierdag, *Discrimination,* at 48-82.

[67] See also the UN Charter, Articles 13(1)(b) and 55(c). Generally, see McKean, *Equality,* at 52-62; Kamminga, *Inter-state Accountability,* at 74-7; Vierdag, *Discrimination,* at 86-95.

[68] See particularly the UDHR, Articles 2 and 7; the ECHR, Article 14; the ICCPR, Articles 14(1) and 26; the ACHPR; Articles 2 and 3. See generally Naldi, *Constitutional Rights,* at 55.

[69] These conventions entered into force on 4 January 1969 and 1980 respectively.

[70] Naldi, *Constitutional Rights,* at 53-61; Id, "Namibian Bill of Rights," at 56-7; Diescho, *Namibian Constitution,* at 63.

Prohibition of any discrimination or adverse differential treatment based on economic status in Namibia is also important. It is novel in Namibian national law. This factor should be viewed within the wider context of Namibian colonial rule. It underlines the adverse economic position and conditions of the great majority of the Namibian people particularly the Black population caused by the erstwhile colonial regime. It, therefore, seeks to ensure that nobody should be discriminated against simply because he or she is poor or economically disadvantaged.

Clearly, with the exception of discrimination based on economic status, the main Namibian non-discrimination clause: Article 10 resembles similar clauses embodied in major human rights instruments. As with these instruments, the Namibian clause mandatorily prohibits broadly and variously discrimination on such grounds as race, sex, language, religion, ethnic origin, political or other opinion. In theory, this clause domestically incorporates concepts, principles and norms encapsulated in, and prohibited by, these treaties. The form and content of non-discrimination in the Namibian clause correspond to international standards. It thus domestically effectuates Namibia's monist theory.

Most importantly, Article 10(2) of the Constitution of Namibia, as with international human rights instruments, reflects an attempt to adhere to the rule of law. It enshrines the notion that every person is equally subject to the law of the land as administered by the courts. Individuals must be treated without discrimination in both civil and criminal judicial proceedings. In order to underline its commitment to uphold these principles, Namibia has ratified treaties abolishing discrimination such as the Convention on the Elimination of all Forms of Discrimination against Women, 1979 and most notably the ACHPR.

The factors of discrimination in Article 10(2) are multifaceted. Their primary objective is the protection of individuals against adverse differential treatment by any person acting privately or officially. Importantly, some of the enumerated grounds reveal special circumstances of Namibia. It is thus appropriate to examine these grounds individually particularly those which have been the subject of judicial activity.

Ethnicity and racialism Namibian municipal law in general and Article 10(2) in particular prohibits discrimination on the related grounds of ethnicity and racialism. As regards ethnicity, of the fore-cited international human rights treaties, only the ACHPR mentions ethnicity as a ground of discrimination and corresponds to Article 10(2).

Discrimination on ethnicity becomes significant for Namibia if viewed in a wider context of ethnic frontiers in Africa whose borders were arbitrarily and artificially, or rather geometrically divided during colonialism. Consequently, most countries in Africa contain different ethnic or tribal groupings within their borders. Moreover, there is a fixed hierarchy of status between the various groups and individuals within groups.[71] Thus ethnicity in many African countries is fully embedded in society and often causes intra-tribal low key conflicts which have the potential to destabilise the society. The inclusion of ethnicity as a discriminatory factor in the Constitution of Namibia is a realisation of the potential problem the phenomenon may cause. It also reflects Namibia's ethnic diversity.

As regards discrimination on the ground of race, it is submitted that it is apposite that Namibia should flatly outlaw racialism in order to express its revulsion against the practice. Racism is outlawed both under customary international law[72] and treaty law particularly the Convention on the Elimination of All Forms of Racial Discrimination, 1965 which binds Namibia as a State party. The ratification of this and other related international treaties reinforces Namibia's commitment to outlaw and deprecate, at least theoretically, the practice of racial discrimination.

To reinforce Namibia's philosophy against racism and the anti-discrimination clause, racial discrimination and the practice and theory of apartheid are specifically outlawed in Article 23(1) of the Namibian Constitution. In addition, this clause criminalises the practice and propagation of these practices.

---

[71] In Namibia, the Bushmen or San are accorded by dominant Namibian tribes or ethnic groups a markedly and overall lower status which is not expressed in any legal terms but through attitudes and beliefs. See Naldi, *Constitutional Rights*, at 55; Diescho, *Namibian Constitution*, at 90-3.

[72] South West Africa Cases 1966 I.C.J. Reports, 6 at 313-4 (dissenting view of Judge Tanaka); Barcelona Traction Case 1970 I.C.J. Reports 3; Naldi, *Constitutional Rights*, at 54-5; Mckean, *Equality*, at 264-84; Brownlie, *Principles*, at 598.

The issue of non-discrimination particularly Article 23(1) was at stake in *Kauesa v. Minister of Home Affairs*.[73] Importantly, in resolving this issue, the High Court of Namibia made eloquent reference to international human rights standards and sources particularly the ECHR, UDHR, ACHPR, ICCPR, American Convention on Human Rights (hereafter ACHR) and Convention on the Elimination of all Forms of Racial Discrimination. The applicant, a police officer, stated in a television programme that the white command structure of the Namibian police force was responsible for the corruption and all-pervading irregularities in the force. He was subjected to disciplinary action under existing police regulations. He subsequently made an application to the Namibian High Court to have the regulations declared null and void, and for an order protecting his freedom of speech and expression. One of the issues to be decided by the Court was whether the statement uttered by the applicant was discriminatory against the respondents, the white members of the police force.

In determining whether the statement was discriminatory and thus contrary to Articles 10(2) and 23(1) of the Constitution, the Court relied upon the above-cited human rights treaties and said, per O'Linn, J., that "The aforesaid international instruments recognise that the protection of the dignity of all persons, equality before the law, including the equal protection by the law, and non-discrimination are and should be the main components in societies emerging from oppression to democracy as well as those intending to maintain democracy."[74] Justice O'linn proceeded to stress that "The Namibian Courts have expressed themselves very strongly on the importance of the fundamental rights to equality and non-discrimination in the Namibian Constitution."[75] Finally, the Court held that the applicant's statement constituted a breach of the fundamental right of the

---

[73] 1995 (1) S.A. 51 (Nm HC).

[74] Ibid., at 87. It is also important to note that the Court made a specific reference to Article 144 of the Constitution which makes international law, customary and conventional, part of Namibian municipal law. It also said, referring to the ACHPR, that by formally recognising the Charter, Namibia has made its provisions part of Namibian law. Ibid., at 86.

[75] Ibid., at 87.

respondents not to be discriminated against on the basis of race. The above mentioned international human rights instruments constituted, in part, the basis of its decision.

With respect to Article 23(1) of the Constitution, the Court observed that it is a specific constitutional authority for legislation by an Act of Parliament to render criminally punishable, and to provide for punishment that will express the revulsion of the Namibian people at practices of racial discrimination and the practice or ideology of apartheid. In this regard, it is worth noting that paragraphs (2) and (3) of Article 23 provide for affirmative action, or positive discrimination legislation. Both clauses enjoin the Namibian parliament to enact legislation specifically aimed at redressing the ills and prejudices caused by racial discrimination and apartheid.

Crucially, in 1991 the Namibian parliament enacted the Racial Discrimination Prohibition (Amendment) Act, 26 of 1991 in order to give effect to Article 23 and in particular its paragraphs (2) and (3). The Act criminalises acts and practices of racial discrimination and apartheid in relation to provision of public services and amenities, and acts involving incitement of racial disharmony and victimisation. The significance of this Act not only in municipal law of Namibia but also in relation to international law has been underscored by the Namibian High Court in the fore-cited *Kauesa v. Minister of Home Affairs*. According to the Court, "When the provisions of s 11(1)(b) read with s 14 of the Racial Discrimination Prohibition (Amendment) Act, 26 of 1991(Nm) are seen in the context of ...international treaties and conventions, it can safely be said that this provision ..is..in line with the constitutions and/or penal codes of many other democratic countries and international treaties and conventions."[76] In the Court's view, the Act reflects international standards on prohibition of racial discrimination embodied, inter alia, in international human rights treaties and instruments.

However, in so far as the Act criminalises racial discrimination, it is contended that it should be construed in the light of human rights provisions of the Constitution of Namibia. It should not be applied in a way that undermines the human rights friendliness of the Constitution. As the Court observed in *Kauesa v. Minister of Home*

---

[76] Ibid., at 95.

Affairs, this Act is only a corrective measure, but not revenge; not discrimination in reverse; not the mere changing of the roles of perpetrators and victim.

The vehement condemnation of racial discrimination by the Namibian courts as not only a criminal law matter but also as offending against the Constitution was echoed in the *Government of the Republic of Namibia v. Cultura 2000*. As highlighted earlier on in this study, at stake was whether the State (Repudiation) Cultura 2000 Act 32 of 1991 violated Cultura 2000 right to culture. The Supreme Court referred briefly and cursorily to the international law clause (Article 144) of the Constitution and noted that the Constitution articulates a jurisprudential philosophy which, in express and ringing tones, repudiates legislative policies based on the criteria of race and ethnicity. It also observed that the constitutional jurisprudence of a free and independent Namibia is based on total repudiation of the policies of apartheid.[77] It is clear that the Court's approach is influenced by institutional racism under the colonial State. It is also a reflection of the Constitution's emphatic approach against racism.

Sex discrimination   Adverse differential treatment on the basis of sex in Namibia is explicitly outlawed by Article 10(2) of the Constitution. This provision has been fortified by Article 95(a) of the Constitution. The latter promotes, as State policy, legislation aimed at securing equal opportunity for women. However, these clauses do not define sex discrimination.[78] A comparison is here made with Section 8(2) of the new South African Constitution which outlaws discrimination not only on the basis of sex but also gender. It is submitted, however, that sex discrimination in Namibia should cover all sexes. But, it should be

---

[77]   1994 (1) S.A. 407 (Nm SC). For a detailed discussion of the approach of the Namibian Supreme Court to racism, Generally, see Naldi, *Constitutional Rights*, at 54-61.

[78]   By contrast, the International Convention on the Elimination of all Forms of Discrimination, Article 1(1) defines sex discrimination as any distinction, exclusion, restriction or preference which has the purpose or effect of nullifying or impairing the recognition, enjoyment or exercise on an equal footing, of human rights and fundamental freedoms of women, irrespective of marital status. See Naldi, *Constitutional Rights*, at 58; Kauesa v. Minister of Home Affairs 1995 (1) S.A. 51. (Nm HC).

136

underlined that not all sorts of different treatment are automatically outlawed on the ground of sex. Different treatment based on reasonable and objective criterion, say, in the name of positive discrimination is permissible.

Different treatment based on reasonable and objective factors is recognised by the Namibian law with respect to women particularly their equality with men. It should, in the first instance, be observed that women have traditionally been subjected to discrimination by Namibian customary law and practices. There are entire systems of customary law co-existing with official rules which discriminate against women in areas such as succession and family law, property, finance and contracts.[79] Secondly, there is a body of general legal norms and national legislation which discriminate against women and limit their equality with men. Statutory law and the inherited Roman-Dutch law have generated barriers that detrimentally affect women's social, economic and political opportunities. Legislation affecting the rights and status of women was a feature of the pre-1990 legal order.[80] In this vein, Article 18(3) of the ACHPR imposes a legal obligation on Namibia, as state party, to eliminate every discriminatory practice against women. This clause also obliges Namibia to protect the rights of women as stipulated in international declarations and conventions.

Against the backdrop of the ACHPR in particular and Namibia's pre-independence racist laws and reality generally, tremendous improvements have been made since independence to better the legal status of women. Presently, in addition to Article 23(3) of the Constitution of Namibia on affirmative action in favour of women, legislation has been enacted which ensure equality of women

---

[79] Customary law of succession does not recognise the rights of female children to succeed to their father's property on his death. Similarly, where the father dies intestate, his property devolves only upon his eldest son. In the absence of the latter, property devolves upon the younger son. This occurs even where he is survived by other children including eldest sisters. Moreover, unless the husband makes a specific bequest to his wife, she does not inherit from his estate. See Becker, "Women," in Malan, *Communal Land*, at 56-8.

[80] The pre-independence legislation which gave men more equality than women in Namibia included the Marriage Act No. 25 of 1961 and the Administration of Estates Act No. 66 of 1965. For instance, in the latter, section 72 denied a mother of an illegitimate child the right to be curator of his/her property.

with men. The most important legislation is the Married Persons Equality Act, No. 1 of 1996. Section 2 thereof abolishes the marital power of the husband over the person and property of the wife. This provision removes restrictions placed by the marital power on the capacity of the wife to enter into contracts and litigate including, but not limited to, registration of property in her own name, to bind herself as a surety, act as executrix of the deceased estate and trustee of the insolvent estate. In all these transactions, consent of the husband is not required.

Further, according to Section 5 of the Act, spouses married in community of property have equal power over the administration of the community of property, contract debts incurred by the joint estate and disposal of the assets of the joint estate. Under Section 12, the domicile of a married women is not determined only in relation to her husband's domicile. It is ascertainable by the same factors applicable to any individual capable of acquiring domicile of choice. These legislative safeguards are designed to improve the status of women in all aspects of life. They are aimed at removing discrimination against the female sector of Namibian society. They also complement and effectuate Namibia's non-discriminatory laws. Most significantly, they reinforce Namibia's monist theory.

The issue of discrimination against women arose tangentially in *S v. D and Another*.[81] The two appellants were each convicted of rape and sentenced to three years' imprisonment part of which was conditionally suspended. At stake was the cautionary rule in sexual assault cases which required the court to consider allegations of sexual assault with abundant caution despite the sex of the complainant. The Court, per Frank, J., noted that in an overwhelming majority of cases of this nature the complainants are female and in Namibian social fabric this state of affairs is hardly likely to change. In the Court's view, the so-called cautionary rule has no other purpose than to discriminate against female complainants. The Court concluded that "This rule is thus probably also contrary to art 10 of the Namibian Constitution which provides for the equality of all persons before the law regardless

---

[81]   1992 (1) S.A. 513 (Nm HC). See generally Naldi, *Constitutional Rights*, at 60.

of sex."[82] This statement is a judicial recognition that the cautionary rule in question infringes national human rights law. As a corollary, this rule is also contrary to international human rights norms.

It is demonstrably clear that the domestic enforcement of the principle of non-discrimination by the Namibian judiciary has started to take account of international human rights standards. The Namibian courts are increasingly relying on these standards to construe non-discrimination clauses of the Constitution and related laws. This approach has the beneficial effect of enriching national human rights law with international standards. It also offers the courts an opportunity to broaden the national protection system in this area of Namibian national law.

The Right to Property

The right to property is firmly protected under general international law.[83] It is also specifically recognised and protected by various international human rights instruments. Article 17(1) of the UDHR guarantees to everyone "the right to own property either alone as well as in association with others." Paragraph (2) thereof prohibits arbitrary deprivation of property. According to Article 14 of the ACHPR "the right to property shall be guaranteed." Under the European human rights system the right to property is guaranteed not in the ECHR but its First Protocol. Article 1 thereof provides that "every natural or legal person is entitled to the peaceful enjoyment of his possessions." These possessions include property rights.

A comparable Namibian clause on property rights is Article 16(1). This clause commands that "all persons shall have the right in any part of Namibia to acquire, own and dispose of all forms of immovable and movable property individually or in association with others and to bequeath their property to their heirs or legatees..." Article 16(1) articulates the individual right to property more positively. It

---

[82]   1992 (1) S.A. 513 (Nm HC) at 516. However, the Court emphasised that all depends on the nature and circumstances of the alleged offence which should be considered carefully. See also Naldi, *Constitutional Rights*, at 60.

[83]   See Harris et al, *European Convention*, at 516-38; Lindholt, *University of Human Rights* at 139-44; Ankumah, *African Commission*, at 142; Naldi, *Constitutional Rights*, at 82-5; Alfredsson, "Article 17," in Eide, *Human Rights*, at 255-62.

brings out the natural-law component of this right by protecting the right of "all persons."[84] Moreover, it mandatorily recognises the right or interests therein of all persons not only to acquire, own and dispose of property of whatever form; whether movable or immovable, but also their right to bequeath property to other individuals irrespective of the manner of acquisition. The latter aspect is not found in, and is thus an improvement on, the international human rights instruments. It is a recognition of the fact that in modern times the law must secure this right, as with all other rights, more firmly and establish a positive right of an individual to own property and bequeath it to others.

Furthermore, by protecting "all forms of immovable and movable property," Article 16(1) includes protection of traditional or community property rights of black people in Namibia in the same way that it protects the fee simple property rights of white Namibians. It protects communal lands which are held under traditional customary law.[85] Thus despite differences in articulation, the substantive content and scope of this clause reflects, by and large, international standards. It incorporates international property standards in Namibian law and provides additional protective standards.

The Namibian property clause gives the State the right to limit the acquisition of property by foreign nationals despite the fact that Article 99 of the Constitution encourages foreign investment. This clause is in line with the general rule that the ownership of property is subject to municipal law. Moreover, it serves a valid public purpose.[86]

The Namibian property clause has been supplemented by the Agricultural (Commercial) Land Reform Act.[87] This Act provides

---

[84]   Harring, "Constitution of Namibia," at 472.

[85]   Harring, "Constitution of Namibia," at 472. See also Becker "Women and Land Rights" in Malan and Hinz, *Communal land*, at 56.

[86]   Naldi, *Constitutional Rights*, at 82-4. See also Harring, "Constitution of Namibia," at 467-84.

[87]   Act No. 6/1995. According to the Preamble, the Act is meant to provide for the acquisition of agricultural land for land reform purposes and allocation of such land to Namibian citizens who do not own or otherwise have the use of any or adequate agricultural land.

necessary details for the acquisition and disposal of agricultural land. It also provides for control mechanisms of land allocation.

Property rights in general and Article 16(1) in particular were in contention in *De Roeck v. Campbell and Others*.[88] The case involved an application for a rule *nisi* for the attachment of certain immovable property, namely erf 107, Olympia Township, in Windhoek, owned by the first respondent pending the outcome of an action to be instituted by the applicant against the respondents. The question was whether or not property in question fell within the ambit of Article 16(1) of the Constitution. The Namibian High Court interpreted Article 16(1) broadly and held, per Levy, J., that Olympia Township falls within the ambit of Article 16(1). It further noted that the right to own property is a fundamental human right found in the Namibian common law and now entrenched in the Constitution. According to the Court, ownership of property includes the right to possess one's own property, to dispose of it and even to destroy it. Any person who interferes with this right has the onus to justify his or her claim. It is clear that the Court interpreted property rights broadly and liberally. The interpretation adopted by the Court is indeed appropriate. It is in line with the human rights spirit of the Namibian Constitution. It is submitted, however, that this approach should have been informed with international jurisprudence and treaty clauses on property rights in order to reinforce the Namibian right to property clause and lend support to and underscore Namibia's monist theory.

There are several crucial but controversial issues associated with the right to property. The main issues are expropriation and compensation. As a general rule, a State may expropriate or compulsorily acquire property either of its citizens or foreigners subject to payment of compensation.[89] Thus Namibia has a sovereign right to expropriate property subject to payment of compensation. Once expropriation is determined as lawful, compensation follows. Both concepts are inter-connected.

---

[88]   1990 N.R. 353 (Nm HC).

[89]   Mapp, *Iran-US Claims Tribunals*, at 170; Brownlie, *Principles*, at 531-8; Charter of Economic Rights and Duties of States, 1974, GA Res. 3281(XXIX), Article 2(2)(c). *Reprinted* in 14 ILM 251(1975). See also the ACHPR, Articles 14 and 21(2); First Protocol to ECHR, Article 1; UDHR, Article 17(2).

Expropriation Article 16(2) of the Constitution of Namibian embraces the notion of expropriation of property under certain conditions. It empowers the State or a competent body or organ authorised by law to expropriate individual property in the public interest provided the expropriation is not arbitrary or discriminatory. This clause corresponds to Article 14 of the ACHPR which also subjects property rights of individuals to encroachment by the State in the general interest of the community.

The recognition of the sovereign right of the Government of Namibia to expropriate property provided it is in the general societal or public interest is in stark accord with general international law. In the *Case Concerning Certain German Interests in Polish Upper Silesia* the Permanent Court of International Justice observed that expropriation was permissible in international law if necessary for reasons of public utility, judicial liquidation and similar measures.[90] This principle has been reiterated in the Resolution on Permanent Sovereignty Over Natural Resources of 1962.[91] It now forms part of customary international law. But the ECtHR has noted in *Sporrong and Lonnroth v. Sweden* that a fair balance should be struck in expropriating individual property between the fundamental right, interest and welfare of the individual to own and be in continued and peaceful enjoyment of his or her right to property and the obvious need of the general public interest.[92]

The need to maintain this balance arose in *Freiremar S. A. v. Prosecutor General of Namibia*.[93] The appellant was convicted for illegally fishing in Namibian territorial waters. His fishing vessel was forfeited to the State. The Court held that confiscation of the fishing

---

[90] P.C.I.J (1926), Ser A, No 7 at 22. See also Naldi, *Constitutional Rights*, at 82; Shaw, *International Law*, at 520; Hlatshwayo, "Expropriation laws in Zimbabwe," at 50; Brownlie, *Principles*, at 537-8; Mapp, *Iran-United States Claims Tribunal*, at 175. Cf the Constitution of South Africa, Section 28(3) which recognises that property may be expropriated "for public purposes only."

[91] GA Reso. 1803 (XVII), Article 4.

[92] (1984) 7 E.H.R.R. 256.

[93] Criminal Case No. 2/1994 (unreported).

vessel as a penalty for crime was permissible under international law and hence legislation authorising forfeiture was not unconstitutional. It was in the general interest of the public to forfeit such property. It is clear that the Court's decision was influenced partly by the fact that expropriation of property for public interest is recognised by international law.

The issue of expropriation of property arose in the *Cultura 2000 case.* The High Court nullified the State Repudiation (Cultura) Act, 1991 attempting to recover donations of monies and property made by the previous government to the applicant on the ground that the Act empowered the State to take property without providing just compensation. According to the High Court, the State action of recovering monies donated to the applicant amounted to expropriation of property and was therefore contrary to Article 16(2). However, on appeal, the Supreme Court took the view that Section 2(1) of the Act does not deal with expropriation. It relates to repudiatory acts of the State according to Article 140(3) of the Constitution.

In realisation of the fact that under apartheid riddled Namibia, the vast majority of the African population was dispossessed of their land through racial laws, the Namibian Government has adopted the National Land Policy (hereafter the NLP) which guarantees to every Namibian equal protection of land rights.[94] The NLP further aims at redressing the social and economic injustices inherited from the colonial period and seeks to secure and promote the interests of the poor and especially to ensure equity in access to land.[95] Consequently, the Agriculture (Commercial) Land Reform Act was enacted to achieve these aims. The Act authorises the Minister responsible for land to acquire land for public purposes and in particular to give it to the disadvantaged communities. The extent to which this law will ensure that the disadvantaged communities have access to land in fulfilment of the basic right to property will depend on the Government's commitment to implement the NLP.

Compensation   Compensation for expropriated property is a controversial aspect of the right to property. It has led countries to

---

[94]   National Land Policy, White Paper, September 1997, principle 11.

[95]   Ibid., principles 8 and 12.

design various standards of compensation to suit their own local circumstances and conditions. In Namibia, Article 16(2) of the Constitution requires that expropriation of property should be subject to payment of "just compensation." By contrast, the UDHR and the First Protocol to the ECHR neither mention compensation for deprivation of property nor indicate the standard of measurement. Compensation is only mentioned in Article 21(2) of the ACHPR. This clause diverges from the Namibian clause by declaring that dispossessed people shall have the right to "...an adequate compensation."

The traditional rule supported by Western countries is that compensation for compulsory acquisition of property should be prompt, adequate and effective.[96] This rule effectively requires full compensation. Its rationale is to compensate the owner a "going concern value" or "fair market value" whose total amount is fixed promptly but payment of which may be spread over a reasonable period provided such payment is guaranteed and allowance for interest for late payment is made and that the compensation should be freely transferable from the country paying it.[97] This standard has, however, been challenged by developing States as too rigid. They maintain that a less rigid standard of adequate compensation be adopted.[98] The standard sought by developing nations is contained in United Nations

---

[96] Brownlie, *Principles*, at 532-5; Naldi, *Constitutional Rights*, at 83; Texaco v. Libya 17 ILM 1 (1978). See also Mapp, *Iran-United States Claims Tribunals*, at 179. According to Mapp, the compensation issue arises in three different contexts. First, compensation for particular property. For this property there must be full compensation according to the traditional prompt, adequate and effective principle. Secondly, illegal expropriation for which the owner of property receives either full compensation, including consequential loss, or *restitutio in intergrum*. Thirdly, large-scale nationalisations where the affected individuals are entitled to appropriate compensation. It is with respect to the latter where opinion is divided especially between Western and developing nations. *Id*, at 176-82.

[97] Mapp, *Iran-United States Claims Tribunals*, at 177; Harris DJ *Cases and Materials on International Law*. 4th ed. (London: Sweet & Maxwell, 1991) at 543; Hlatshwayo, "Expropriation Laws," at 50; Aldrich, *Iran-United States Claims Tribunal*, at 218-76.

[98] This standard seems to have acquired some status of *de lege ferenda*. See Naldi, *Constitutional Rights*, at 83; Texaco v. Libya 17 ILM 1 (1978).

Resolution 3281 of 1974.[99] Article 2(c) thereof confirms the right of States to nationalise foreign property subject to compensation being determined solely under the domestic law of the nationalising State. However, Western nations have opposed this standard of compensation. They insist upon full compensation despite international law consensus for appropriate and adequate compensation.[100]

The opportunity to interpret and test Namibia's standard of just compensation arose in *Cultura 2000 case* where the applicants argued, inter alia, that acquisition of property made by the previous government to the applicants by the post-independence Government of Namibia without providing just compensation was contrary to Article 16(2). The Supreme Court having ruled that the government's action did not amount to expropriation meant that the issue of compensation also fell away. An opportunity was therefore missed to judicially examine what Namibia's standard of just compensation really entails and the extent to which it should reflect or be brought in line with the international standard of prompt, adequate and effective payment.

The important point, however, is that Namibia's adoption of a just standard of compensation clearly demonstrates a radical departure from the international standard of prompt, adequate and effective payment. This dichotomy reflects Namibia's own domestic conditions and historical experiences which were characterised by the fact that most Namibians were dispossessed of property especially land during colonial rule. The just standard of compensation is an attempt to ensure justice in the distribution and acquisition of property. This process demands the adoption of much lesser strict requirements of compensation assessment. In any event, international law is not against States adopting standards of compensation depicting local conditions.

The Right to Education

The right to education constitutes one of the main basic rights in international law. It is protected by several human rights treaties and instruments. Article 17(1) of the ACHPR guarantees every individual

---

[99] G.A. Res. 3281 (XXXIX), 12 December 1974. See also Mapp, *Iran-United States Claims Tribunals*, at 165.

[100] Mapp, *Iran-United States Claims Tribunals*, at 181.

the right to education. However, this clause does not specify conditions and criteria of achieving this right. By contrast, Articles 26 and 13 of the UDHR and the International Covenant on Economic, Social and Cultural Rights (hereinafter ICESCR) respectively do not only recognise everyone's right to education but recognise that primary education shall be compulsory and available free to all, and higher education shall, with restrictions based on capacity, be widely expanded. These clauses are analogous to Article 2 of the First Protocol to the ECHR, albeit, the latter guarantees the right in negative terms.

Similarly, the Constitution of Namibia protects the right to education.[101] Article 20(1) thereof provides that "All persons shall have the right to education." Paragraph (2) makes primary education compulsory and guarantees free education at State schools. Paragraph (3) guarantees all children of school-going age the right to attend school until they reach sixteen years, or finish primary, whichever is the sooner.[102] These clauses correspond, in content and scope, to international human rights instruments particularly Articles 13(1) of the ICESCR and 26(1) of the UDHR. They incorporate the international standards of the right to education in Namibian municipal law and thus effectuate Namibia's monist theory. In particular, Namibia domestically implements its international obligation under the ICESCR as a State party to protect the right to education. However, unlike the international human rights instruments, the Namibian clause is silent on free education in secondary and higher education.

Article 20(1) enjoins Namibia, in line with international human rights instruments, to provide education to its citizens. This clause protects the right to education in positive and mandatory terms. By

---

[101] Generally, see Fourie, "Economic rights," at 363; Naldi, *Constitutional Rights*, at 96-102; Diescho, *Namibian Constitution*, at 64. In terms of Article 5 of the Namibian Constitution, economic, social and cultural rights are also enforceable in domestic courts. This clause states that, "The fundamental rights and freedoms enshrined in this Chapter shall be respected and upheld by the Executive, Legislature and Judiciary and all organs of the Government and its agencies and, where applicable by them, by all natural and legal persons in Namibia, and *shall be enforceable by the Courts in the manner hereinafter prescribed.*" (emphasis supplied).

[102] Diescho, *Namibian Constitution*, at 64.

guaranteeing this right to "All persons," Article 20(1) brings out the natural-law foundation of the right to education. Subject to reasonable exceptions, this right inheres in every human being. The cornerstone of this right is to provide individuals with opportunities of access to education institutions. With the exception of primary education, the right to education does not guarantee to everyone the right of admission at educational institutions.[103]

According to Article 20(4) of the Namibian Constitution, individuals are free to establish and maintain private schools, colleges and kindred institutions of tertiary education at their own expense provided they maintain standards obtaining in State schools. This clause is comparable to Section 25(3)(c) of the Constitution of Malawi. Namibia's limited resources makes it reasonable to permit these schools. The institution may, however, appear to be discriminatory against pupils whose families cannot afford high fees charged by these schools.

An important aspect of the right to education is parents' right to ensure education and teaching of children in conformity with their own religious and moral beliefs.[104] There is no equivalent protection in the Namibian clause. This right is an adjunct to the right to education. It ensures that the State respects the rights of parents while exercising its functions in education. However, generally, the full and effective implementation of the right to education in Namibia is affected by limited resources.

The right to education was considered in *S v. Namseb*.[105] The Namibian High Court declared that a child's right to schooling is a fundamental right. It is not a mere privilege. Clearly, the Court adopted a broad and liberal interpretation of the right to education. This approach is a reasonable construction of the right to education. It gives substance to this right.

However, the Court did not draw inspiration from international human rights instruments protecting the right to education in

---

[103] Cf Section 32(a) of the Constitution of South Africa which guarantees individuals equal access to educational institutions.

[104] See ICCPR, Article 15(4); Second Protocol to the ECHR, Article 2. See also the Constitution of South Africa, Section 32(c).

[105] 1991 (1) SACR 223 (SWA).

interpreting the Namibian clause. The issue was determined mainly on the basis of Namibian national law and jurisprudence. It is submitted that in line with Namibia's monist theory, the Court should have utilised the international human rights instruments and jurisprudence to buttress its decision. It is a rarity that educational rights and indeed economic, social and cultural rights in general become a subject of litigation before municipal courts. It is even more so for the courts to declare that educational and similar rights, which are often called mere privileges, are indeed rights. This case presented a rare opportunity for the Court to place reliance on international human rights norms in interpreting the right to education. It would have given an added legal force to the Court reasoning and reinforced Namibia's friendliness to international law.

Cultural Rights

Cultural rights enjoy international recognition. Article 27(1) of the UDHR confers everyone the right "freely to participate in the cultural life of the community, to enjoy the arts and to share in scientific advancement and its benefits." Analogously, Article 17(3) of the ACHPR states that "every individual may freely take part in the cultural life of his community." This clause, additionally, imposes a duty on States to promote and protect this right in line with duty-oriented approach of the Charter.[106] Both clauses are similar to Article 15(1)(a) to (c) of the ICESCR. These protective clauses are fortified by Article 27 of the ICCPR which ensures that minorities are not denied the right to their culture, religion or language.[107]

The right to culture is similarly accorded constitutional recognition and status in Namibian municipal law. Article 19 of the Constitution entitles every person "to enjoy, practice, profess, maintain and promote any culture, language, tradition or religion." This clause implements Namibia's obligation under the ICESCR and the ACHPR as a state party to protect cultural rights of individuals. It transforms international cultural normative standards embodied in these treaties

---

[106] Makua wa Mutua, "The Banjul Charter," at 339-80; Gittleman, "The African Charter," at 667-714; Umozurike, *The African Charter*, at 63-5.

[107] Generally, see Nettheim, "Peoples," in Crawford, *Rights of Peoples*, at 107-26.

into Namibian municipal law. These cultural rights include arts, music, dance and literature.

Protection of language in Article 19 is particularly significant. With the exception of Article 27 of the ICCPR,[108] most international human rights instruments do not expressly and positively guarantee the right to use one's own language. Thus the Namibian clause offers an additional and more progressive safeguard than international instruments. It recognises the different languages in the country.

The additional safeguards embodied in Article 19 are tradition and religion. As regards tradition, the clause ensures that the traditional lives of the various ethnic groups are safeguarded. This accords with Article 17(3) of the ACHPR which enjoins States to promote and protect traditional norms. The protection of religion also ensures that religious groups practice and propagate their religion.

These rights are, however, not protected absolutely. Against the background of colonialism, tribalism and apartheid, Article 19 makes the enjoyment of cultural rights subject to the Constitution, the rights of others and the national interest. While it may be clear what these other conditions entail, that is not the case with national interest. All sorts of circumstances may be used to justify an erosion of this right under the guise of national interest. The crucial point, however, is that any cultural practices that impinge upon these conditions are invalid.

The opportunity to elaborate on cultural rights in general and particularly Article 19 presented itself in the *Cultura 2000* case.[109] The High Court of Namibia held that the State Repudiation (Cultura) Act of 1991 authorising the government to confiscate monies and donations advanced to the applicants was contrary to Article 16(1) of the Constitution of Namibia protecting cultural rights. The Court arrived at its decision by relying on what it called broad and universal cultural human rights norms. According to the Court, the effect of Article 144 of the Constitution of Namibia was to assign these norms a domestic status. Clearly, Article 144 influenced the Court to rely on international

---

[108] Cf the Constitution of South Africa, Section 32(b) which provides that educational instructions should wherever possible be in the language of one's choice. See further Constitution of Malawi, Section 26 which entitles every person the right to use the language of his or her choice.

[109] 1994 (1) S.A. 407 at 412.

human rights norms to interpret Article 19 of the Constitution of Namibia. These norms constituted the basis of the Court's decision.

Conclusion

It is abundantly clear from the preceding analysis that despite differences in the drafting style, phraseology and formulation of human rights clauses, the juridical substantive content and scope of the protective clauses of the Namibian Bill of Rights reflects, by and large, the influence of international human rights standards contained in major human rights treaties and instruments such as the UDHR, ICCPR, ECHR, ICESCR and the ACHPR. By replicating human rights norms embodied in these instruments, the Bill of Rights essentially incorporates these norms into Namibian domestic law. It domestically effectuates Namibia's monist theory. However, the Bill contains additional safeguards with respect to rights such as the right to property, education and non-discrimination. The additional protection of these rights reflects Namibia's local conditions. The Bill was greatly influenced by the colonial dispensation under which human rights especially land rights were denied the vast majority of the Namibian people. Racial discrimination was also pervasive. Moreover, the bulk of the Namibian population especially the Africans were denied basic educational rights. The Bill recognises this reality and marks a positive and progressive approach as well as an improvement upon the domestic human rights protection system. It gives an added impetus to Namibia's monist theory.

Additionally, Namibia has, at least in theory, attempted to remedy some of the practices which militate against the implementation of human rights norms such as sex discrimination and whipping of male offenders under customary law and practices. These practices reveal a conflict between cultural relativism and cultural imperialism and universalism. They collide with universal norms. But to the extent that the cultural practices place individuals in disadvantageous positions, it is submitted that they should give way to norms which enhance the status of individuals. Significantly, as an expression of revulsion against these practices, the Namibian municipal law not only prohibits sex discrimination but also encourages positive discrimination in favour of women and similarly placed individuals. It has also abolished the death penalty. The removal of these practices also gives additional force to Namibia's newly adopted monist theory.

The monist theory has, however, been compromised at the enforcement level particularly by the judiciary. Namibian courts are yet to implement this theory in domestic law. International human rights law, both customary and conventional, has been invoked and relied upon in relatively few and isolated cases in interpreting national law. For example, one situation where the theory was given effect to is in relation to whipping. The Namibian Supreme Court relied on Article 3 of the ECHR and the ECtHR decision in *Tyrer* case to outlaw whipping in Namibian national law. The monist theory has also been domestically effectuated with respect to the principle of non-discrimination and cultural rights. Even with respect to these norms, the theory has been given a cursory and perfunctory attention. In most cases such as those dealing with trial within a reasonable time, judicial independence, expropriation of property and the right to education, the courts have reached their decisions mainly on the basis of national law and jurisprudence. They have yet to actively use rich international jurisprudence in the general area of human rights law to build upon national jurisprudence. This approach effectively compromises Namibia's monist theory. It is submitted that in order to effectuate this theory internally, national courts should actively invoke and rely on international law and sources in legal proceedings. This approach also serves a useful purpose of enriching national law with international standards. It further broadens the national human rights protection system.

6 Botswana:
Dualism Reinforced

This chapter examines the extent to which Botswana's inherited monist-dualist approach has been implemented in the post-independence legal order with respect to human rights law. It thus analyses the human rights norms in the Bill of Rights against similar rights in major international human rights instruments in order to determine whether national human rights norms not only reflect and, domestically incorporate, international standards for the protection of such norms, but also reinforce the dualist or monist approach regarding the inter-relations between international law and Botswana national law. It also examines the manner in, and extent to, which courts have handled the inherited approach. In particular, it examines whether, and the extent to which, the courts have utilised international human rights norms in enforcing national human rights law. It concentrates on those national human rights issues where international human rights norms have, explicitly or implicitly, arisen. As such, the chapter deals mainly with the process of translating international human rights law into Botswana municipal law.

Judicial Practice

The Right to Life

The right to life is recognised and protected in municipal law of Botswana. According to Section 4(1) of the Constitution "No person shall be deprived of his life intentionally save in the execution of the sentence of the court in respect of an offence under the law in force in Botswana of which he has been convicted."[1] This clause does not

---

[1]   See Lindholt, *Universality of Human Rights*, at 94-7; Maope, *Human Rights*, at 36-7; Neff, *Human Rights*, at 65-7; Takirambudde, "Botswana," in Baehr et al, *Human Rights*, at 139. The right to life is also recognised along with other rights by the

protect the right to life in positive terms. It protects this right in negative terms by merely preventing the intentional deprivation of life. This contrasts starkly with provisions in international human rights instruments especially the ACHPR and ECHR. Respective Articles 4 and 2 of both conventions protect the right to life in positive terms.

As under the ACHPR and ECHR, the right to life in Botswana is recognised and protected subject to limitations. However, the ACHPR does not specify instances under which this right may be limited. It only prohibits arbitrary deprivation of the right to life. Section 4(a) to (d) of the Constitution of Botswana recognises that this right may be violated in the execution of a sentence of the court, in self-defence, to suppress a riot or prevent the commission of an offence. This clause corresponds to Article 2(2) (a) to (c) of the ECHR.[2] These exceptional instances ensure legality when deprivation of life is contemplated. This means that these exceptions should be narrowly interpreted in order to protect life.

Despite phraseological technicalities, the Botswana right to life clause, in line with international law, firmly protects the right to life. It implicitly incorporates international standards for the protection of the right to life into municipal law of Botswana. It further imposes a legal obligation on Botswana to protect this right. The practical importance of this clause is, however, minimised by the institution of the death penalty.

The death penalty   As indicated earlier on, the death penalty is categorically outlawed at the international level by Article 1(1) of the Second Optional Protocol to the ICCPR Aiming at the Abolition of the Death Penalty. However, in Botswana, as in many other countries, capital punishment is a legally permissible and competent sentence.

The Penal Code of Botswana explicitly and unambiguously declares that "...any person convicted of murder shall be sentenced to

---

preambular Section 3 of the Constitution of Botswana entitled "Fundamental Rights and Freedoms of the Individual."

[2]   Generally, see Harris et al, *European Convention*, at 45-54. Also, see Barnett, *Constitutional Law*, at 381-2; Novak, *U.N. Covenant*, at 105.

death."[3] Capital punishment is reserved only for most serious offences such as murder, treason[4] and murder committed in the process of committing piracy.[5] In terms of Section 26(1) of the Penal Code, execution is by hanging. In order to limit circumstances under which it may be meted out, the death sentence cannot be imposed on persons below eighteen years[6] and pregnant mothers.[7] It also may not be imposed where there are extenuating circumstances such as provocation, intoxication, youthfulness and absence of actual intention to kill.[8]

It is apposite to note that although international human rights standards have been invoked and relied on to challenge the constitutionality of the death penalty in Botswana, the judiciary has exercised extreme restraint to outlaw it. One of the cases in which it was challenged is *Molale v. The State*.[9] The appellant was convicted by the High Court of Botswana of murdering his girl-friend by inflicting fatal blows on her with an axe. He was sentenced to death. On appeal to the Court of appeal, he argued, amongst other things, that the death penalty imposed on him by the High Court violated his constitutional right to life and, anachronistically, it is an antediluvian and barbaric penalty. Although the Court of appeal reduced the sentence to fifteen

---

[3] Penal Code, Laws of Botswana, Cap. 08:01, Section 203 (1). See generally Nsereko, "Capital Offenses in Botswana," at 239-59; Lindholt, *Universality of Human Rights*, at 97-9.

[4] Penal Code, Laws of Botswana, Cap. 08:01, Section 34(1).

[5] Ibid., Section 63(2).

[6] Ibid., Section 26(2).

[7] Ibid., Section 26(3). See also Criminal Procedure and Evidence Act, Laws of Botswana, Cap. 08:02, Section 298(1).

[8] Other factors which the court can take into consideration are factors, not too remote or faintly or indirectly related to the commission of the crime, which bears upon the accused's moral blameworthiness in committing it. These factors include ill-treatment of an employee, ailment such as epilepsy and economic plight. See Nsereko, "Capital Offenses in Botswana," at 244-60; State v. Lathe, Criminal Trial No. F2/1990 (1 March 1991) (unreported).

[9] Criminal Appeal No. 56/1994 (CA) (unreported).

years imprisonment on different grounds it, however, failed to pronounce on the constitutionality of the death penalty. The Court, per Aguda, J.A., merely held that "following upon the conclusion to which I have arrived as regards the sentence of death, it is no longer necessary for me to consider either of the two grounds filed by Mr Morotsi as regards capital punishment." The pertinent ground read that "the method of execution of the appellant ordered by the learned judge as prescribed by Section 203(1) of the Penal Code was anachronistic, antediluvian and barbaric."

On pure legal technicalities, the Court was justified in not considering the issue of capital punishment. However, capital punishment is an important and topical issue in Botswana on which the view of the highest court in the country is necessary and would influence public opinion. In fact, this case is one of the few cases where the issue was specifically raised. Moreover, the argument that the death penalty is antediluvian and barbaric was an implicit invitation to the Court to take into account international normative standards in determining its constitutionality. But the Court decided the issue mainly on the basis of national law and declined to adjudicate its constitutionality.

Capital punishment was also an issue in *Mosarwana v. State.*[10] The appellant, on substantial evidence, was convicted of murdering the deceased for calling him a thief. The High Court sentenced him to death in accordance with Section 203(1) of the Penal Code. It also found that there were no extenuating circumstances and in accordance with Section 26(1) of the Penal Code, ordered that the appellant be hanged. On appeal to the Court of Appeal, the appellant argued, inter alia, that Section 203(1) permitting the death penalty was *ultra vires* the Constitution since Section 4 thereof prohibits the intentional taking of life. The Court failed to analyse the general import and content, and the precise limits of Section 203(1). It merely held that, on proper construction, Section 203(1) prescribing the death penalty was not inconsistent with, and thus not *ultra vires*, the Constitution. The Court noted that, while there was international sentiment, as reflected at the United Nations, to abolish the death penalty, it could not rewrite the Constitution in order to give effect to such sentiment. Its function in

---

[10] [1985] B.L.R. 258.

the interpretation of the Constitution was adjudicatory and not legislative. Relying strictly and narrowly on national law and jurisprudence, the Court confirmed the death sentence. It is submitted that this case presented an opportunity for the Court to utilise international human rights norms to determine the constitutionality of the death sentence. If it had adopted this approach, it would have found out that current thinking on the international plane is increasingly moving towards the abolition of the death penalty. Also, the approach would have influenced the Court to reach a different conclusion and if need be substitute the death sentence with a term of imprisonment.

The death penalty was also a contentious issue in *State v. Ntesang*.[11] The appellant was convicted of murder and sentenced to death by hanging. He appealed against sentence on the grounds, inter alia, that the death penalty breached the constitutional right to life clause. The Court of Appeal dismissed the appeal and confirmed the death sentence imposed by the High Court. It thus refused to declare capital punishment unconstitutional. However, the Court took judicial notice of developments to abolish the death sentence at the international level and invited parliament to consider effecting appropriate changes at national level. It, nevertheless, refused to use these developments to determine the constitutionality of capital punishment and if need be outlaw it.

These pronouncements clearly demonstrate judicial restraint in Botswana to invoke and rely on international human rights standards to outlaw the death penalty. This form of restraint is an indirect judicial confirmation of the classical dualist theory that international and national law are distinct legal orders each governing a different legal sphere.

It is important to note that Botswana has not signed the Second Optional Protocol to the ICCPR Aiming at the Abolition of the Death Penalty and the ICCPR. It is, therefore, not legally obliged to outlaw the death sentence or submit reports under both conventions to the Human Rights Committee.[12]

---

[11]   [1995] L.R.C. (Const) 338.

[12]   Articles 3 and 40 of the Second Optional Protocol to the ICCPR Aiming at the Abolition of the Death Penalty and the ICCPR respectively oblige states parties to submit reports to the Human Rights Committee on the measures they have adopted to give effect to both conventions.

Significantly, there is national debate to abolish the death penalty. The debate centres around two approaches: abolitionism and retentionism.[13] Abolitionists such as human rights activists and defence lawyers contend that evidence is lacking that capital punishment deters crime and as such it should be abolished. Retentionists especially members of the public and few politicians, on the other hand, defend capital punishment as a deterrent. They argue that although capital punishment does not prevent crime, it has a deterrent effect.

There seems, however, to be no easy solution to this debate. Seemingly, capital punishment in Botswana will continue to be lawful and permissible for some time. This is because the debate is both emotionally and politically charged, and the greater part of the public does not appear to be ready to endorse its abolition. It is submitted that the gradualist approach is the only preferable approach, at least, at the present time. Significantly, capital punishment has been sparingly imposed. According to Amnesty International Report, in 1995 only one man whose death sentence was confirmed by the Court of Appeal was awaiting execution, two men convicted of murder and sentenced to death had their death sentences set aside by the Court of Appeal and another man's death sentence, Boiki Mokholo, was commuted to a fifteen-year prison term.[14]

Personal Liberty

Personal liberty in Botswana is recognised and protected by Section 5(1) of the Constitution. This provision declares that "no person shall be deprived of his personal liberty save as may be authorised by law." Section 5(1) corresponds to Article 6 of the ACHPR, Article 3 of the UDHR and Article 9(1) of the ICCPR except that it does not also

---

[13] See generally Nsereko, "Capital Offenses in Botswana," at 235-68; Barry and Williams, "Russia's Death Penalty," at 248-58. The mid-way approach to capital punishment is gradualism. This approach advocates the gradual and step by step elimination of the death penalty. Its rationale is based on the reduction of the number of crimes in respect of which the death penalty may be imposed. See Barry and Williams, Ibid., at 256.

[14] Amnesty International 1997 Report, "Botswana," at 95-6. See also Takirambudde, "Botswana," in Baehr et al, *Human Rights*, at 139; Granberg and Parkinson, *Botswana*, at 333.

protect security of person. Moreover, unlike the international human rights instruments, the Botswana clause does not protect this freedom positively. It adopts a negativist approach. Nevertheless, it incorporates, both in form and content, the basic international standards for the safeguard of personal liberty. It extends procedural fairness and guarantees to the individual in ordinary criminal process. It encompasses freedom from arbitrary arrest and detention. This clause safeguards individual physical liberty.[15]

The Constitution of Botswana, as with international instruments,[16] does not guarantee the right to liberty in absolute terms. It recognises executive powers of the State to deprive the individual of his liberty, for instance, in execution of the lawful sentence of the court, on reasonable suspicion of a person having committed an offence and to protect the rights of others or the society.[17] However, its deprivation must be authorised by law. This means that it is not the deprivation of liberty in and of itself that is objectionable but rather that which is arbitrary and unlawful.

It is in this vein that Section 5(2) of the Constitution provides that an individual whose right to personal liberty is threatened or who is arrested or detained should be informed as soon as practicable, in the language that he understands, of the reasons of his arrest or detention. In paragraph 3, any person who is arrested or detained on reasonable suspicion of having committed an offence should be brought as soon as is reasonably practicable before court usually within forty-eight hours. If he is not tried within a reasonable time, he shall be released unconditionally or upon reasonable conditions to ensure that he appears at a later date for trial. These safeguards guarantee the right of

---

[15] See Nowak, *U.N. Covenant*, at 159; Dinstein, "Life, Physical Integrity and Liberty," in Henkin, *Bill of Rights*, at 128-35.

[16] The Constitution of Botswana, Section 5 (1) (a) to (k). The limitations are spelt out in the same terms as in 5(1) (a) to (f) of the ECHR, to include, inter alia, limitations designed to execute the sentence of the court, to secure the attention of the person in court, in order to prevent the unlawful entry of a person in the country or for the purpose of expulsion, extradition or other lawful removal of the person from the country and limitations based on reasonable suspicion of a person having committed an offence.

[17] Generally, see Section 5(1) (a) to (K).

habeas corpus. They correspond to Article 5(2) to (5) of the ECHR. They are designed to ensure legality when this freedom is curtailed. In practice, these safeguards are generally respected by government authorities.[18]

The most controversial issue concerns arrest or detention by police officers on reasonable suspicion of the person having committed an offence. Generally, police officers have powers to arrest any person on reasonable suspicion or grounds of having committed a crime.[19] The question that emerges is, what amounts to reasonable grounds or suspicion that a person has committed a crime? Or, what is the test of reasonableness in these cases? This issue was a point of contention in *Oakametse v. Attorney-General and Another.*[20] The applicant was arrested by the Police in Serowe in the Central Administrative District on allegations that she called the complainant a witch. She was detained. She challenged her detention in the High Court on the basis of Section 5(2) of the Constitution. The Court held that to arrest and detain someone but without evidence of any offence which she has or was suspected to have committed is unlawful and intrusion of her physical liberty. It further held that, where an individual is arrested or detained on suspicion that she has committed an offence, the suspicion must be reasonable and based on real evidence but not mere allegations. It ordered her release. The Court did not, however, indicate whether the test of reasonableness should be judged by national or international human rights standards. It, nonetheless, based its decision only on the constitutional provision protecting individuals right to liberty.

---

[18] Takirambudde, "Botswana," in Baehr et al, *Human Rights*, at 140; Granberg and Parkinson, *Botswana*, at 333.

[19] For instance, see Criminal Procedure and Evidence Act, laws of Botswana, Cap. 08: 02, Section 28 (b)(1) to (111).

[20] Civil Trial No (F) 52 of 1987 (unreported).

Section 10 of the Constitution of Botswana elaborates the right of individuals to a fair trial.[21] It is analogous to Article 14 of the ICCPR and Article 6 of the ECHR. It resembles Article 7 of the ACHPR. It is also equivalent to Articles 10 and 11 of the UDHR. As with the international human rights treaties and instruments, the Botswana fair trial clause contains the Anglo-saxon concept of due process of law.[22] This right entails the minimum guarantees of the accused in criminal proceedings. These guarantees include trial by an independent and impartial court, trial within a reasonable time, presumption of innocence, trial in the accused's language or the language that the accused understands, public trial and legal representation. It is important to examine the extent to which Botswana courts have drawn inspiration from international human rights norms and sources in the enforcement of these laudable principles.

Reasonable time   The concept of trial within a reasonable time is embraced by municipal law of Botswana. Section 10(1) of the Constitution provides that "any person charged with a criminal offence shall, unless the charge is withdrawn, be afforded a ...hearing *within a reasonable time.*" This clause resembles Article 6(1) of the ECHR and Article 7(1)(d) of the ACHPR. However, the equivalent Article 14 (3)(c) of the ICCPR talks of "trial without undue delay." Essentially, this phrase also captures the substantive elements of trial within a reasonable time. Thus the Botswana clause, as with the international human rights instruments, encapsulates the concept of a speedy trial. It ensures that trials commence and finish speedily. This right includes not only the right to a speedy trial but also to a judgment within a reasonable time.[23]

The problematic issue concerns the guiding rule in determining whether trial should take place within a reasonable time. Judicial

---

[21]   For an analysis of this provision, see Lindholt, *Universality of Human Rights*, at 113-30; Neff, *Human Rights*, at 29-31.

[22]   Generally, see Harris, "Fair Trial," at 352-78; Nowak, *U.N. Covenant*, at 257-8; Byre and Byfield, *Commonwealth Caribbeans*, at 63-75.

[23]   Nowak, *U.N. Covenant*, at 258.

activity on this issue was attracted in *The State v. Merriweather Seboni*.[24] On 31 December, 1967 the accused was charged with theft of Government funds totalling 1, 257 South African Rands. The trial took place on 3 February, 1969. It effectively meant that there was a delay of more than a year. The delay was wholly attributable to the State in that a lot of time was taken in transmitting the record from the Magistrate, who presided over preparatory proceedings, to the Attorney-General for his decision whether to prosecute the accused in the High Court or remit the case to the Subordinate Court for trial. It was finally decided that trial should take place at the High Court. At the commencement of the proceedings, the accused raised a preliminary issue concerning his right to be tried within a reasonable time as provided for under Section 10(1) of the Constitution. He argued, inter alia, that this provision had been infringed in relation to him because he had to wait for approximately one year before his trial could commence. The State argued that the delay was not attributable to it. Rather, it was caused by the shortage of staff and administrative inefficiency and as such the accused could not seek the benefit of Section 10(1).

The Court construed Section 10(1) and noted that although the question whether or not there has been unreasonable delay depends on the circumstances of each case, nonetheless a delay of this magnitude was extremely unreasonable. It flagrantly violated Section 10(1) of the Constitution and thus prejudiced the accused. The Court observed that administrative deficiency cannot be invoked as justification for failure to comply with this clause. Clearly, the Court's decision cannot be faulted in the light of the inordinate delay involved. It gave substance to Section 10(1). Significantly, the Court decided the matter not only on the basis of Section 10(1) of the Constitution. It also sought guidance from comparative national decisions particularly *Baker v. Wingo* case and Article 5(3) of the ECHR dealing with trial within a reasonable time to reinforce its decision. With respect to the latter, the High Court, per Dendy Young, C.J., as he then was, observed that "Article 121, paragraph 1 of the German Criminal Procedure Code provides that no one may be kept in detention on remand for more than six months...The provision is supposed to take account of Article 5,

---

[24] (1966-70) B.L.R. 153. For an analysis of this case, see Neff, *Human Rights*, at 29-30.

paragraph 3, of the European Convention on Human Rights."[25] Justice Dendy Young proceeded to note that "In my view, these two decisions throw some light on the problem before me."[26] The Court dismissed the State's application and ordered a retrial. Article 5(3) of the ECHR formed, in part, the basis of the Court's decision.

However, subsequent court decisions do not reveal the same readiness to seek guidance from international human rights law and sources to construe Section 10(1) of the Constitution. In *Rapula Sello v. State*[27] the accused was convicted of malicious damage to property and sentenced to three years imprisonment. One year lapsed before his appeal against sentence was heard by the High Court of Botswana. The Court, per Heyfron-Benjamin, C.J., as he then was, pointed out that trial within a reasonable time did not end on conviction in the court of first instance. It also applied on appeal. The Court held that the delay in question was unreasonable. However, the Court relied purely on Section 10(1), and not international human rights norms, to declare that the delay was unreasonable. Similarly, in *S v. Makwekwe*[28] a delay of two years and eight months was held to be unreasonable. The Court retorted that it is no small matter for a man to live for years with a serious charge hanging over his head. The delay of this nature inflicts mental suffering and must of necessity interfere with the freedom of movement, employment opportunities and social life of the accused. However, as in *Rapula Sello v. State*, the Court decided the matter purely and only on the basis of national law. It did not inform its decision by international human rights standards in order to reinforce its reasoning and broaden its approach to the concept of trial within a reasonable time.

Be that as it may, international human rights standards and sources were invoked and utilised to interpret Section 10(1) in *Johannes Kgolagano v. Attorney-General*.[29] On 2 December 1992 the

---

[25]   (1966-70) B.L.R. 153 at 155.

[26]   Id.

[27]   Criminal Appeal No. 121 of 1977 (unreported). For a detailed discussion of this case, see Sanders, "Constitutionalism," at 356.

[28]   (1981) B.L.R. 196.

[29]   Criminal Case No. F.34/1996 (unreported).

accused was charged with murder. He was released on bail. His trial in the High Court only commenced on the 8 June, 1995. This meant that there was a two and half years delay in bringing him to trial. At the commencement of the trial, his attorney invoked Section 10(1) of the Constitution and argued that the applicant had been denied the right to trial within a reasonable time. In determining whether the delay in question was unreasonable, the Court sought assistance and guidance from comparative case law in Zimbabwe and the United States interpreting similar clauses[30] as well as international human rights instruments.

With respect to international human rights instruments, the Court noted that "the right to be tried within a 'reasonable time' is also guaranteed by Article 6(1) of the European Convention for the Protection of Human Rights and Fundamental Freedoms. This right is also embodied in the African Charter on Human and People's Rights... (see Article 7(1))."[31] The Court then concluded that the embodiment of this principle in different constitutions and international instruments reflects a universal acceptance of the right to a speedy trial as an important factor in the concept of fair trial. It held that two and half years delay was extremely unreasonable. Thus unlike in previous cases, the determination that there was unreasonable delay in this case was partly inspired by human rights treaties particularly Article 6(1) of the ECHR and Article 7(1) of the ACHPR.

It should be pointed out that there is a lack of consistency in the jurisprudence of Botswana courts regarding the available remedy when trial within a reasonable time safeguard is breached. In *Rapula Sello v. State* case, the accused was acquitted but, in *Seboni's* case, the Court ordered a retrial. In *Makwekwe's case*, the Court observed that a delay of two years and eight months was a factor to be taken into account when determining sentence whereas in *Johannes Kgolagano v. Attorney-General,* because of the seriousness of the charge, the Court could not order the stay of the proceedings.

Most significantly, the decisions demonstrate the fact that instances in which international law and sources in general and

---

[30]   Ibid., at 10-15. The Court also made reference to the Canadian Charter of Human Rights and Fundamental Freedoms.

[31]   Ibid., at 10-11.

particularly human rights treaties have been invoked and relied upon to construe the right of accused persons to be tried within a reasonable time in Botswana have been irregular and inconsistent. They have also not been uniform. The courts have yet to develop a clear and consistent pattern of invoking international human rights norms to interpret this right. This approach lessens the effectiveness of international law in protecting the right of individuals to be tried within a reasonable time in national law. It further reinforces Botswana's inherited classical dualist theory. These cases presented an opportunity for the courts to actively invoke international human rights law to interpret the concept of trial within a reasonable time so as to reinforce national human rights law and jurisprudence, and broaden the national protection system.

Language   In terms of Section 10(2)(b) of the Constitution of Botswana, the accused is entitled to be informed of the nature of the offence charged in the language that he understands and in detail. This clause corresponds to Article 14(3) (a) of the ICCPR and 6(3) (a) of the ECHR. Interestingly, the ACHPR is silent on the issue of language notwithstanding the co-existence of various ethnic languages in many African countries. Nonetheless, in line with other international human rights instruments, Section 10(2)(b) accords individuals the right to be informed of the offence not in their own language but in the language that they understand. Although this clause speaks only about information relating to the nature of the charge but not the actual conduct of the proceedings, it is submitted that the language facility also applies to the conduct of the trial.

The importance of using the language an accused understands in Court was underscored in the Kenyan case of *Andrea v. The Republic.*[32] In this case, the accused's language was Swahili. His statement was recorded in English. The trial was also conducted in English. He complained that he did not understand English but could only speak Swahili and Portuguese. His objection was upheld by the High Court noting that the possibility of the accused misunderstanding the proceedings was very great. The facility is designed to ensure that the accused follows the proceedings fully. In this regard the courts

---

[32]   (1970) E.A. 46.

have warned against raising the issue of language to ventilate matters that are irrelevant to the issue in the trial such as propaganda.[33]

Trial in the language understood by the accused is especially crucial in Botswana and it is to be welcomed. Despite the fact that Botswana is generally proclaimed to be a homogenous society, there are several other ethnic groups in the country each speaking its own language.[34] This makes the issue of language comprehensible to the accused all the more necessary. But, this safeguard is watered down by the fact that the different ethnic languages in the country are not official languages of the court. The official language of the court is English. This factor poses greater difficulties in enforcing this safeguard since many people speak their vernacular languages and do not fully understand English. Thus many may not understand the nature of the charge or even follow the trial fully.

In view of the difficulties inherent in enforcing the language safeguard, the protective clause in Botswana, as with the international human rights instruments,[35] guarantees the accused the right to an interpreter without payment if he cannot understand the language used at the trial.[36] This safeguard is implemented in practice. However, it is not expressly clear whether this safeguard extends to provision of interpreters during pre-trial interrogations. It is submitted that the right to an interpreter should not only be available at the trial. It should also be made available in pre-trial interrogations of the accused and suspects. Further, one issue that the Botswana clause does not cover, and has yet to be judicially determined, is whether interpretation also covers translation of relevant written documents such as evidence and judgments. It is further submitted that in order to guarantee the accused

---

[33]   R v. Merthyr Tydfil, Ex parte Jenkins [1967] 1 All E.R. 636.

[34]   Apart from the Tswana language which is predominantly and widely spoken in the country, the other ethnic languages are kalanga, subia, sesarwa, seyei and kgalagadi. Generally, see Nsereko, "Religious Liberty," at 843.

[35]   For instance, see ECHR, Article 6(3)(e). This clause provides that "everyone charged with a criminal offence has the minimum right to have the free assistance of an interpreter if he cannot understand or speak the language used in court." Generally, see Harris, "Fair Trial," at 368-9.

[36]   Section 10(2)(f). See also Neff, *Human Rights*, at 73.

a fair trial, written materials relevant in court should also be translated into the language that he/she understands.

The critical question relates to the effectiveness of the right to an interpreter in ensuring that the accused fully understands and follows the proceedings. This issue may arise where, for instance, the interpreter has an interest in the proceedings or he being the only person who speaks the accused's language does not also understand English very well. The former issue has arisen mainly within the context of using police officers as interpreters who almost invariably play a larger part in investigation of crimes. It arose in *State v. Galeboe*.[37] The police officer, who was an investigating officer in the case, was used by the Magistrate as an interpreter despite objection from the defence that he, the police officer, had an interest in the case. The appellant had also indicated that there was some misinterpretation on the part of the interpreter. Relying strictly on Section 10(2)(b) of the Constitution and evidence before it, the High Court observed that the use of an interpreter who had taken part in the investigation was an irregularity. It, however, held that because there was no evidence that the accused had suffered prejudice it could not overturn the decision of the lower court.

Similarly, in *Mokwena v. State*[38] the Court used a police officer as an interpreter. Relying entirely on Section 10(2)(b), the Court observed that the practice of using the police as interpreters in court was undesirable but sometimes unavoidable. In both cases, the Court decided the matter purely on national law, that is, Section 10(2)(b) of the Constitution of Botswana. It made no reference at all to international human rights law and jurisprudence dealing with the right to interpreters. This approach could have informed the Court about the importance attached to this right in international arena and its potential effects on the individual and, it is submitted, could have persuaded the Court in both cases to vitiate the proceedings.

Independent and impartial court or tribunal The municipal law of Botswana embraces the concept of trial by an independent and impartial court or tribunal. Section 10(1) of the Constitution accords

---

[37] (1968-70) B.L.R. 364.

[38] (1975) 1 B. L. R. 24. Generally, see Neff, *Human Rights*, at 74.

any person charged with a criminal offence the right to be tried by "an independent and impartial court." This clause resembles Article 10 of the UDHR and Article 6(1) of the ECHR. It also resembles Article 14(1) of the ICCPR except that the latter further requires that the tribunal should be competent. Article 7(1)(d) of the ACHPR only requires the tribunal to be impartial. Thus, by and large, the concept of trial by an independent and impartial court in Botswana reflects international safeguards. It is an institutional guarantee that the rights and duties of individuals in civil suits and criminal charges are not to be heard and decided by political institutions.[39]

This institutional guarantee embodies two main over-lapping concepts: independence and impartiality. First, independence. Judicial independence relates primarily to the relationship between the courts and the executive. It dictates that the accused must be heard by a tribunal which does not reach its decision due to pressure from the executive and outside forces. Secondly, impartiality. This concept entails two main sub-rules. First, the rule against bias (*nemo judex in causa sua*). This sub-rule dictates that the tribunal should not have an interest in the proceedings or be biased against one of the parties thereon.[40] The court is biased if, for instance, it or one of its members has an interest, pecuniary or otherwise, in the proceedings. Secondly, is the right to be heard (*audi alteram partem* rule). This rule requires that the accused be given the opportunity to be heard. Consequently, trial *in absentia* may constitute a violation of the right of the accused to a fair hearing. This rule may, however, be waived by the accused if, for instance, he or she conducts himself or herself in a way that makes trial in his or her presence practically impossible.

Of the two concepts, it is impartiality especially the most problematic rule against bias that has attracted the attention of Botswana courts. It arose in *Ali Khan and Another v. State*.[41] The appellants were charged, inter alia, with contravening the Fauna Proclamation of 1961 and Central Kalahari Game Reserve (Control of

---

[39]   Nowak, *U.N. Covenant*, at 244-6; Harris, "Fair Trial," at 354-7.

[40]   This rule has been emphasised in several English cases. For instance, see R v. Sussex Justices, Ex parte McCarthy [1924] 1 K.B. 256; R v. Cambora Justices, Ex parte Pearce [1955] 1 Q.B. 41. Also, see Sunday Times v. United Kingdom (1979) 2 E.H.R.R. 245.

[41]   (1968-70) B.L.R. 4.

Entry) Regulations of 1963 in that they entered the Central Kalahari Game Reserve and hunted therein without permits. The Presiding Officer who tried the case was also the District Commissioner for the area and in charge of the administration of the proclamation and regulations thereunder and in particular with the issuance of entry and hunting permits. The appellants made an application for his recusal on the basis that he was likely to be biased against them. He refused to recuse himself. The issue was raised on appeal.

In determining whether the District Commissioner infringed Section 10(1) of the Constitution on the right of the accused to be tried by an impartial tribunal or court, the High Court sought assistance from comparative decisions especially South African and English cases[42] and held that the Presiding Officer ought to have recused himself. The Court further emphasised how this rule is strictly enforced by noting that it does not require actual bias but a likelihood of bias. It is sufficient if an impression is reasonably created in the minds of the appellants that they would not have a fair trial. The predication of rule is that justice must not only be done, but must manifestly and undoubtedly be seen to be done.[43] The case was remitted to the trial court for re-trial.

The concept of judicial impartiality also arose in *State v. Mack*.[44] The appellant was convicted of attempted rape contrary to Section 138 of the Penal Code of Botswana. He pleaded guilty. The prosecutor stated the facts which the accused admitted. But then the judicial officer, taking the view that the facts did not disclose the crime charged, that is, the intention necessary to commit the crime of rape, summarily acquitted the accused. The Attorney-General, being dissatisfied with the decision of the Magistrate, appealed to the High Court. The High Court allowed the appeal and referred the case back to the Magistrate for re-trial. When the case re-opened, the Magistrate forthwith recused himself on the ground that the accused would be

---

[42]   Ibid., at 6.

[43]   Cf Elliot Mochochoko v. Regina (1961-62) H.C.T.L.R. 42. In this case the High Court of Basutoland Protectorate emphasised that the test whether or not the accused would be afforded a fair trial is based on the viewpoint of a reasonable person.

[44]   (1968-70) B.L.R 323.

prejudiced if he presided because he was not clear about some aspects of the law on rape.

Convinced that the Magistrate was refusing to try the case, the Attorney-General applied to the High Court and asked it to direct the Magistrate to try the case. He argued that the Magistrate was biased against the State. The Attorney-General invited the High Court to invoke "its inherent power to see that justice is done not only to the accused but also to the state, and to deal with the matter by way of review." After considering the point raised by the Attorney-General, the High Court concluded that it could not compel the Magistrate to re-try the case because he was entirely entitled to determine whether or not the accused was going to receive a fair trial. There was no bias on the part of the Magistrate. It accordingly dismissed the appeal.

It is evidently clear from both cases that the Court did not take into account international human rights standards particularly human rights treaties enshrining the concept of impartiality when interpreting this right. It decided the issue purely on the basis of the constitutional clause on fair trial. It is unclear whether factors which constitute bias should be judged only according to national conditions or whether they should take on board international normative standards.

Legal counsel Section 10(2)(d) of the Constitution of Botswana proclaims that "every person who is charged with a criminal offence shall be permitted to defend himself before the court in person or, at his own expense, by a legal representative of his own choice." Paragraph (e) thereof further requires that a person be "afforded facilities to examine in person or by his legal representative the witnesses called by the prosecution..." These clauses firmly guarantee the right to legal representation in criminal proceedings. They are similar to Article 11(1) of the UDHR, Article 14(3) (d) of the ICCPR, Article 6(3)(c) of the ECHR and Article 7(1)(c) of the ACHPR.[45] This right should be available to the individual as soon as he or she gets in contact with the criminal justice system, that is, soon after the arrest.

Legal counsel safeguard in Botswana, as in international human rights instruments, encompasses numerous individual rights.[46]

---

[45] Generally, see Nowak, *U. N. Covenant*, at 258-60.

[46] Nowak, *U. N. Covenant*, at 258.

First, the right to defend oneself in person. It is the primary, unrestricted right of everyone charged with a criminal offence to be present at the trial and to defend himself or herself. He should not be tried *in absentia*. If he is unable to do so, he can forgo this right and then, as his second right, he can make use of defence counsel. The court is required to inform him of this right. In principle, he may engage an attorney of his own choosing. This implies that legal counsel should not be imposed on the accused.[47] The third issue, relates to expenses. If the accused can afford it, he should meet his own legal expenses. Here the Botswana clause diverges from the international human rights instruments in that it does not expressly guarantee the accused free legal assistance if he lacks financial means. However, depending primarily on the seriousness of the offence and the potential maximum punishment the accused is likely to receive such as in murder and manslaughter cases the State renders free legal assistance.

An opportunity to examine the juridical content of the right to legal representation arose in *Tshipo v. State*.[48] The appellant was charged with careless driving. His application for postponement of the case so that he could engage an attorney was refused by the presiding Magistrate. On appeal, the High Court observed that legal representation becomes even more significant if failure to engage an attorney would result in prejudice to the accused. In *Richard Macha v. State*[49] the Court warned that the courts must always act reasonably and must not over-act or be carried away or seen to be carried away by the circumstances of any particular case. They must weigh the rights of the individual, as enshrined in the Constitution, against the rights of the State and the people as a whole to have justice done fairly by affording the accused legal counsel.

In both cases, the Court made reference to comparative national judicial decisions particularly South African decisions in determining whether or not the accused right to legal representation has

---

[47] In interpreting Article 6(3)(c) of the ECHR, the Strasbourg organs have formulated a strict approach and affirmed the right of the States to assign a defence counsel against the will of the accused if it is in the interest of administration of justice. See Nowak, *U.N. Covenant*, at 259.

[48] Criminal Appeal No. 171/1984 (unreported).

[49] (1982) 1 B.L.R. 98. See Nsereko, "Legal Representation," at 211-27.

been infringed.[50] However, no reference was made at all to international judicial decisions and international human rights treaties and instruments protecting the right to legal counsel to reinforce the Court's decision in both cases.

By contrast, in *Agnes Bojang v. State*,[51] the Court did not only invoke and rely on comparative national judicial decisions, but it also sought assistance and guidance from provisions of international human rights instruments in determining whether the Magistrate Court was under a legal obligation to inform the applicant of her right to legal counsel on a charge of stealing by a person employed in the public service. The Court noted that "due to paucity of case law in our courts which should guide this court in solving the question which faces it, it should not be surprising that assistance is sought from... some of the international conventions designed to provide guarantees similar or near to those found in our Constitution or laws."[52] After referring to these international conventions, the Court emphasised that the right to legal counsel is meant to ensure a fair hearing. Failure to protect this right renders other constitutional safeguards meaningless. It quashed the conviction. Thus the court's decision was partly influenced by human rights normative standards in these treaties.

A peculiar aspect of the right to legal counsel in Botswana but which is not found anywhere in the international human rights instruments concerns the right to legal representation in customary or traditional courts.[53] Section 10(12)(b) of the Constitution excludes the right to legal representation in customary courts or proceedings in a

---

[50] For instance, in Tshipo v. State the Court referred to R v. Joannon 1957 (4) S.A. 385. In Richard Macha v. State recourse was made to the English decision in Galos Hired and Another v. R [1944] A. C. 144; R v. Mary Kingston 32 Cr. App. R. 183.

[51] Criminal Case No. 6/1993 (unreported).

[52] Ibid., at 7. International Conventions that the Court referred to are the American Convention on Human Rights (hereafter ACHR), ECHR and ACHPR.

[53] The domestic law of Botswana distinguishes between two types of courts. There are the ordinary and customary courts. The ordinary courts includes the Court of Appeal, High Court and the various grades of Magistrates Courts. These courts administer the general law: mainly Roman-Dutch common law and statute law. Customary Courts administer customary or traditional law of the various tribes in the country. See generally Nsereko, "Legal Representation," at 211-15.

subordinate court for an offence under customary law. This inroad into the right to counsel is further embodied in Section 27 of the Customary Courts Act.[54] Persons appearing before these courts who wish to exercise this right must apply to court to have their cases transferred to the magistrate's courts.[55] Failure by the court to accede to the application renders the trial a nullity. The reason for this is that the concept of legal representation does not form part of Botswana indigenous system of jurisprudence. Moreover, the officers who preside over these courts are not formally trained in the law or procedure which lawyers practice.[56]

Significantly, a great number of people in Botswana, and indeed in most countries in Southern Africa, are subject to, and governed by, customary law. Criminal and civil cases of a minor nature, which constitute the majority of cases before courts in these countries, are dealt with in customary or traditional courts. This essentially means that exclusion of legal representation in these courts curtails and further compromises the accused's guarantee of a fair trial. The practice adversely affects the right of individuals to legal representation especially those living under the system of customary law. This practice illustrates a conflict between international human rights norms and customary practices.[57] Most importantly, it shows that Botswana does not fulfil its obligation under international human rights law and specifically the ACHPR to ensure the enjoyment of this

---

[54] The Laws of Botswana, Cap 04:05. Section 27 provides as follows: "Notwithstanding anything contained in any other law, no advocate or attorney shall have a right of audience - (a) in any customary court; or (b) in any subordinate court in any criminal proceedings or in any civil proceedings which fall to be determined by customary law. Generally, see Sanders, "Constitutionalism," at 366-7.

[55] Customary Courts Act, Cap 04:05, Section 30(1).

[56] Nsereko, "Legal Representation," at 220; U.S. Department of State, "Botswana," in *1996 Human Rights Country Reports,* at 3.

[57] For a detailed discussion of difficulties concerning the interaction between international human rights norms and customary practices, see Preis, "Cultural Practice," at 287; Neff, "Human Rights in Africa," at 331-47; Beyani, "Women's Rights," in Cook, *Human Rights*, at 285-306.

freedom by its citizens. Its municipal law diverges from international normative standards.

Legal representation under customary law has been questioned in courts. However, the courts have addressed it only on the basis of national law particularly the Constitution and not international law. It was questioned in *Moisakamo v. Moisakamo*.[58] The case did not concern human rights law. Rather, it dealt with the division of matrimonial property following upon divorce. The parties had been married by Christian rites and their property was therefore governed by the Married Persons' Property Act (Cap 29:03 of the Laws of Botswana), specifically by Section 7 of the Act which applies to marriages between "Africans." The effect of Section 7 is that in the absence of another prior arrangement between the parties, their property rights are governed by customary law. Counsel for the defendant argued that this fact effectively excluded the jurisdiction of the High Court to entertain the action. The proper forum was the customary court. However, the High Court was of the view that it had jurisdiction based, inter alia, on the fact that legal practitioners have no right of audience in customary courts. This could compromise legal defence of the parties. The unhappiness of the High Court with exclusion of legal representation in customary courts, particularly in criminal law field was expressed thus: "Of course the provisions of the Customary Courts Act in so far as they purport to bar legal representation of persons charged with offences under the Penal Code before customary courts are of doubtful constitutional firmness and validity."[59]

It is submitted that the right to legal representation must also be accorded the accused in customary courts. The issues before these courts may be complicated for the accused to handle without the assistance of a legal practitioner. The presence of a lawyer may also be beneficial to the court itself in unknotting these issues. The fact that the accused fails to opt out of the customary court's jurisdiction when the case first comes to these courts should not be held against him. He has the constitutional right to legal representation at any stage of the

---

[58] Matrimonial Cause 106/1978 (judgment delivered on 23 September 1980) (unreported). See Sanders, "Constitutionalism," at 366-7.

[59] Ibid., at 22.

judicial process. Legal representation is vital in these courts as in ordinary courts. It is a universal and inherent right of every person whether indigent or rich and irrespective of whatever law he or she is subject.

At the implementation stage, the right to legal counsel is compromised by the fact that most people in the country cannot afford the high fees charged by attorneys. However, the government has a policy of providing free legal assistance to individuals who cannot afford the high fees charged by lawyers. In practice, this policy has been given effect to especially in murder and other serious cases. Moreover, the University of Botswana Legal Clinic and Botswana Centre for Human Rights provide free legal assistance to needy persons. The work of both institutions is, however, limited by lack of adequate financial resources.

Notwithstanding these issues, it is clear that except for *Agnes Bojang v. State* case, Botswana courts have construed the right to legal representation predominantly on the basis of national law and jurisprudence. They have not actively and consistently sought assistance and guidance from international human rights standards and sources when interpreting this right in order not only to enrich national law with international standards but also to utilise these standards to broaden and extend the right to legal counsel to customary law.

Public trial The right to a public trial is recognised and safeguarded in the municipal law of Botswana.[60] Section 10(10) of the Constitution requires that "all proceedings of every court and proceedings for the determination of the existence or the extent of any civil right or obligation... including the announcement of the decision of the court..., shall be held in public." A comparable safeguard is contained in Article 14(1) of the ICCPR and Article 6(1) of the ECHR. The ACHPR does not have an explicit provision protecting the right to public trial. But this right can be implied from Article 7 according every individual the right to have his cause heard.

Section 10(10) of the Constitution of Botswana protects the right to public trial mandatorily and in positive terms. It extends this right both to civil and criminal proceedings. It means that all trials in

---

[60]   Generally, see Lindholt, *Universality of Human Rights*, at 120-1.

civil and criminal matters must, in principle, be conducted publicly and orally.[61] Further, by providing that public trial should be made available in "every court," the Botswana clause envisages customary courts. However, unlike the international human rights instruments, public trial in Botswana encompasses the announcement of the decision in public. The right to a public hearing may, however, be waived by the individual. The waiver should be unequivocal. It also should not conflict with important public interest consideration calling for the public to be present at the trial.[62]

Thus, Section 10(10), largely, incorporates the international human rights standards of trial in public in Botswana municipal law. It accords parties to the proceedings public hearing. In a democratic society, this right further extends to the general public. It is the duty of the State to ensure its observance in practice.

As with the international human rights instruments,[63] the municipal law of Botswana broadly recognises that the right to a public hearing is subject to restrictions. The press and public may be excluded from all or part of the trial in the interest of morals, public order or national security or where publicity would prejudice the interest of justice or if necessary in a democratic society.[64] Moreover, a public hearing may be excluded if necessary to protect the welfare of certain individuals. Section 10(11)(b) of the Constitution refers to "persons under the age of 18 years." This restriction is designed to protect the interest of vulnerable young persons. Under these instances, *in camera* trials would be justified.

The most controversial of these exceptions is exclusion of public hearings in the interest of national security. It was an issue in

---

[61] Fredin v. Sweden (1991) 13 E.H.R.R. 784. See also Nowak, *U.N. Covenant*, at 249.

[62] Hakansson v. Sweden (1991) 13 E.H.R.R. 1. A waiver has been criticised especially where the applicant fails to ask for public hearing before a court that by law conducted its proceedings in private because it requires the applicant to take the initiative to require the application of the exception to the rule requiring a public hearing. See Harris, et al, *European Convention*, at 220.

[63] The ICCPR, Article 14(1); the ECHR, Article 6(1).

[64] The Constitutions of Botswana, Section 10(11). Also, see *State v. Gordon Tokwe* Review Case No. 279/1984, High Court, (unreported).

State v. Gordon Tokwe.[65] The applicant was charged with official corruption contrary to Section 99(a) of the Penal Code of Botswana. When trial commenced, the State made an application for trial to be conducted *in camera* on the ground that the case involved matters of top secret which affected national security. Matters in question concerned receipt of money by a member of the Botswana police from a foreign embassy for providing that embassy with secret information concerning security and political matters. Relying on the English case of *Attorney-General v. Leveller Magazine and others* (1979) 68 Cr. App. R. 342, the Court, per Justice Hannah, as he then was, examined Section 10(10) of the Constitution and noted that it is important that wherever possible courts should conduct their proceedings in public. It stressed that courts should examine carefully any argument advanced in favour of secrecy based on national security.

According to the Court, the rationale of public hearing is to provide safeguards against judicial arbitrariness. It also protects litigants from secret administration of justice with no public scrutiny. Publicity makes the administration of justice transparent. Moreover, it ensures democratic control of the justice system. It is the rational idea of better finding the truth.[66] It further contributes to the maintenance of public confidence in the courts. It thus ensures that justice should not only be done but should manifestly and undoubtedly be seen to be done. However, as in most cases on fair trial, the Court arrived at its decision without seeking any guidance from international human rights standards.

Significantly, except for minor differences in form, it is clear that the substantive content of the Botswana fair trial clause largely reflects international human rights standards. It embodies the main international human rights standards of a fair trial. However, in practice, the judiciary has not actively invoked and utilised international human rights standards in enforcing these guarantees. The

---

[65]   Review Case No. 279/1984, High Court, (unreported).

[66]   Nowak, *U.N Covenant*, at 247-8. According to Nowak publicity entails two precepts. First, it entails dynamic publicity of the proceedings of the judicial organs in the formal-procedural sense, that is, the manner in which a court arrives at its decision. Secondly is static publicity of the judgment. This precept involves the means by which the court is able to supervise the proceedings once they have been completed. Id.

judiciary has interpreted these clauses mainly on the basis of national law and jurisprudence. References to comparable clauses in international human rights instruments and international decisions has been minimal, inconsistent and irregular. Put differently, Botswana courts have accorded international human rights norms a limited role in interpreting national fair trial guarantees.

Torture and Inhuman or Degrading Punishment or Treatment

The prohibition of torture and related practices is articulated in the municipal law of Botswana.[67] Section 7(1) of the Constitution categorically and unambiguously declares that "no person shall be subjected to torture or to inhuman or degrading punishment or other treatment." This clause is comparable to Article 5 of the UDHR and Article 7 of the ICCPR. The latter, additionally, prohibits subjection of anyone without his free consent to medical or scientific experimentation. Similar directive proscriptions appear respectively in Articles 3 and 5 of the ECHR and the ACHPR. Additionally, the latter prohibits generally all forms of exploitation and degradation of man. Thus Section 7(1) is literally equivalent to clauses in international human rights instruments. It translates international normative standards on prohibition of torture and kindred conducts into the domestic law of Botswana.

It is worth noting that although there is no documentary evidence, incidents of torture in Botswana especially by police and other security forces have been alleged particularly during detentions of suspected criminals.[68] The practice has been revealed in a number of

---

[67] Lindholt, *Universality of Human Rights*, at 103-9; Neff, "Human Rights in Africa," at 338-40; Id, *Human Rights*, at 14-20; Takirambudde, "Botswana," in Baehr, et al, *Human Rights*, at 139; Maope, *Human Rights*, at 68-9.

[68] Generally, see Nsereko, "Legal Representation," at 213; Takirambudde, "Botswana," in Baehr et al, *Human Rights*, at 139; Neff, *Human Rights*, at 14-16; Maope, *Human Rights*, at 68. Allegations of torture are usually made during police interrogation of suspected offenders. Police use a variety of interrogation techniques and there is great emphasis is on secrecy and the leaving of no traces of injury that makes it difficult to prove. This practice is especially rife in cases involving theft of cars and diamonds. See Amnesty International 1997 Report, "Botswana," at 96.

judicial pronouncements. In *George Khoza and Another v. Attorney-General and Another*[69] the accused were convicted by a Magistrate Court on a plea of guilty for kidnapping a South African citizen. They were given a custodial sentence. They applied to the High Court for their release arguing that their plea of guilty was extracted through torture and violence by the police and threats that if they refused such treatment would be repeated. The Court believed their story, quashed the conviction and set them free.

A method of torture reportedly used by Botswana Police is known as "riding the jack." It was employed in *Mosotho Masina and Mogosi v. State.*[70] The appellants were questioned by the police for three days. They were taken to the entrance of the toilet, made to undress, handcuffed behind their back, made to sit on the bare floor, a piece of plastic held over their mouths and noses which was removed whenever they were near suffocation when they would be asked the whereabouts of the deceased and the appellants' knowledge of his death. Each time they denied the process was repeated. The Court of Appeal struck out the confession obtained as a consequence of this practice. This practice obviously violates Botswana's obligation under international law and should be avoided. Police interrogations should be supervised by independent persons and individuals.

It is apposite to observe that while the international human rights instruments mandatorily prohibits any form of torture and associated treatment without exceptions, Section 7 does not. Paragraph (2) thereof preserves any punishment that was permissible before the Constitution came into operation, that is, before independence in 1966. Any punishment that was lawful before this date is excluded from the prohibitions. This clause creates an exception to the prohibition of torture and similar practices.

This raises the question whether practices such as whipping and hanging which predate the adoption of the Constitution of Botswana are excluded from torture and similar practices? Do these practices amount to inhuman or degrading treatment? Attempts to

---

[69] Civil Case No. 94/1982 (unreported).

[70] Criminal Appeal No. 14/1983 (unreported). Generally, see Nsereko, "Legal Representation," at 213.

implement prohibitions against torture and inhuman or degrading punishment or treatment have been confronted with these major issues.

Whipping Whipping, both judicial and non-judicial, has been a major concern in an attempt to implement prohibitions against inhuman or degrading punishment or treatment in Botswana. This punishment is reserved for offences such as rape, assault occasioning actual bodily harm, housebreaking and robbery. It can be imposed on adult males but not female offenders, males sentenced to death and those over forty years.[71]

The constitutionality of whipping has been challenged in Botswana courts. Significantly, in trying to resolve the issue, the courts have invoked and relied on international human rights law. It was an issue in *Clover Petrus v. State*.[72] The two accused were charged with and convicted by a Magistrate for house breaking and theft contrary to Section 305(10)(a) of the Botswana Penal Code (Amendment) Act of 1982. Each of the accused was sentenced to three years imprisonment and to corporal punishment as provided for by Section 301(3) of the Criminal Procedure and Evidence Act (hereinafter the CPEA). This clause authorises the administration of corporal punishment at delayed and repeated intervals. The accused lodged an appeal against both the conviction and sentence with the High Court. On the issue of corporal punishment, they argued that such a penalty was contrary to Section 7(1) of the Constitution of Botswana outlawing torture or inhuman or degrading punishment or other treatment and as such unconstitutional.

In arguing that the institution of corporal punishment or caning is unconstitutional, the appellants relied on the decisions of the ECtHR in *Tyrer v. The United Kingdom* and other relevant international human

---

[71]   Maope, *Human Rights*, at 78; Neff, *Human Rights*, at 18; Lindholt, *Universality of Human Rights*, at 106. See also State v. Keakitse Review Case No. 4/1982 (unreported) in which a fourteen-year old boy was convicted of theft and sentenced to be caned with two light strokes. On appeal, the High Court enhanced the sentence to six strokes stressing that, for deterrence purposes, the circumstances of the case dictated a severe sentence. For an analysis of this case, see Neff, "Human Rights in Africa," at 338.

[72]   [1985] L.R.C. (Const) 699. This case is fully discussed in Lindholt, *Universality of Human Rights*, at 106; Coldham, "Human rights," at 91; Mbao, "Constitutional Government," at 194.

rights instruments, to wit, the ECHR and the ACHPR.[73] In essence, the appellants wanted the Court to determine the constitutionality of corporal punishment against international human rights law embodied in these sources.

In resolving this point, the Court, per Aguda, J. A., also invoked and relied, in part, on these human rights treaties, that is, Article 5 of the ACHPR, Article 5 of the UDHR, the ACHR and the ECHR.[74] Justice Aguda noted that he relied on these instruments to demonstrate that human rights have matured into customary international law binding on all States including Botswana.

The Court also referred to the ECtHR decision in *Tyrer v. United Kingdom*. Maisels, J.P., as he then was, said, "I now deal with the reasons for the court's finding that corporal punishment as prescribed in section 301(3) of the CPEA is *ultra vires*...We were also referred to a decision of the European Court of Human rights, *Tyrer v. United Kingdom*, 2 EHHR 1...and to the decision of the German Court on 10 June 1963... A reading of the *dicta* in the various judgments ...leaves me in no doubt that the repeated and delayed infliction of strokes as enjoined by section 301 (3), would be regarded as inhuman or degrading."[75]

The Court proceeded to observe that there is a universally recognised normative prohibition against corporal punishment. Moreover, as a "member of a comity of civilised nations," Botswana is legally bound to proscribe this form of punishment.[76] The Court finally held that the infliction of whipping in a delayed and repeated manner was inhuman and degrading punishment. It, however, held that whipping *per se* is not an inhuman or degrading punishment.[77] The

---

[73] [1985] L.R.C. (Const) 699 at 721-2.

[74] Ibid., at 722.

[75] Ibid., at 713-4.

[76] Ibid., at 714. (emphasis supplied).

[77] However, Justice Akinola Aguda observed that he was convinced "beyond any shadow of doubt that the mere imposition of corporal punishment is under any circumstances at this time and age certainly degrading if not inhuman." Ibid., at 724-5.

important point for the present study is that the Court relied on international human rights treaties and *Tyrer v. United Kingdom* in which the ECtHR declared birching to be inhuman to outlaw instalmental whipping. The international human rights norms embodied in these sources constituted part of the basis for declaring instalmental whipping unconstitutional.

The ECtHR decision in *Tyrer v. United Kingdom* was also used to challenge whipping in *Desai and Modi v. The State.*[78] The case involved an appeal to the High Court of Botswana against both conviction and sentences from a decision of the Senior Magistrate for Gaborone Administrative District in which the appellants were charged with unlawful possession of habit-forming drugs, mandrax, contrary to the Habit Forming Drugs Act of Botswana. Both appellants were each sentenced to ten years imprisonment. But the second appellant, Modi, received an additional three strokes with a cane and the first appellant, because of his age, sixty-two years, was spared the strokes. As in *Clover Petrus v. State*, the second appellant argued against the sentence of corporal punishment that the imposition of a long term of imprisonment in addition to corporal punishment amounted to an inhuman and degrading treatment and as such contravened Section 7(1) of the Constitution prohibiting that form of punishment. Both appellants also argued that the provisions of domestic legislation empowering the courts to impose a sentence of whipping were unconstitutional hence null and void.

The Court rejected the argument that a sentence of strokes was inhuman and degrading. However, after referring to *Clover Petrus v. State* case and the ECtHR's decision in *Tyrer v. United Kingdom*,[79] it noted that to combine strokes with a term of imprisonment amounted to an inhuman and degrading treatment. It ordered the deletion of the strokes.

It is demonstrably clear that Botswana courts have been hesitant to outlaw corporal punishment notwithstanding the fact that

---

[78]   (1985) B.L.R 582.

[79]   Ibid., at 587. (Per O'Brien Quinn, formerly Chief Justice of Botswana). See further *Raditlhose v. State* Criminal Appeal, No. 14/1990 (unreported) where the Court of Appeal confirmed the inappropriateness of combining strokes with imprisonment by deleting six strokes from four years imprisonment on a conviction for shopbreaking and theft.

they have sought guidance from international human rights law to determine its constitutionality. What is objectionable, according to the courts, is the mode of executing it in a repeated and delayed manner and its combination with other similarly severe sentences such as long term of imprisonment rather than the institution itself. International norms have not played any role in determining the constitutionality of this practice.

Hanging The second problematic issue regarding prohibition against degrading and inhuman punishment or treatment is the institution of hanging. The question that arises is whether hanging, as a mode of executing the death penalty, in itself constitutes a degrading and inhuman punishment or treatment? This institution was challenged in *Mosarwana v. State.*[80] The appellant contended, inter alia, that hanging to be visited on him on a murder conviction and subsequent death sentence contravened Section 7(1) of the Constitution prohibiting torture or inhuman or degrading punishment and was as such unconstitutional. He drew the Court's attention to the fact that the United Nations has urged its members, of which Botswana is, to restrict the number of offences for which the death penalty might be imposed with a view to its final and complete abolition throughout the world. However, the Court simply ignored the submission premised on what was happening at the international level. It merely said that its function was adjudicatory but not legislative and cursorily held that execution by hanging was a lawful punishment.

Similarly, in the fore-cited *State v. Ntesang,* it was argued on behalf of the appellant that hanging that he was ordered to undergo by the High Court amounted to an inhuman and degrading punishment and therefore contrary to Section 7(1) of the Constitution. The Court of Appeal construed this provision narrowly and restrictively, and held that hanging was saved by Section 7(2) of the Constitution. According to the Court, Section 7(2) created an exception to the prohibition on inhuman or degrading punishment or treatment which was lawful immediately before the Constitution came into operation. Thus since hanging was a lawful mode of execution immediately before the Constitution came into force it was not an inhuman or degrading

---

[80]   [1985] B.L.R 258. See also Molale v. The State Criminal Appeal No. 56/1994 (CA) (unreported).

punishment. It was *intra vires* the Constitution. Again, the Court took the view that since its functions were merely adjudicatory but not legislative, it could not outlaw hanging.

Democracy

The legal system of Botswana recognises the right to democratic governance. This right is, however, not enshrined in the Bill of Rights. It is protected by Section 67 of the Constitution. This clause stipulates that a person shall, unless he is disqualified for registration as a voter under the law, be entitled to be registered as a voter for electing members of the National Assembly. However, unlike the international human rights instruments such as Article 21 of the UDHR, Article 25 of the ICCPR and Article 13 of the ACHPR,[81] Section 67 does not positively accord to everyone the right to vote. It merely stipulates conditions which a person shall satisfy in order to be registered as a voter. These are citizenship, age, and residence.[82] Section 67 is reinforced by the Electoral Act.[83] The Act prescribes procedures for registration of voters, elections, polling and election petitions. Section 30 thereof specifically requires an intending voter to be registered in a given constituency and to produce the voter's registration card in order to be permitted to vote. These provisions are underscored by the requirement of periodic presidential and parliamentary elections. Presidential and parliamentary elections are authorised by Sections 32 and 61 of the Constitution respectively.

These provisions, in line with international human rights instruments, are designed to accord universal suffrage internal domestic effect. They encapsulate the pluralist and democratic nature

---

[81] For a detailed discussion of the concept of democracy in international law, see Crawford, "Democracy" at 113-33; Reisman, "Sovereignty" at 866; Franck, "Democratic Governance" at 46-91; Id, *Fairness in International Law*, at 83-139.

[82] The Constitution of Botswana, Section 67(1)(a) to (c). But for a discussion of these conditions and their implication in the electoral process in Botswana, see Tshosa, "Political Activity," at 371-83; Otlhogile, "Electoral Process," at 222-33; Danevad, "Do Elections Matter," at 381-402.

[83] Laws of Botswana, Cap. 02:07. Generally, see Lindholt, *Universality of Human Rights*, at 148.

of Botswana through a representative government. They spell out in detail the essential elements and minimum content of democracy as the right of all citizens to be governed according to their will and to participate in the political life of their societies. The authority of a government, elected by a majority to conduct the public affairs of the society is a consequence of the exercise of the right of participation in public life by all citizens, whether they belong to the majority or the minority.[84]

The right to democracy in Botswana has arisen mainly within the context of the right of female citizens married to foreigners to pass their Botswana citizenship to their children. This is because according to Section 61(1)(a) of the Constitution, only citizens of Botswana are entitled to vote. The question is, are children of these women also entitled to vote? To put the issue into proper context, in 1987 Parliament enacted the Citizenship Act which stripped Botswana female citizens married to foreigners of their rights to pass their Botswana citizenship to their children. This means that because they are not citizens of Botswana, having assumed the citizenship of their fathers, children of these women could not enjoy the human rights, including the right to vote, enjoyed by children born to Botswana men. This Act was successfully challenged in *Attorney-General v. Unity Dow*.[85] Relying on international human rights treaties such as the ACHPR and Convention on the Elimination of Discrimination against Women of 1967,[86] the Court of Appeal of Botswana declared the 1987 Citizenship Act unconstitutional. Most importantly, the case led to an enactment of the Citizenship (Amendment) Act No. 14 of 1995. Section 4(1) thereof extends citizenship to children of Botswana women married to foreigners. As a corollary, children of Botswana women now enjoy universal suffrage in Botswana.

---

[84]   Crawford, "Democracy" at 114-5. Crawford argues that the concept of democracy reflected in these instruments is not a simple majoritarian one. It is a reflection of the idea that every person, whether a member of a majority or a minority, has basic rights, including rights to participate in public life. Ibid., at 115.

[85]   (1992) L.R.C. (Const) 632. For a discussion of this case in relation to the right to vote in Botswana, see Tshosa, "Political Activity," at 377.

[86]   (1992) L.R.C. (Const) 632 at 656. See also Maluwa, "Malawian Constitution of 1995," at 77-8.

Clearly, the above human rights treaties were instrumental in influencing the Court to declare the Citizenship Act unconstitutional. They also prevailed upon the National Assembly to enact the Citizenship (Amendment) Act. The Court's approach seeks to shift away from Botswana dualist conception of international law and its municipal law. It complements Botswana's standards of protection with international standards. It is submitted that if the judiciary can vigorously and consistently pursue this approach it can cross-fertilise national law with international standards and accord these standards a firm and solid place in Botswana municipal law.

Non-discrimination

The principle of non-discrimination enjoys a prominent status in the normative order of Botswana. It features in two clauses in the Constitution. Section 3 thereof guarantees every person in Botswana the fundamental rights and freedoms of the individual whatever his race, place of origin, political opinions, colour, creed or sex.[87] This provision should be examined conjunctively with Section 15 which regulates discrimination in greater detail. Its paragraph 1 prohibits discriminatory law either of itself or in its effect. Paragraph 2 forbids discrimination of any person by a person acting by virtue of written law or in performance of public function or authority. It defines discrimination in paragraph 3 as affording different treatment to different persons attributable wholly or mainly to their respective descriptions by race, tribe, place of origin, political opinions, colour or creed whereby persons of one such description are subjected to disabilities.

The main non-discriminatory clause in Botswana: Section 3 corresponds mainly to Articles 14 of the ECHR except for the omission of concepts of religion, language and birth embodied in this instrument. It slightly resembles Article 2 of the ACHPR. It clearly reveals the

---

[87] For a detailed discussion of this clause, see Lindholt, *Universality of Human Rights*, at 186-211. See also Takirambudde, "Botswana," in Baehr, et al, *Human Rights*, at 146-7; Maope, *Human Rights*, at 112-22; Neff, "Human Rights in Africa," at 334-8; Id, *Human Rights*, at 11-3; Sanders, "Constitutionalism," at 354-5; Quansah, "A Woman's Servitude Removed," at 195-204.

influence of the European non-discrimination clause.[88] It is its replica. Thus the content of this right corresponds to international human rights standards. It entails the concept that individuals are equally subject to the law of the land as administered by ordinary courts.

Botswana's commitment to abide by the principle of non-discrimination is underlined by the fact that it has ratified treaties abolishing discrimination notably the Convention on the Elimination of All Forms of Discrimination against Women, 1979, the Convention on the Elimination of All Forms of Racial Discrimination, 1965 and the ACHPR, though it has yet to ratify others. It has, in theory, incorporated the non-discrimination normative standards encapsulated in these treaties into its municipal law. The non-discrimination clause of Botswana, in line with the main international human rights treaties, prohibits discrimination based on a variety of grounds. It is appropriate to examine whether in adjudicating these grounds the judiciary has sought guidance and assistance from international human rights law to reinforce its decisions.

Racialism Racialism, as a ground of discrimination, does not only feature conspicuously in international law but it also appears prominently in the Bill of Rights of Botswana. It is prohibited by both Sections 3 and 15(1) of the Constitution. Moreover, Botswana's ratification of the ACHPR and the Convention on the Elimination of All Forms of Racial Discrimination, 1965 has underlined its commitment to outlaw and deprecate, at least theoretically, the practice of racial discrimination.

It is worth observing that Botswana courts have not, unlike courts in countries such as South Africa and Namibia, ardently attacked racism. But they too hold similar views against the practice. A rare occasion presented itself in *S v. Zweiger.*[89] The accused, a white South African, was charged with unlawful possession of firearms and ammunition, and uncut diamonds valued at 6000 Botswana Pula

---

[88] Generally, see Heyns, "Human Rights Law," at 252-63; Moagi v. Attorney-General Criminal Appeal 28/ 1979 (8 April 1981) (unreported), per justice Baron, at 5.

[89] Review Case No. 522/1978 (12 October 1978) (unreported) discussed in Sanders, "Constitutionalism," at 354-5. See also Barend van Niekerk, "Mentioning the unmentionable: Race as a Factor in Sentencing." *South African Journal of Criminal Law and Criminology* (1978), 3: 151-58.

(equivalent of £1000 British Sterling). He was fined and given a non-custodial sentence. On review, the High Court noted that the sentence was too lenient in view especially of a similar case tried by the same magistrate six months ago of two poor blacks charged with possession of diamonds valued at 22 Botswana Pula who were each given three years jail term two of which were suspended conditionally.

Relying only on Section 3 of the Constitution, the Court noted that there was no evidence that the Magistrate took into account the fact that the accused was white but felt that the decision projected such a picture. It observed that "nothing is more calculated, or more likely to induce a sense of outrage than an impression that an accused is being given special treatment on account of his race." However, the Court made no reference to similar clauses in international instruments and comparative international jurisprudence in order to buttress its reasoning and give municipal effect to Botswana's international obligations to outlaw racism.

Sex discrimination   The main non-discriminatory clause of the Constitution, that is, Section 3, flatly outlaws adverse differential treatment based on sex. However, Section 15(3) does not include sex as one of the of discriminatory factors. But both the High Court and the Court of Appeal of Botswana in the *Unity Dow case* conclusively held that Section 15(3) was not restrictive and definitive, unless this was clearly so from the intention of the Legislature, of discrimination. Rather, it extended the meaning or is explanatory of the word discrimination. Thus sex discrimination is also outlawed in Section 15(3).[90]

Discrimination on the ground of sex has arisen mainly in relation to women's equality with men. This is a central issue in Botswana. In this regard, Article 18(3) of the ACHPR legally obliges Botswana, as a State party to this Convention, to ensure the elimination of every discrimination against women.

Discrimination against women arises in two areas. First, customary law. Secondly, legislation. With respect to customary

---

[90] Quansah, "A Woman's Servitude Removed," at 195-204; Takirambudde, "Botswana," in Baehr et al, *Human Rights*, at 146. See further Neff, "Human Rights in Africa," at 335; Simon, "Botswana," at 91-2; Rembe, " Sex Discrimination," at 158-9.

practices, there are customary rules existing alongside official rules which discriminate against women. For example, women are discriminated against under succession, property and family law. Thus unless the husband makes a specific bequest to his wife, she does not inherit from his estate. The estate devolves upon the eldest son. Moreover, where the father dies intestate, customary law of succession does not recognise the rights of female children to succeed to his property on his death. The property devolves only upon his eldest son but not other children.[91]

The question that arises is, are these customary practices compatible with the non-discrimination norms? Or rather, can the non-discrimination norms be derogated from on the basis of these practices? These questions become pertinent when analysed within the context of Section 15(4)(d) of the Constitution. This clause makes customary law an exception to equality and non-discrimination in addition, for instance, to derogations reasonably justifiable in a democratic society. This poses the question, is the exclusion of the principles of equality and non-discrimination under customary law justifiable in a democratic society? This issue arose specifically in a Swaziland case of *Ross-Spencer and Another v. Master of the High Court*.[92] The case involved the constitutionality of a statute exempting the estates of Africans, but not Europeans, from death duties despite the constitutional guarantee of equality of protection before the law subject to the exception that the law could make discriminations where reasonably justifiable in a democratic society. The Swaziland High Court held that this kind of differential treatment was reasonably justifiable in a democratic society since the Swazi society comprised classes or groups of people living under different social and economic conditions. Thus it was reasonable to construe the law to effectuate this factual reality.

On a pure question of reasonable interpretation of the law in question, the approach of the court is appropriate. It is not a derogation

---

[91] Schapera, *Handbook on Tswana Law*, at 230-57; Van Niekerk, "Customary law of Botswana", at 242-7. See also Takirambudde, "Botswana," in Baehr et al, *Human Rights*, at 147. See further Maope, *Human Rights*, at 119-22.

[92] [1970-76] Swazi. L. R. 58. For an analysis of this case, see Aguda, "Discrminatory Statutory Provisions," at 299-308; Neff, "Human Rights in Africa," at 335-6.

from the principle of non-discrimination. Rather, it is a recognition of the fact that society in countries like Swaziland, and certainly in Botswana, live under customary law and practices which oftentimes are antagonistic to, and in conflict with, the universal norms but without in themselves being discriminatory provided they reflect practical reality and do lead to social cohesion.

This case is, however, contrasted with the fore-cited *Unity Dow* case in which the Attorney-General argued that the omission of the word "sex" among the discriminatory grounds in Section 15(3) of the Constitution did not breach the non-discrimination clause because it had been intentionally omitted so as to reflect the fact that under the customary law of Botswana society is based on patrilineal structure. This means that discrimination of this nature was reasonably justifiable in Botswana democratic society. Drawing inspiration from court decisions in other countries and international human rights treaties especially the ACHPR, which is an embodiment of African human rights normative values and standards,[93] the Court rejected this argument holding that it was impossible to accept the argument that Botswana is a discriminatory society. According to Bizos, J.A., "If the makers of the Constitution of Botswana intended it to discriminate against women because it is a patrilineal and male oriented society, they could not have missed the opportunity of expressly debarring them from holding office as President, minister, deputy minister or member of Parliament."[94]

Obviously where the customary practices are not only unreasonable as the Court observed in *Unity Dow* case but are also utterly discriminatory, in content and effect, it is submitted that preference should be given to universal norms. Of course, this approach engenders a situation where customary norms give way to universal rules resulting in cultural imperialism where norms are

---

[93] Umozurike, *The African Charter*, at 87-96. Professor Umozurike notes: "There are provisions and procedures that are different from those of earlier charters. Some of them are merely a natural development, a greater elaboration; others are unique and peculiar, so that they may be said to be autochthonous." Ibid., at 87.

[94] [1992] L.R.C. (Const) 623 at 682. See also Beyani, "Women's Rights," in Cook, *Human Rights of Women*, at 294-8.

imposed on the public by vanguard elite groups.[95] But whatever the effect of these imposed norms may be, especially with respect to the notion of cultural imperialism, an unreasonable customary practice would have to be construed and if need be corrected and modernised to effectuate universal standards which advance the status of the womenfolk.

Second is the question of discriminatory legislation. There is a body of laws which limits equality of women with men. The inherited Roman-Dutch and statutory law have generated barriers that adversely affect women's social, economic and political opportunities. There is an array of legislation on areas such as citizenship, family law and labour law which discriminate against women.[96] In family law sphere, the Deeds Registry Act is the most pertinent legislation.[97] Under Section 18(4) thereof, a woman married in community of property is deprived of her right to have immovable property transferred or ceded to her except where the property has been exempt from community of property. This clause denies women the most important commodity in the country. Section 5 thereof gives the husband power alone to deal with their joint estate. Thus the husband is given the right, which is not available to the wife, to dispose of their joint property. Further, under the Administration of Estate Act, a married woman cannot be granted letters of confirmation without the husband's consent.[98]

These pieces of legislation and customary practices are incompatible with the principle of non-discrimination. They are, on strict application of Article 18(3) of the ACHPR, discriminatory against women. Significantly, the whole question of sex discrimination in Botswana especially in relation to the womenfolk was resolved by

---

[95] Preis, "Cultural Practice," at 294-7; Neff, "Human Rights in Africa," at 337-8; Beyani, "Women's Rights," in Cook, *Human Rights of Women*, at 285-9.

[96] Takirambudde, "Botswana," Baehr et al, *Human Rights*, at 146; Lindholt, *Universality of Human Rights*, at 195-211; Ng'ong'ola, "Land Tenure Reform," at 5-6. As regards citizenship, that is, the right of Botswana women to pass citizenship to their children, the legal impediment has been removed by the Citizenship (Amendment) Act of 1995. The Act gives Botswana women the right to pass their citizenship to their children even where they are married to non-citizens.

[97] Act No. 84/1966.

[98] Act No. 20/1972, Section 91(2).

the *Unity Dow* case. Relying heavily on international human rights conventions such as the ACHPR, UDHR and ECHR and Convention on the Elimination of all Forms of Discrimination against Women of 1967, the Court of Appeal outlawed sex discrimination. According to Justice Aguda, these instruments must be resorted to whether or not they "have been specifically incorporated into our law."[99]

The Court stressed that discrimination based wholly on sex is not only unconstitutional but is violative of universally recognised human rights norms. According to Justice Aguda, "more than ever before, the whole world has realised that discrimination on grounds of sex, like that institution which was in times gone by permissible both by most religious and the conscience of men of those times, namely, slavery, can no longer be permitted or even tolerated, more so by the law."[100] It is, therefore, clear that the prohibition of sex discrimination in major human rights treaties and general norms of international human rights law played a central role in influencing the Court to declare sex discrimination unconstitutional in Botswana.

Most significantly, the *Unity Dow* case compelled the Government to announce in 1994 its intention to commission a consultancy to review all the relevant laws of the country and recommend changes in order to improve the status of women.[101] However, this still remains an aspiration only.

Property Rights

Two clauses in the Constitution of Botswana protect basic property rights. In Section 3(c) of the Constitution "every person in Botswana is entitled to the.. protection for the privacy of his home and other property and from deprivation of property without compensation." Section 8(1) thereof emphatically states that "no property of any description shall be compulsory taken possession of, and no interest in or right over property of any description shall be compulsorily

---

[99] [1992] L.R.C. (Const) 623 at 673.

[100] Ibid., at 640. See also Attorney General of Botswana v. Moagi, Criminal Appeal No. 73/1978 (unreported). For an analysis of this case, see Sanders, "Constitutionalism in Botswana," at 50-2.

[101] Takirambudde, "Botswana," Baehr et al, *Human Rights*, at 147.

acquired..." This clause is the main property clause in Botswana. It does not only protect the right to property. It also protects "interest in or right over property." It protects a legally recognised interest or right in property. This relates to any interest of a proprietary or pecuniary nature, which if not immediately held or claimed in the property is nevertheless so associated with the property. It excludes any remote interest or right in the property.[102] Protection of property or interest therein of *any* description includes both movable and immovable property including land held on freehold title and communal land held under customary law.[103] Thus Section 8(1) offers a secure protection of property rights irrespective of the manner of acquisition.

Section 8(1) does not, however, employ the language of the international human rights instruments such as Article 17(1) of the UDHR, Article 14 of the ACHPR and Article 1 of the First Protocol to the ECHR and formulate the classical right to property positively. It does not categorically prescribe individuals entitlement to property. It adopts a negativist approach and merely protects property or interest or right therein from compulsorily acquisition. The international human rights instruments employ mandatory terms by providing that the right to property shall be protected and shall not be arbitrarily expropriated or compulsorily acquired. Nonetheless, Section 8(1) constitutes the legal basis for the protection of individuals' right to property in Botswana. To ensure its practical application, this clause has been supplemented by the Acquisition of Property Act[104] and Land Control Act.[105] The latter Act aims at creating for citizens of Botswana a statutory 'right of pre-emption' in the acquisition of land in freehold sector including agricultural land. The former empowers the President

---

[102] Pieter Bruwer and Others v. The President of Botswana and Others, Misca. No. 478/96, at 13-4, per Justice Nganunu (unreported). See also Ng'ong'ola, "Land Rights in Botswana," at 12.

[103] See generally Bishop, "Squatters on their Own Land," at 92-121; Ng'ong'ola, "Land Rights" at 1-26; Alice Mogwe, "Who Was There first?, at 1-10.

[104] Laws of Botswana, Cap. 32: 10. See Generally Ng'ong'ola, "Compulsory Acquisition," at 298-317; Pieter Bruwer and Others v. The President of Botswana and Others, Misca. No. 478/96(unreported).

[105] Act No. 23/1975, Cap 31:11. For an analysis of this legislation, see Ng'ong'ola, "Land Tenure Reform," at 1-29; Id., "Land Rights in Botswana," at 11-26.

to acquire property or interest therein if he deems it necessary or expedient in the public interest.

It is clear that both the substantive content and scope of Botswana property clauses are in line with international law. They, by and large, reflect international standards for the protection of property rights. They recognise everyone's right to own property or interests therein irrespective of the manner of acquisition. The main controversial issues associated with property rights are expropriation and compensation. It is apposite to examine whether in dealing with these issues the judiciary has been inspired by international human rights law and sources.

Property expropriation   In line with international law, Botswana property clauses authorise the State to invoke its executive powers to expropriate property of any kind or description. Section 3(1) of the Acquisition of Property Act empowers the President to expropriate any property if he deems it expedient or necessary in the interest of defence, public safety, public health, public morality, town and country planning or land settlements and for purposes beneficial to the community. Section 8(1)(a) of the Constitution authorises compulsory acquisition of property if it is injurious to the health of human beings, animals or plants; for purposes of securing the development; in the general public interest and where reasonably justifiable in a democratic society.[106] Additionally, property may be expropriated for purposes of exploitation, development or utilisation of mineral resources.[107] This limitation broadens areas in which the State may expropriate property. It takes into account special and peculiar circumstances of Botswana economic needs. The economy of Botswana is dependent on mineral resources. It is, therefore, reasonable to allow the State to acquire property for development or utilisation of mineral resources.

---

[106] This clause also provides that this right may be limited where the law provides for the acquisition of property, inter alia, to satisfy any tax or rate; by way of penalty for breach of the law whether under civil process or after conviction for a criminal offence and to prevent removal or attempted removal of property out of or into the country in contravention of any law. Generally, see Ng'ong'ola, "Compulsory Acquisition," at 298-317; The President of Botswana and Others v. Pieter Bruwer and Others Civil Appeal No. 13/1997 (unreported).

[107] The Constitution of Botswana, Section 8(i)(a)(ii).

These limitations are designed to serve a significant societal need. However, they should be balanced against the welfare and interest of the individual to own and be in continued and peaceful enjoyment of his or her right to property.[108] This means that expropriation of property should not be arbitrary or discriminatory. In order to ensure legality, it should be according to law.

Unlike most African countries, Botswana did not embark on massive property expropriation after independence. As such no major inroads have been made into the property clauses. Consequently, expropriation laws have not attracted much judicial activity. One of the few cases in which these laws were challenged is *The President of Botswana and Others v. Pieter Bruwer and Another.*[109] On 10 July 1996, the Minister of Local Government, Lands and Housing issued a notice in the Government Gazette expressing its intention to acquire for public purposes the respondents' farm (Molopo Ranch) together with improvements thereon, which included livestock (15, 000 head of cattle) pursuant to the Acquisition of Property Act. The respondents contested the acquisition. Their main complaint related not to the President's power to acquire immovable property, in this case the farm, but the moveable property especially livestock in the farm.

The main issue for the Court was, therefore, whether the President's power to acquire property under the Acquisition of Property Act extended to moveable property. The Court did not question the general authority of the President to compulsorily acquire immovable property for public purposes. With respect to moveable property, the Court interpreted Section 8(1) of the Act which forbids compulsory taking of possession of private property or interest in or right over property of any description in order to determine whether the President's power extends to such property. It held that the President had no power under the Act to acquire livestock in the farm. Amissah, J.P. said, "Clearly, the Acquisition of Property Act empowers Government to compulsorily acquire immovable property only. Government is incompetent to acquire moveable property. A notice of

---

[108] Lindholt, *Universality of Human Rights*, at 139.

[109] Civil Appeal No. 13/1997 (unreported).

intention to compulsorily acquire cattle, which are moveables, as well as land, as the notice under consideration shows, is invalid...''[110]

This case was, of course, decided strictly and purely on the basis of the Acquisition of Property Act which applies to immovable property only. It is significant to note that in arriving at its decision, the Court invoked and relied on comparative jurisprudence from South Africa and England. Jurisprudence from these countries influenced it to conclude that moveable property could not be expropriated under the Act. However, no reference was made to property clauses in human rights treaties. Moreover, no recourse was had to international jurisprudence on the subject. The Court confined itself only to national legislation and jurisprudence. It did not broaden its interpretation by relying on international norms and jurisprudence. As such, it reinforced Botswana's inherited dualist theory.

The standard of compensation As highlighted elsewhere, neither the UDHR nor the First Protocol to the ECHR mention compensation for deprivation of property and the standard of compensation. Compensation is only mentioned in Article 21(2) of the ACHPR. This clause provides: "In case of spoliation the dispossessed people shall have the right to the lawful recovery of its property as well as to adequate compensation." In so far as it requires adequate compensation for expropriated property, Article 21(2) approximates partially to Section 8(b)(1) of the Constitution of Botswana which requires that any expropriation of property must be accompanied by "prompt payment" of "adequate compensation."

Again, as indicated earlier on, the traditional rule supported by Western countries is that compensation for compulsory acquisition of property should be prompt, adequate and effective.[111] This means that Botswana's standard of compensation diverges from the international standard in so far as the requirement of effective, or rather full compensation is concerned. But it conforms to the adequate

---

[110] Ibid., at 28 of the judgment.

[111] Brownlie, *Principles*, at 532-5; Naldi, *Constitutional Rights*, at 83; Texaco v. Libya 17 ILM 1 (1978). See also Mapp, *Iran-United States Claims Tribunals*, at 179.

compensation standard favoured by developing States.[112] In fact, within the context of economic and social conditions in Botswana, the full compensation standard is too high and unsupportable. Local conditions demand the adoption of much lesser strict requirements of compensation assessment. This is within its sovereign right.

The opportunity to interpret and test the standard of compensation arose in *Attorney-General of Botswana v. Western Trust (Pty) Ltd*, commonly called the Bonnington Farm case.[113] On 28 August, 1978 the Government compulsorily acquired two properties, Bonnington Farms, used for grazing and farming purposes, belonging to the respondent in terms of the Acquisition of Property Act. No dispute arose as regards the necessity of the acquisition since the land was clearly needed for use in town and country planning in the outskirts of Gaborone, the capital city of Botswana. When it became clear that the views of the two parties as regards the appropriate amount of compensation were irreconcilable, a Board of Assessment was constituted in terms of Section 11(4) of the Act to assess compensation. Being dissatisfied with the level of compensation awarded by the Board to the expropriatee, the Government appealed to the High Court of Botswana.

As regards the preferred method of determining compensation, the Court interpreted the "adequate compensation" provided for by Section 8(b)(1) of the Constitution to mean the total market value of the property or what a "willing seller and purchaser would most probably have done in an open market sale" together with potentialities such as the industrial development value and hope value. In arriving at this method of assessment, the Court interlaced its decision with decisions from other countries interpreting similar provisions. It noted that "... we consider that reading the constitution, and the South African and English authorities on the point, the only fair method of valuation is one based on the principle that the expropriatee should be compensated adequately for the land, and in so far as money can do it, be put back into the same position as he would have been had the land

---

[112] This standard seems to have acquired some status of *de lege ferenda*. See Naldi, *Constitutional Rights*, at 83; Texaco v. Libya 17 ILM 1 (1978).

[113] Civil Cause No 37/1981 (Civil Appeal No. 12/1981) (unreported). Generally see Ng'ong'ola, "Compulsory Acquisition," at 298-317.

not been expropriated."[114] However, the Court did not adopt the same approach and refer to comparative international norms and decisions of bodies such as the ECtHR interpreting similar clauses.

In sum, it is clear that Botswana courts have not actively invoked international human rights norms to construe Botswana expropriation and compensation laws. International norms have played no role in assessing and reviewing the legal interpretation and application of Botswana's expropriation and compensation laws against a backdrop of rapid urban expansion. They have underscored Botswana's dualist theory by relying primarily on national provisions and jurisprudence.

Educational Rights

The right to education, as with most human rights norms traditionally treated as economic, social and cultural rights; the so-called second generation rights,[115] enjoys no constitutional status and recognition in Botswana municipal law. It effectively means that, legally speaking, there is no basis for Botswana citizens to assert the right to education in municipal law.

At the international stage, educational rights are enshrined in Article 26 of the UDHR, Article 13 of the ICESCR and Article 17(1) of the ACHPR. These clauses are analogous to Article 2 of the First Protocol to the ECHR, albeit, the latter guarantees the right in negative terms. The former articles do not only recognise everyone's right to education but recognise that primary education shall be compulsory and available free to all, and higher education shall, with restrictions based on capacity, be widely expanded. These instruments enjoin States Parties to provide education to its citizens not as a privilege but as a right. The cornerstone of this right is to provide individuals with

---

[114] Civil Cause No 37/1981 (Civil Appeal No. 12/1981) (unreported) at 4-5 of the judgment.

[115] Human rights are traditionally trichotomised into the first generation rights (civil and political rights), second generation of rights (economic, social and cultural rights) and third generation rights (the so-called right to peace, development and environment). Literature on this categorisation is extensive. See for example, Ankumah, *The African Commission*, at 143-44; Makua wa Matua, "The Banjul Charter," at 339-80; Gittleman, "The African Charter," at 667-714.

opportunities of access to educational institutions. However, with the exception of primary education, the right to education does not guarantee to everyone the right of admission at educational institutions.[116]

Of these instruments, Botswana has expressed consent to be bound by the ACHPR. This means that internationally, Botswana is legally bound to respect educational rights of its citizens except that they cannot assert and claim these rights at municipal level as the ACHPR has not been translated into municipal law. In practice, however, individuals enjoy the right to education. Despite the fact that the educational system inherited at independence particularly at the post-primary level, was among the least developed in Africa,[117] Botswana has taken steps to provide education at primary, secondary, technical and vocational, and university levels. The current National Development Plan is poised to attaining universal access to the first nine years of education: seven and two years of primary and secondary education respectively and to increasing access to other higher levels of education. The Department of Non-formal education, set up in 1978 as part of a national strategy to widen access to education, administers a national literacy programme as well as correspondence courses.[118]

In stark contrast to international human rights instruments, there is no legal provision in Botswana allowing individuals to establish and maintain private schools and kindred institutions of tertiary education. Notwithstanding, in principle, private schools are permitted at owner's expenses. Limited resources makes it reasonable

---

[116] Cf the Constitution of South Africa, Section 32(a). This clause guarantees individuals equal access to educational institutions.

[117] At independence, there was only one government-financed secondary school and such educational and training facilities as existed were largely the outcome of missionary endeavours and self-help initiatives. Beyond the secondary level, all professional and technical education had to be pursued outside the country particularly in South Africa. See generally Granberg and Parkinson, *Botswana*, at 79-90.

[118] In 1990 the Government spent 8% of the total GNP on education. This percentage has improved considerably as a result of the increase of approximately 60% in budgetary allocations for education in the period 1991-1994. See Takirambudde, "Botswana," in Baehr et al, *Human Rights*, at 145; Granberg and Parkinson, *Botswana*, at 86-7.

to permit these schools even though some families cannot afford to send their children to these schools because they charge high fees. Furthermore, parents have the right to ensure education and teaching of children in conformity with their own religious and moral beliefs and convictions.

The enjoyment of the right to education is, however, limited by law in certain instances. Section 29 of the Education Act, No. 40 of 1966 which deals with Teacher Training College Regulations compels pregnant students to withdraw from colleges. Their return to college is conditional upon approval by the Permanent Secretary of the Ministry of Education. Further, students cannot write examinations during pregnancy. They can only write after six months of pregnancy. These regulations were challenged by students in *SRC, Molepolole College of Education v. Attorney-General of Botswana*.[119] The Court of Appeal noted that the regulations were not, as claimed by the College and accepted by the High Court, protective measures to the mother and child, and an encouragement of a well planned maternity leave. Rather, they were designed to punish unmarried young mothers. This is particularly so since the recurrence of pregnancy results in permanent exclusion from colleges. Moreover, married students are not subjected to similar measures. Their cases are considered "particular cases."

Although, the Court did not make any specific reference to international human rights norms in general and treaties protecting the right to education to arrive at its conclusion, nonetheless, it approvingly referred to and relied upon *Unity Dow* case wherein eloquent and extensive reference was made to human rights treaties to outlaw sex based discrimination. Relying on this case, the Court underlined the fact that the whole intention of making regulations specifically for women was unreasonable and unfair, and struck down the Teacher Training College Regulations. The human rights treaties formed, albeit indirectly, part of the basis of the Court's decision.

---

[119] Civil Appeal No. 13/1994, Misca No. 396/1993 (unreported). Judgment delivered on 31 January, 1995. See Quansah, "The Right to Get Pregnant," at 97-102; Lindholt, *Universality of Human Rights*, at 207-211.

Conclusion

Despite differences in the drafting style, phraseology and formulation, it is evidently clear that the various human rights norms embodied in the Bill of Rights of Botswana bear influence of Western liberal-oriented international human rights standards. Their juridical substantive content and scope are, by and large, in line with international human rights standards. They were influenced by, and thus domestically effectuate, standards embodied in international human rights instruments. Even the attendant derogation and claw-back clauses are crafted in terms similar to those contained in international human rights instruments. This was a clear, albeit implicit and indirect, attempt to accord international human rights norms a role in municipal law of Botswana. By replicating human rights norms in international instruments, the Bill of Rights implicitly incorporates international standards in these instruments into Botswana national law.

The practical application and enforcement of human rights norms by courts has, however, not been consistent with the idea mirrored in the Bill of Rights. When interpreting the various human rights norms in the Bill of Rights, Botswana courts have not actively and consistently referred to and relied upon similar provisions in international human rights instruments and international norms generally. Their interpretation has mainly been based on national law and jurisprudence. Admittedly, there are instances where reliance has been placed on human rights treaties such as the UDHR, ICCPR, ECHR and ACHPR as well as international customary law, for instance, in cases of non-discrimination, concepts such as trial within a reasonable time, inhuman and degrading treatment or punishment, democracy and the right to life. But, even in these instances such reference has been cursory. It has also occurred in few and isolated cases. Moreover, it has not been consistent and uniform.

It is also significant to note that even in cases where international norms are invoked and relied on to interpret domestic human rights law especially with respect to practices which *ex facie* are repugnant to human rights norms contained in the Constitution, the courts have not actively relied on international norms to invalidate these practices. For example, international human rights norms have been relied on to challenge the death penalty, corporal punishment and hanging as a mode of executing the death penalty. In some of these instances the courts consulted international sources *mero motu* and acknowledged their importance in interpreting national law. But, they were not prepared to use norms in these sources to nullify these practices. Instead, they invoke national standards to endorse them.

Thus it is evident that despite being authorised by the Interpretation Act to construe national law on the basis of international treaties, Botswana courts have restrained themselves from actively invoking international law to enhance domestic human rights protection and enrich national jurisprudence. They have not been active enough to employ the rich legal resource provided by international standards to interpret national law and accord these standards a firm and solid place in Botswana national law. This approach reinforces the classical dualist, not monist, theory inherited from the United Kingdom. It endorses the conception that international law and Botswana national law are separate legal regimes. The adverse effect of this approach is that it limits the role and effectiveness of international human rights law in national law. Perceptibly, courts will continue to adopt this approach in the foreseeable future in the light of the few cases and inconsistent manner in which the subject is being handled unless, statutorily or constitutionally, the legal position is explicitly clarified and courts empowered to invoke directly international law in general when enforcing national law including human rights law.

7 Zimbabwe:
Dualism Challenged

It has been demonstrated in the previous discussion that Zimbabwe, like Botswana, inherited from Britain the dualist theory with respect to treaties and monism in relation to customary international law. This chapter examines the post-independence practice in order to find out whether this legacy still obtains. The exercise is undertaken by examining human rights norms embodied in the constitutionally entrenched Bill of Rights. These norms are compared and contrasted with similar norms in major human rights treaties and instruments in order to find out not only whether national norms reflect international standards, but also whether they embrace the inherited legal legacy. In the process, the chapter examines how the Zimbabwean courts have treated the subject in practice in the enforcement of human rights norms. In particular, it examines whether, and to what extent, the courts have utilised international human rights law and sources in enforcing human rights especially in trying to resolve some of the critical issues that arise in the enforcement process.

Judicial Practice

The Right to Life

The municipal law of Zimbabwe recognises and protects the right to life.[1] According to Section 12(1) of the Constitution "no person shall be deprived of his life intentionally save in execution of the sentence of a court in respect of a criminal offence of which he has been convicted." This protective clause corresponds to Article 3 of the UDHR, Article 6 of the ICCPR and Article 4 of the ACHPR. In

---

[1] Generally, see Hatchard, *Individual freedoms*, at 83-5; Human Rights Watch, *Zimbabwe*, at 23-39; Zimmerli, "Human Rights," at 239-300; Austin, *Legislation of Rhodesian Front*, at 1-21.

particular, it is equivalent to Article 2(1) of the ECHR. The Zimbabwean, as with the similarly drafted Botswana, right to life clause, but unlike the international human rights instruments, does not protect the right to life positively. It protects this right in negative terms by merely forbidding the intentional deprivation of life. It does not express its natural-law foundation as an inherent and inalienable right. By contrast, the international human rights instruments protect this right in directory and positive terms. They also articulate its inalienability.[2]

Nevertheless, the Zimbabwean clause recognises the sanctity of life by prohibiting its intentional deprivation. This right is supreme. As Dinstein points out, it "is incontestably the most important of all human rights. Civilised society cannot exist without legal protection of human life. The inviolability or sanctity of life is, perhaps, the most basic value of modern civilisation."[3]

However, unlike most international human rights instruments, and certainly the UDHR and ICCPR, the right to life is not accorded absolute protection in municipal law of Zimbabwe. Section 12(2) (a) to (d) of the Constitution recognises that this right may be limited in self-defence; defence of any person or property; in order to effect a lawful arrest or prevent the escape of a person lawfully detained; for purpose of suppressing a riot, insurrection or mutiny; in order to prevent the commission of an offence or if a person dies as a result of lawful act of war. With the exception of the latter limitation, the Zimbabwean clause corresponds to Article 4 of the ACHPR and, in particular, Article 2(2) (a) to (c) of the ECHR. It is a transplant of the ECHR both in its formulation of the right to life and circumstances under which this right may be limited or curtailed. These clauses recognise that under exceptional circumstances, the State can use its executive powers to derogate from the right to life. However, in order to ensure legality, the

---

[2]   Generally, see Nowak, *U.N. Covenant*, at 105.

[3]   Dinstein, "Life, Physical Integrity, and Liberty," in Henkin, *The International Bill of Rights*, at 114. See also Nowak, *U.N. Covenant*, at 104; Umozurike, *The African Charter*, at 34.

deprivation of life should be unintentional. Also it should not be arbitrary.[4] It should be in accordance with the law.

Thus, in line with international human rights instruments, the Zimbabwean municipal law recognises and protects the right to life. Its right to life clause incorporates international standards for the protection of the right to life into municipal law. It, together with the international human rights treaties such as the ICCPR and the ACHPR which Zimbabwe has ratified, also imposes a legal obligation on Zimbabwe to protect an individual's life.

It is significant to note that Zimbabwean courts have yet to analyse the right to life clause especially in relation to equivalent clauses in the international human rights instruments. It is thus not possible to assess whether and the degree to which the courts have been, and will be, guided by international human rights standards when interpreting the right to life. However, one issue that arises in connection with the implementation of this right is the death penalty.

The death penalty   The death penalty is a lawful and competent sentence under the national law of Zimbabwe. Its imposition is authorised by Section 12(1) of the Constitution. As in Botswana, execution in Zimbabwe is by hanging. It is reserved only for the most serious offences such as murder, treason, rape, murder committed in the process of committing piracy and robbery or attempted robbery where there are aggravating circumstances.[5] However, its application may be excluded but only in exceptional cases where there are extenuating circumstances, for instance, where a person kills in self-defence or under provocation. Except for persons below eighteen years and pregnant mothers, the death penalty can be imposed on anybody convicted of these offences. The exclusion of the death sentence in

---

[4]   As to the difference between "arbitrary" in the ICCPR and "intentional" in the Zimbabwean clause and other human rights treaties, see Nowak, *U.N. Covenant*, at 110-13.

[5]   The death sentence is also provided for under the Law and Order Maintenance Act, 1983, Sections 24(1) to (2), 27 and 50. Under this Act, offences for which the death sentence may be imposed include possession of any arms of war and carrying out, or involvement in, acts of terrorism or sabotage. See Hatchard, *Individual freedoms*, at 84-5.

respect to these categories of people is designed to limit circumstances under which it may be meted out.

As observed earlier on, Article 1(1) of the Second Optional Protocol to the ICCPR Aiming at the Abolition of the Death Penalty categorically and explicitly outlaws the death penalty. However, Zimbabwe has yet to sign this convention. As such, Zimbabwe is not legally obliged to observe it.

Significantly, in the early 1990s the debate, probed by the public and civil society, both national and international such as Amnesty International, ensued on the abolition of the death sentence in Zimbabwe due to a number of prisoners who were condemned to death and awaiting execution. The debate was, however, aborted when Parliament impetuously passed the Criminal Laws Amendment Act of 1992 which retains capital punishment for murder, treason and military offences. This means that capital punishment in Zimbabwe will continue to be lawful and permissible for some time in the future. As a matter of fact, it is carried out in practice. A number of prisoners who were condemned to death and awaiting execution have since been executed. According to Amnesty International Report, seven people were executed in Zimbabwe in 1997, which represented a significant increase over previous years, five others were sentenced to death and twenty-two remained under sentence of death at the end of the year.[6]

It is significant to observe that the death penalty has not *per se* attracted active judicial attention in Zimbabwe. However, the Supreme Court of Zimbabwe has expressed its view regarding its constitutionality and appropriateness in Zimbabwean municipal law. In *Catholic Commission for Peace and Justice in Zimbabwe v. Attorney-General, Zimbabwe and Others* the Court, per Gubbay, Chief Justice, expressly and categorically noted that "It was not sought, nor could it reasonably be, to overturn the death sentences on the ground that they were unlawfully imposed. The judgments of this Court dismissing the appeals of the condemned prisoners cannot be disturbed. They are final, and the constitutionality of the death penalty *per se*, as well as the mode of its execution by hanging, are also not susceptible to

---

[6] Amnesty International 1997 Report, "Zimbabwe," at 346-7. See further Hatchard, *Individual freedoms*, at 84.

attack."[7] This approach clearly marks a judicial confirmation of the institution of the death penalty in Zimbabwean municipal law. It is ample evidence of self-restraint exercised by the Zimbabwean courts to outlaw the death penalty. It underlines the fact that so long as the judiciary hold this view, the death penalty will continue to be institutionalised in Zimbabwe.

It is submitted that this case presented an opportunity for the Supreme Court to authoritatively determine the appropriateness of the death penalty in Zimbabwean municipal law both against the Constitution of Zimbabwe and indeed current international human rights standards. The fact that the legislature passed a law preventing its attack does not usurp the power of the judiciary to determine its constitutionality. The Supreme Court has inherent powers to determine whether or not the death penalty is constitutional in municipal law of Zimbabwe.

Personal Liberty

Section 13(1) of the Zimbabwean Constitution provides that "No person shall be deprived of his personal liberty save as may be authorised by law..." The specific safeguards protected by this clause are the right of the accused or detainee to be informed as soon as practicable, in the language that he understands, of the reasons of his arrest or detention; the right of any person who is arrested or detained for purposes of bringing him to court or on suspicion of having committed an offence and who is not released, to be brought as soon as is reasonably practicable before court, and if he is not tried within a reasonable time, to be released unconditionally or upon reasonable conditions and the right to compensation for unlawful arrest and detention.[8] Section 13(1) corresponds to Article 3 of the UDHR, Article 9 of the ICCPR and Article 6 of the ACHPR. It is also

---

[7] 1993 (4) S.A. 239 at 243. This case is discussed in detail below in relation to the "death row" phenomenon. Generally, see Nherere, "Bill of Rights," at 44; Madhuku, "European Court of Human Rights," at 939-40.

[8] The Constitution of Zimbabwe, Section 13(3), (4) (a) to (b) and (5). See Hatchard, *Individual Freedoms*, at 46-58; Gubbay, "Fundamental Human Rights," at 244-6.

analogous to Article 5 of the ECHR.[9] These conventions similarly prohibit unlawful arrest and detention of individuals. However, unlike the international human rights instruments, Section 13(1) does not protect security of persons.

Section 13 recognises that personal liberty is subject to exceptions. The limitations are crafted in almost the same terms as in the ECHR. They include, inter alia, limitations designed to execute the sentence of the court, to secure the attention of the person in court, based on reasonable suspicion of a person having committed an offence, in order to prevent the unlawful entry of a person in the country or for the purpose of expulsion, extradition or other lawful removal of the person from the country.[10] These limitations are not peculiar to Zimbabwe. They are also found in most international human rights instruments. They are designed to serve a significant societal purpose.

It is evidently clear that Section 13(1) of the Constitution of Zimbabwe, in line with international human rights instruments, protects individuals physical freedom subject to restrictions. It largely bears influence of international safeguards. It guarantees individuals procedural fairness against unlawful intrusion with their liberty. This provision imposes a legal obligation on State authorities to respect and observe the liberty of the individual.

The right to personal liberty constitutes a scheme for providing arrested individuals and detainees with proper safeguards. It ensures protection of the individual physical liberty. Any restrictions on this right must be authorised by law. The law relied upon must be consistent with civilised and international norms and standards. Its rationale is to avoid arbitrary deprivation of personal liberty.[11]

The most controversial issue, however, concerning restrictions on personal liberty concerns arrest by police officers on reasonable suspicion that a person has committed an offence. Generally, the police

---

[9] Harris, et al, *European Convention*, at 128-9. See further Nowak, *U.N. Covenant*, at 158-82; Dinstein, "Life, Physical Integrity, and Liberty," in Henkin, *The International Bill of Rights*, at 128-35.

[10] The Constitution of Zimbabwe, Section 13(2)(a) to (i).

[11] Minister of Home Affairs v. Dabengwa 1984 (2) S.A. 345 at 350-1 (per Beck, J.A.); Harris, et al, *European Convention*, at 97.

in Zimbabwe have powers to arrest any person on reasonable suspicion of having committed a crime. The question that emerges is, what amounts to reasonable grounds or suspicion that a person has committed a crime? This issue has been entertained in the courts in Zimbabwe. It arose in *Moll v. Commissioner of Police and Others*.[12] The Zimbabwean High Court emphasised that the arresting police officer must take reasonable care before effecting an arrest. He must personally have reasonable grounds to suspect that the person being arrested has committed a crime. If he has difficulties in determining whether suspicion is reasonable on the basis of the information to hand, he should confirm it with superior officers. Otherwise the arrest is unlawful. In *S v. Miller*[13] the Court held that failure by an arresting police officer to take steps to confirm or allay the suspicion makes the suspicion unreasonable and the consequent arrest unlawful.

It is clear that in both cases, the Court gave life and substance to the right to liberty. It adopted a broad and liberal interpretation of this right. However, the Court decided the issue entirely on the basis of Section 13 of the Constitution. It did not inform its reasoning by any reference to international human rights standards or sources. It is not clear whether the grounds of suspicion should take account only of local conditions or should also have regard to international normative standards.

Another issue that has arisen in relation to the Zimbabwean personal liberty clause relates to imprisonment for inability to fulfil a contractual obligation or civil debt. The question is, does civil imprisonment infringe the right to personal liberty? In this regard, Section 13(2)(c) of the Constitution provides that no person shall be deprived of liberty save "in execution of the order of a court made in order to secure the fulfilment of an obligation imposed on him by law." This clause authorises derogation from the right to personal liberty in cases where it is necessary for purposes of civil imprisonment. This issue arose in *Chinamora v. Angwa Furnishers and Others*.[14] Importantly, in trying to resolve this issue, the Court made eloquent

---

[12] 1983 (1) Z.L.R. 238 (ZHC) at 242-4.

[13] 1973 (2) R.L.R. 387.

[14] Civil Application No. 240/1995 (unreported).

reference to international human rights instruments and sources. The respondent, Angwa Furnishers Ltd, obtained a default judgment in the Magistrates Court against the applicant, Chinamora, for an amount of money, being a debt incurred through the purchase of goods from the respondent. The applicant was unable to pay. The respondent made and obtained a decree of civil imprisonment against him. The applicant challenged the Magistrate's order in the Supreme Court arguing, inter alia, that the civil imprisonment ordered against him violated his personal liberty guaranteed under Section 13(1) of the Constitution. He also based his case partly on the fact that imprisonment for a civil debt is prohibited by Article 11 of the ICCPR which binds Zimbabwe as a State party, Article 1 of the Fourth Protocol to the ECHR, Article 7(7) of the ACHR and on the ACHPR to which Zimbabwe is also a party.[15]

Significantly, the Supreme Court also relied on these treaties in order to determine whether the Magistrate Court (Civil) Rules, 1980 (Statutory Instrument No. 290 of 1980) which authorise the Magistrates Court to order civil imprisonment were contrary to Section 13(1) of the Constitution. The Court noted that to adopt any other construction, always acknowledging that an inroad into the substantive protection afforded by Section 13(1) should be interpreted restrictively *in favorem libertatis*, would be to render the provision superfluous. However, although the Court acknowledged the important constitutional issue raised by the case and the prohibition of civil imprisonment in international law, it remained unpersuaded by the argument that civil imprisonment violates Section 13(1). According to the Court, the argument was purely an academic exercise devoid of any practical realities. It dismissed the application and ordered the applicant to honour the judgment.

It is submitted that the Court approached the issue in a simplistic way. It also accorded the international human rights instruments and sources relied upon by the applicant less weight and consideration especially if, by its own admission, any inroad into the right to physical liberty should be interpreted in favour of the liberty of the individual. An argument based on international human rights law and particularly human rights treaties far from being an academic exercise, serves significant practical benefits. It gives additional

---

[15] Ibid., at 15-16.

practical force and impetus to the protection in question and ensures that the liberty of the individual is indeed safeguarded.

Personal liberty has been the main focal issue in cases of arrest and detention without trial or preventive detention especially during state of emergencies.[16] Under the Zimbabwean Constitution, primary powers to declare a state of emergency resides with Parliament. But the actual power to declare the state of emergency reposes in the President after obtaining parliamentary approval.[17] The state of emergency may be declared if the President thinks it is necessary or expedient for public safety, public order and essential services and preservation of peace, order and good government. Since independence, the President has exercised these emergency powers due to constant threats posed by the erstwhile South African regime in pursuit of its destabilisation campaign of its neighbouring Southern African States. To realise its aim, the South African Government sponsored espionage agents against its neighbours. Disturbances in Matebeleland areas in the late 1980s also forced the government of Zimbabwe to declare states of emergency in these areas. Consequently, the police arrested and detained several people under emergency laws.[18]

These arrests and preventive detentions were challenged in courts. One case in which they were challenged is *Minister of Home Affairs v. Dabengwa*.[19] The respondent was charged with high treason. He was detained under Section 17 of the Emergency Powers (Maintenance of Law and Order) Regulations of 24 May 1983. According to paragraph 2(1)(b) of the Second Schedule of the Constitution, his detention was subject to review "forthwith" after the expiry of thirteen days by a review tribunal. His detention was,

---

[16]   Generally, see Hatchard, *Individual Freedoms*, at 46-58; Id, "Emergency Powers" at 35-70; Gubbay, "Fundamental Human Rights," at 244-6.

[17]   The Constitution of Zimbabwe, Section 66. Provisions for declaration of state of emergencies in Zimbabwe predate independence. They were instituted in the early 1960s and re-enacted in 1966 in Southern Rhodesian following the Unilateral Declaration of Independence. They were retained in 1980 when Zimbabwe attained independence and reviewed in 1986. See Hatchard, "Emergency Powers" at 35-6.

[18]   Hatchard, "Emergency Powers" at 35-9.

[19]   1984 (2) S. A. 345 (ZSC).

however, not reviewed. He applied to the High Court for an order directing his release. The High Court, in granting the writ *de homine libero exhibendo* observed that the respondent's continued detention in the face of the failure to effectuate review provisions constituted an illegality which could not be allowed to perpetuate. It declared his detention illegal. On appeal, the Supreme court reversed this order reasoning that it is not in every case that failure to afford personal liberty safeguards results in the granting of this order. The Court may compel the authorities to comply with the regulations. Nevertheless, the Court emphasised the crucial importance of the right to personal liberty of persons especially those under preventive detention. According to the Court, state authorities are under a legal duty to safeguard this freedom.

Further, in *Minister of Home Affairs v. Austin and Another*,[20] the respondents were accused of spying against Zimbabwe for the former apartheid government of South Africa. They were arrested and detained under Section 17 of the Emergency Powers (Maintenance of Law and Order) Regulations and the Official Secrets Act of Zimbabwe. They challenged the detention order signed by the first appellant, Minister of Home Affairs, on the ground that it did not "inform" them of the reasons for the detention as required by Section 17(2) of the Emergency Regulations. The High Court, per Blackie, J., as he then was, held that the respondent's detention was unlawful by reason of the first appellant's failure to supply adequate reasons for their detention. On appeal, the Supreme Court endorsed and upheld the decision of the High Court. It held that the detention order was defective in the information as to the reasons of the detention. The appeal was dismissed.

Dumbutshena, C.J., as he then was, stressed that in drawing up the grounds of detention, it is incumbent upon the detaining authority to appreciate that the detainee must be furnished with sufficient particulars to enable him to prepare his case and to make effective representations before a review tribunal. A bare and bold statement that the detainee was a spy was not sufficient to warrant his detention. In arriving at its decision, the Court referred to Indian, English and South African decisions interpreting similar provisions on preventive

---

[20] [1987] LRC (Const) 567. Generally, see Gubbay, "Fundamental Human Rights," at 245.

detention.[21] Although the decision of the Supreme Court was sound in that it gave effect to the right to personal liberty, it, however, did not rely on international human rights treaties to reinforce its decision. It also did not draw inspiration from decisions of international tribunals interpreting emergency provisions embodied in human rights treaties in the same way that it did with comparative national jurisprudence. Decisions of these tribunals such as the ECtHR, the European Commission of Human Rights (hereafter the European Commission) and the Human Rights Committee (hereafter the HRC) are also useful in assisting the Court to determine how these provisions have been interpreted at the international level. They guide the Court in interpreting national clauses. They also broaden its approach towards interpretation of national human rights law in this area.

By contrast, international human rights law and sources were invoked and relied upon in *Bull v. Minister of Home Affairs* to interpret Section 13 of the Constitution.[22] The petitioner, a legal practitioner, petitioned the High Court for an order declaring that Section 106(2) of the Criminal Procedure and Evidence Act (hereafter CPEA), Cap. 59 which empowered the Minister of Home Affairs to oppose any application for bail the granting of which would be prejudicial to national security was contrary to Section 13(1) of the Constitution. He made the petition after his clients had been denied bail by a Magistrate Court on the basis of Section 106(2) of the CPEA. The Minister opposed the application arguing, inter alia, that Section 106(2) could not be tested against Section 13(1) of the Constitution since the denial of bail to the accused was in the interest of national security. After construing both clauses, the Court concluded that Section 106(2) could be tested against, and was indeed contrary to, Section 13(1) of the Constitution. It held that Section 106(2) was unconstitutional.

Crucially, the High Court arrived at its conclusion by, inter alia, relying on decisions of the ECtHR interpreting Article 5 of the ECHR. It noted that its conclusion was "fortified by the passage in the judgment of the European Court on Human Rights in the case of *Stogmuller v. Austria* 1 EHHR 155 at 190-91...speaking of Article 5 of the European Convention on Human rights and Fundamental Freedoms

---

[21] Ibid., at 576-9.

[22] [1987] LRC (Const) 547.

(which article is the parent of Section 13 of the Constitution of Zimbabwe) and more specifically of Article 5(1)(c)..." The ECtHR decision in *Stogmuller v. Austria* influenced the Supreme Court to declare that Section 106(2) was contrary to Section 13(1). This decision is one of the few cases in which the Zimbabwean courts have invoked and relied on international human rights standards to interpret preventive detention regulations in relation to the right to personal liberty. It reinforced the Court's decision that Section 106(2) of the CPEA was unconstitutional.

It is apparent from these pronouncements that in those cases that were decided immediately after Zimbabwe's independence, the courts were reluctant to invoke and rely upon international human rights standards and sources to declare unlawful emergency laws and regulations. These courts were staffed by pre-independence judges. Their approach towards human rights law was still guided and influenced by discriminatory and apartheid-like laws of the former Southern Rhodesia. They had not yet developed a human rights culture. The decision in *Bull v. Minister of Home Affairs* made a significant inroad into this approach.

Fair Trial Guarantees

The municipal law of Zimbabwe embraces fair trial safeguards. These guarantees are elaborately recognised and protected by Section 18 of the Constitution. The clause is in line with Article 10 of the UDHR and Article 7 of the ACHPR. In particular, the safeguards in Section 18 are replicated and amplified in detailed and all-embracing Articles 14 and 6 of the ICCPR and ECHR respectively. Thus, as with international human rights instruments, the Zimbabwean fair trial clause protects rights such as public hearing, trial by an independent and impartial tribunal, trial within a reasonable time, the right to legal counsel and right of the accused to have proceedings conducted in the language that he/she understands. It is in direct accord with international human rights standards.

The clauses reveal most of the standard principles and norms evolved for the protection of the right to a fair trial or guarantees of due process of law. They encapsulate most of the necessary safeguards and minimum acceptable standards of justice associated with a fair hearing. The basic aim of these standards is to protect the individual interest in fundamental criminal justice and legal certainty.[23] The examination that follows focuses on some of the specific guarantees embodied in the right to a fair trial.

Trial within a reasonable time   In terms of Section 18(2) of the Constitution of Zimbabwe "If any person is charged with a criminal offence, then, unless the charge is withdrawn, the case shall be afforded a fair hearing within a reasonable time..."[24] This protection ensures that there is minimum delay in determining the lawfulness of the arrest of an individual. The central issue is, what does trial within a reasonable time really entail?[25]

This issue was at stake in *In Re Mlambo*.[26] The applicant had been arrested on 3 October, 1986 and charged with theft. He was released on bail after two weeks in custody. He subsequently appeared in court on twelve different occasions up to August 1987 when charges were withdrawn. However, in August, 1990, he was summoned again to appear in court on substantially the same charges. He applied to the Supreme Court alleging that his right to be tried within a reasonable time had been infringed. The overall length of delay was approximately four years and seven months.

The Court considered several points. In resolving these points, it sought guidance and assistance from the ECtHR decisions. The first point concerned the meaning of the term "charged." The Magistrate in the court of first instance interpreted this term to mean the moment when the accused person is brought to plead in court. The Court Supreme disagreed with this interpretation. Relying on two cases of the ECtHR, namely *Eckle v. Germany (Federal Republic) and Foti v. Italy,*

---

[23] Harris, et al, *European Convention*, at 128-9; In re Mlambo 1992 (4) S.A. 144 (ZSC) at 149. See also Naldi, *Constitutional Rights*, at 61; Nowak, *U.N. Covenant*, at 236-73; Harris, "Fiar Trial," at 352-78.

[24] The ICCPR, Article, 14(3)(c); the ACHPR, Article 7(1)(d); the ECHR, 5(3)(a). Generally, see Byre and Byfield, *Commonwealth Caribbeans*, at 63-75.

[25] See generally Barker v. Wingo 407 US 514 (1972) at 519-20; Musoke v. Uganda (1972) E.A. 137.

[26] 1992 (4) S.A. 144. Generally, see Madhuku, "European Court of Human Rights," at 938-9; Gubbay, "Fundamental Human Rights," at 246-48.

dealing with an analogous Article 6(1) of the ECHR the Court, per Gubbay, C.J., noted that "I have no hesitation in holding that the time frame is designed to relate far more to the period prior to the commencement of the hearing or trial than to whatever period may elapse after the accused has tendered a plea."[27] This observation was in line with what the ECtHR had said in *Eckle v. Germany (Federal Republic)*, namely, that " 'charge' for the purpose of art 6(1), may be defined as 'the official notification given to an individual by the competent authority of an allegation that he has committed a criminal offence...'"[28] Finally, the Court held that the appellant was charged either upon arrest or on the first remand by the Magistrates' Court in October 1986.

The second point related to factors which the court is legally to take into account in determining whether or not the accused person has been accorded trial within a reasonable time. The Court again relied on the judgment of the ECtHR, namely, *Konig v. Federal Republic of Germany,*[29] dealing with Article 6(1) of the ECHR. It noted that each case had to be considered on its own surrounding circumstances particular regard being paid to the complexity of the case, the applicant's behaviour, the manner in which the case was handled by state authorities, the very administration of justice and the interest of the society. As regard the latter factor, the Court broadened the accused "presumptively prejudicial" approach to societal interest. It held that four and half years was extraordinarily inordinate delay. It further held that the delay was attributable to the State. Accordingly, Section 18(2) was infringed. The Court ordered a permanent stay of the proceedings. It also ordered the Attorney General to pay the costs of the application.

This pronouncement clearly demonstrates that in interpreting the protective clause on speedy trial, the Zimbabwean Supreme Court drew inspiration from international sources especially the ECHR and decisions of the ECtHR enforcing the right to be tried within a reasonable time provision of the ECHR. They formed the basis for determining the meaning and juridical content of the right of the

---

[27] 1992 (4) S.A. 144 at 149-50.

[28] Ibid., at 150.

[29] Ibid., at 153.

accused to be tried within a reasonable time. The Court used these sources to interpret this right liberally and broaden its scope.

Legal counsel Section 18(3)(d) of the Constitution of Zimbabwe proclaims that "every person who is charged with a criminal offence shall be permitted to defend himself in person or, save in proceedings before a local court, at his own expense by a legal representative of his own choice." Paragraph (e) further declares that such a person "shall be afforded facilities to examine in person or, save in proceedings before a local court, by his legal representative the witnesses called by the prosecution..."[30] These clauses accord individuals the right to legal representation in line with international human rights instruments such as Article 11(1) of the UDHR, Article 14(3) (d) of the ICCPR, Article 6(3)(c) of the ECHR and Article 7(1)(c) of the ACHPR. They guarantee, in mandatory language, that the accused or defendant should be represented by counsel or accorded an effective legal defence.[31] The Zimbabwean clause adopts the tone of the international human rights instruments by according the right to legal representative to "every person." It recognises the inalienable nature of this right. It thus gives expression to its natural law origin. Individuals must represent themselves *in person*. They can, however, decide not to represent themselves in person and instead make use of defence counsel. But this should be at their own, and not the State, expense.

The importance of the right to legal representation in Zimbabwe municipal law was stressed in *S v. Woods and Another*.[32] The police extracted extra-curial confessions and statements from the accused persons despite the fact that they, the accused persons, had demanded to first consult their lawyers. The trial court did not exclude evidence obtained as a result of these confessions when convicting the accused. On appeal, the Supreme Court held that the police conduct was so serious a violation of the appellants' right to legal representation that the confessions should have been ruled to be

---

[30] Gubbay, "Fundamental Human Rights," at 250; Feltoe, "Lawyers," at 10-17; Hatchard, "Legal Representation," at 135-49.

[31] Golder v. United Kingdom (1975) 1 E.H.R.R. 524. See also Ankumah, *The African Commission*, at 126-9; Nowak, *U.N. Covenant*, at 258-61; Harris, "Fair Trial," at 364-7.

[32] 1993 (2) Z.L.R. 258 See Gubbay, "Fundamental Human Rights," at 250.

inadmissible evidence. According to the Court, legal representation is an important safeguard in the criminal justice system.

Moreover, in *Minister of Home Affairs v. Dabengwa,* Fieldsend, C.J., as he then was, underlined this safeguard when he said, "it is contrary to any true concept of justice that at the discretion of a police officer a detained person should be unable to obtain legal advice and consult with his legal representative. To allow that right in turn to be suspended when there is a state of emergency would be to render it entirely nugatory."[33] However, in both cases, the Court did not make use of international human rights standards to reinforce its decision. It based its decision only on national law of Zimbabwe.

The requirement that individuals should defend themselves at their own expence is not peculiar to Zimbabwe. It is in line with international human rights standards. Generally, individuals meet their own legal fees. However, free legal assistance is provided by the State to individuals who cannot meet high legal fees charged by lawyers particularly for serious cases such as murder and manslaughter. But in other cases of a minor nature, this right is circumscribed by high legal fees charged by attorneys. Thus for those accused who cannot afford these charges, the right is illusory.

It worth noting that, unlike the international human rights instruments, Section 18(3) paragraphs (d) and (e) of the Constitution of Zimbabwe exclude legal representation in proceedings before "local" or traditional courts.[34] This is based on the assumption that the concept of legal representation does not form part of the traditional justice system and that the officers who preside over traditional courts have no formal training in the law and procedure of ordinary courts. As in Botswana and indeed most African countries, a great number of people in Zimbabwe live under customary law and practices. The majority of cases are dealt with in these courts. Clearly, denial of representation by legal counsel in these courts curtails the accused's guarantee of a fair trial.

---

[33] 1982 (4) S.A. 301 at 307.

[34] The Zimbabwean Constitution defines a local Court as "any court constituted by or under any written law for the purpose of applying African customary law." See Constitution of Zimbabwe, Section, 113(1).

It is submitted that legal representation must be made available in local courts. Individuals who come to these courts are entitled to justice in the same way as individuals who go to ordinary courts. Clearly, Zimbabwe's municipal law diverges from international human rights standards. Its municipal law is incompatible with the obligation Zimbabwe assumed under the ICCPR and ACHPR to protect the right to legal counsel of persons living under this system of law.

Torture and Kindred Practices

The domestic law of Zimbabwe outlaws torture and related practices.[35] The relevant Section 15(1) of the Constitution of Zimbabwe provides that "No person shall be subjected to torture or to inhuman or degrading punishment or other such treatment." Although this clause prohibits these practices by adopting a negative, as opposed to a positive, approach, it nevertheless captures the sentiment of international human rights instruments by outlawing these conducts in mandatory terms. It is literally equivalent to Article 5 of the UDHR and Article 7 of the ICCPR. The latter additionally prohibits subjection of anyone without his free consent to medical or scientific experimentation.[36] Similar proscriptions appear respectively in Articles 3 and 5 of the ECHR and the ACHPR. Under these instruments, torture and the related conducts are non-derogable.[37] Thus the Zimbabwean protective clause translates international human rights norms on the prohibition of these conducts into domestic law.

At the implementation stage, observance of prohibitions against torture in Zimbabwe has been compromised by the activities of the police and security forces particularly during state of emergencies in the Matebeleland provinces and the outlying areas after the 1980

---

[35] Generally, see Gubbay, "Fundamental Human Rights," at 235-8; Madhuku, "European Court of Human Rights," at 936-8; Hatchard, "The Cane in Zimbabwe," at 198-204.

[36] The prohibition of medical or scientific experimentation was inserted in this clause as a response to the atrocities of the Nazi concentration camps and was aimed at prohibiting anyone from being subjected against his will to any form of physical mutilation or scientific experimentation. See Nowak, *U.N. Covenant*, at 126-41.

[37] Ireland v. United Kingdom (1978) 2 E.H.R.R. 25; Nowak, *U.N. Covenant*, at 126.

Elections.[38] Following uprising from these regions, the Government accused supporters of the opposition ZAPU (Zimbabwe African Peoples' Unity) party of orchestrating the disturbances. It unleashed attacks through its security forces notably specially North Korean trained force called the Fifth Brigade in these areas. Several people were reported to have been tortured. The action of the security forces were widely condemned by non-Governmental organisations such as the Legal Resources Foundation, the Catholic Commission for Justice and Peace, and Amnesty International.[39]

It is worth noting that under the Zimbabwean municipal law, unlike the international human rights instruments, torture and other similar practices are not prohibited in absolute terms. According to Section 15(2) to (6) of the Constitution, prohibition against torture and other similar practices is not applicable to treatment reasonably necessary to prevent the escape of persons in lawful custody, whipping of eighteen years under *in loco parentis* and in the execution of the death penalty. These practices constitute exceptions to the prohibition against torture and related conducts. Any act falling under these practices is legally permissible. These are issues of major concern regarding prohibition against torture and related conducts. They limit the practical implementation of this safeguard. In this regard, the Zimbabwean protective standards diverges from, and falls below, the international standards.

The question that recommends itself is, do these practices amount to cruel, degrading or inhuman punishment or treatment? It is significant to examine how the Zimbabwean courts have handled these issues and whether in trying to resolve them they have sought any guidance and inspiration from international human rights norms.

Corporal punishment Corporal punishment or whipping, both judicial and non-judicial, has been one of the prescribed modes of penalising persons convicted of criminal offences in Zimbabwe under the

---

[38] In particular, see Africa Watch Report, *Zimbabwe*, at 43-54.

[39] The Amnesty International concerns over torture in Zimbabwe were stated in a memorandum in 1985 to the Zimbabwe Government detailing twenty-one cases of torture. It requested an impartial and independent investigation into the matter. A report of the Lawyers Committee for Human Rights in May 1986 confirmed Amnesty International concerns. See Africa Watch Report, *Zimbabwe*, at 14-20.

customary judicial system.[40] It is still retained even in the contemporary judicial system for certain offences such as rape, assault occasioning actual bodily harm, housebreaking and robbery. Whipping can be inflicted on both adults and minors, but not on female offenders.

The constitutionality of whipping has been challenged in Zimbabwean courts. It was challenged in *State v. Ncube*.[41] The Supreme Court was called upon to decide whether subjecting a male offender to whipping was inhuman or degrading punishment hence contrary to Section 15(1) of the Constitution of Zimbabwe outlawing torture and related conducts. The Court made two observations concerning Section 15(1). In both circumstances it sought guidance from international human rights norms and sources especially the ECtHR decision in *Tyrer v. United Kingdom* interpreting a similarly worded Article 3 of the ECHR. First, the Court noted that Section 15(1) did not cover only torture. It also covers other lesser forms of punishment or treatment. This means that torture has to be construed disjunctively, as the ECtHR noted in *Tyrer v. United Kingdom.* The Court stated that "while the word 'torture' stands alone in the subsection, the nouns 'punishment' and 'treatment' are qualified by the adjectives 'inhuman' and 'degrading.' The use of the word 'or', and not 'and', between 'inhuman' and 'degrading' favours a disjunctive and not a conjunctive interpretation. Certainly that was the construction applied to the identical protection by...the European Court of Human Rights in *Tyrer v. United Kingdom...*"[42]

In the second instance, the Court noted that what had to be examined in order to ascertain whether the punishment was inhuman or degrading was the manner and extent of its application. Relying again on *Tyrer v. United Kingdom*, the Court then held that whipping an adult, by its very nature, was both inhuman and degrading and thus contravened Section 15(1). As Section 15(1) was virtually identical to Article 3 of the ECHR, the Court noted that it was influenced by

---

[40] Madhuku, "The Impact of the European Court," at 936; Hatchard, "The Cane in Zimbabwe," at 198-204.

[41] 1988 (2) S.A. 702 (ZSC). Generally, see Madhuku, "The Impact of the European Court," at 936-8; Hatchard, "The Cane in Zimbabwe," at 198-9; Gubbay, "Fundamental Human Rights," at 235-8; Nherere, "Bill of Rights," at 43.

[42] 1988 (2) S.A. 702 (ZSC), at 714-5. (emphasis supplied).

decision of the ECtHR in *Tyrer v. United Kingdom* where a judicial birching of a 15-year-old youth was held to be degrading hence contrary to Article 3 of the ECHR.

The Court further noted that it had to have regard to the fact that the abolition of whipping in very many countries of the world demonstrates that it is repugnant to the "conscience of civilised men."[43] Justice Gubbay noted that he was persuaded that the whipping which each of the three appellants was ordered to receive was relentless in its severity and "contrary to the traditional humanity practised by most of the whole civilised world, being incompatible with the evolving standards of decency."[44] Moreover, the punishment was so excessive as to shock or outrage contemporary standards of decency.[45] Finally, the court outlawed adult whipping as a form of judicial sentence.

It became clear that this decision related only to whipping of adults. The whipping of male minors or juveniles continued to be regarded as constitutional.[46] Two years later, the constitutionality of whipping male minors was questioned in *State v. A Juvenile.*[47] An eighteen-year-old male was convicted of an aggravated assault and sentenced to receive cuts in accordance with Section 330 of the CPEA of Zimbabwe.[48] The Supreme Court was split on the vexing issue of

---

[43] Ibid., at 721. (emphasis supplied).

[44] Ibid., at 722. (emphasis supplied).

[45] Ibid., at 715.

[46] It is significant to observe that the Zimbabwean courts have expressed serious reservations about the constitutionality of juvenile whipping in several cases. See for instance S v. Ndhlovu 1981 Z.L.R 600. In this case, Gubbay, as he then was, said that "while some judicial officers held differing views on the practice, some, like myself, are generally opposed to it as an inhuman and degrading mode of punishment." See also Hatchard, "The Cane in Zimbabwe," at 199.

[47] 1990 (4) S.A. 151 (ZSC). This case is analysed in Hatchard, "The Cane in Zimbabwe," at 199-200; Madhuku, "The Impact of the European Court," at 937-8; Tshuma, "Spare the Rod," at 214-18.

[48] This clause states that: "(1) As often as any male person who has not attained the age of nineteen years is convicted of any offence, the court before which he is convicted may... sentence such person to receive in private a moderate correction of whipping, not exceeding ten cuts. (2) A moderate correction in terms of

whether or not juvenile whippping is constitutional. Significantly, both camps based their views on the *Tyrer case*. The majority view represented by Dumbutshena, C.J., as he then was, held that even the whipping of minors was inhuman and degrading, and therefore unconstitutional. It needed to be abolished. In particular, Justice Dumbutshena approvingly referred to the ECtHR decision in *Tyrer v. United Kingdom* thus: "The European Court of Human Rights considered in *Tyrer v United Kingdom* (1978) 2 EHRR 1 at 11 part 33, circumstances which made the punishment of whipping 'degrading within the meaning of art 3' of the European Convention for the Protection of Human Rights and Fundamental Freedoms... The European Court of Human Rights was of the view that: 'The very nature of judicial corporal punishment is that it involves one human being inflicting violence on another human being. Furthermore, it is institutionalised violence, that is in the present case violence permitted by the law, ordered by the judicial authorities of the state and carried out by the police authorities of the State.'"[49] To demonstrate that he and his brethren were influenced by this case, Justice Dumbutshena noted that "It would be strange were we to come to a contrary view."[50]

In addition, the Court reinforced its reasoning with United Nations Standard Minimum Rules for the Administration of Justice, 1985. Gubbay, J.A., as he then was, remarked "Although there is no explicit reference in international human rights instruments to corporal punishment as a judicial sanction, a recent inroad has been made by the United Nations Standard Minimum Rules for the Administration of Juvenile Justice, 1985 (the Beijing Rules). According to Rule 17:3: 'Juveniles should not be subject to corporal punishment.' The definition of juvenile is left to national practice."[51] In fact, Gubbay recalls that the decision of the Court in this case to outlaw whipping of juveniles was "influenced by the United Nations Standard Minimum

---

subsection (1) shall be administered by such person and in such place and with such instrument as the court may appoint."

[49]   1990 (4) S.A. 151 (ZSC) at 156.

[50]   Id.

[51]   Ibid., at 169.

Rules for the Administration of Justice (the Beijing Rules)."[52] The Court, per Justice Dumbutshena, questioned whether corporal punishment of juveniles can really be justified in a civilised society with evolving standards of decency that mark the progressiveness of a maturing society such as Zimbabwe?[53] Finally, the majority of the Court concluded that whipping of juveniles was inhuman and degrading, and therefore contrary to Section 15(1) of the Constitution of Zimbabwe.

The contrary view, represented by Justice McNally, noted that the ECtHR did not hold that all violence to the person is *per se* wrong. It merely stressed that the issue involved value judgement. In the minority's view, whipping minors was not inhuman or degrading because it, inter alia, imposed a "short, sharp, salutary and brief painful punishment which achieves in very many cases exactly what is required." For this view, imprisonment in these cases is unacceptable hence the necessity of whipping.

The Court proceeded to consider *mero motu* the constitutionality of whipping in schools. Again, Justice Dumbutshena, as he then was, did not only rely on the decisions of the ECtHR in *Tyrer v. United Kingdom.* He also sought guidance from other decisions of the European Court interpreting Article 3 of the ECHR. He noted that "In *Campbell and Cosans v. United Kingdom* (1982) 4 EHHR 293, the European Court of Human Rights considered that the criteria used in the judicial punishment were applicable in a case concerning school corporal punishment... It appears to me that in a system of education, which has formal rules on corporal punishment drawn upon by a competent authority, the same considerations governing judicial punishment must apply."[54] Justice Dumbutshena proceeded to observe that "The cases from the European Court of Human Rights cited above strengthen my belief that once an authority has enacted legislation for the chastisement of school children by school masters, the authority delegated by the parents to school

---

[52] Gubbay, "Fundamental Human Rights," at 237. See also Tshuma, "Spare the Rod," at 214-18; Hatchard, "The Cane in Zimbabwe," at 201.

[53] 1990 (4) S.A. 151 (ZSC) at 162. (emphasis supplied).

[54] Ibid., at 161.

teachers to inflict reasonable physical chastisement on pupils disappears, that is, the common law no longer applies and with it the delegated authority vanishes."[55] According to Justice Dumbutshena, "An added advantage is that the courts of this country are free to import into the interpretation of Section 15(1) of the Zimbabwean Constitution interpretations of similar provisions in international and regional human rights instruments such as, among others, International Bills of Rights, the European Convention for the Protection of Human Rights and Fundamental Freedoms, and the Inter-American Convention on Human Rights."[56] Clearly, the decisions of the ECtHR and international instruments influenced the Court to also declare whipping in schools unconstitutional.

The decision triggered sharp reaction from the Zimbabwean Parliament. Parliament enacted the Constitution of Zimbabwe Amendment (No.11) Act, 1990 and section 5 thereof authorises whipping of male minors or juveniles. This Act also effected some amendments to the Criminal Procedure and Evidence Act. Section 329 thereof permits moderate whipping of six strokes on males under eighteen years. It is entirely possible that Parliament was influenced by the divergence of opinion in the Supreme Court to override the decision in *S v. A Juvenile* and re-introduce whipping of juveniles. This also explains why Zimbabwe has not ratified the Torture Convention. Significantly, however, the judgments of the ECtHR played a pivotal role in the Zimbabwean Supreme Court's decision to outlaw judicial corporal punishment of both adults and juveniles as well as whipping in schools.

"Death row" phenomenon The second problematic issue regarding prohibition against inhuman or degrading punishment or treatment is the "Death row" phenomenon. The question that arises is whether the "Death row" phenomenon or delays in executing the death penalty, in itself constitute an inhuman and degrading treatment? This issue arose when attempts to challenge the constitutionality of hanging in courts were forestalled in 1990. Parliament took an unprecedented step of amending the Constitution to preclude any argument about the

---

[55]   Ibid., at 162.

[56]   Ibid., at 155.

constitutionality of hanging. Section 5 of the Constitutional Amendment (No. 11) Act stipulates that the sentence of death cannot be declared unconstitutional on the ground that the process of execution is degrading or inhuman.

Consequently, the challenge has been levelled not against whether the death penalty is inhuman or degrading *per se* but rather at delays in carrying out the death penalty or the "death row" phenomenon. The most far reaching decision in which this issue emerged is *Catholic Commission for Peace and Justice in Zimbabwe v. Attorney-General, Zimbabwe and Others.*[57] Importantly, the Zimbabwean Supreme Court resolved the issue by reference to international human rights law and sources particularly decisions of the ECtHR and HRC. The three accused were each convicted of murder separately. They were each sentenced to death and incarcerated for about four and half years while awaiting execution. The applicant, a human rights organisation, brought an application to the Supreme Court on their behalf to have the sentences quashed. It argued that delays in executing the appellants was inhuman and degrading.

The main issue for the Court was whether delays in executing a death sentence could be regarded as an infringement of the right to freedom from inhuman or degrading punishment. The Court referred to several decisions in various jurisdictions and concluded that a delayed execution of the death sentence as in this case was a breach of Section 15(1). It quashed the death sentences and substituted life imprisonment. For purposes of this study, it is illuminating to stress that one of the leading international judicial pronouncements which influenced the Court to quash the death sentences was the ECtHR case of *Soering v. United Kingdom.*[58] In this case, the applicant alleged that the decision by the Secretary of State in the United Kingdom to extradite him to the United States of America to face a trial in Virginia on a murder charge, would contravene Article 3 of the ECHR. The ECtHR held that the delays in executions in Virginia amounted to inhuman and degrading punishment contrary to Article 3. It upheld the application. This case was followed in Zimbabwe.

---

[57] 1993 (4) S.A. 239 (ZSC). Generally, see Madhuku, "The Impact of the European Court," at 940; Hatchard, "The Cane in Zimbabwe," at 199-203.

[58] 1993 (4) S.A. 239 (ZSC) at 261.

In addition, the Supreme Court invoked and relied on decisions of the HRC. It, per Gubbay, C. J., as he then was, noted that, "In recent years the Human Rights Committee, under art 5 para 4 of the Optional Protocol to the International Covenant on Civil and Political Rights, has handed down decisions on whether the length of detention on death row amounted to a violation of the prohibitions against 'torture or cruel, inhuman or degrading treatment or punishment' under art 7 of the Covenant...They are *Earl Pratt and Ivan Morgan*, Communication Nos 210/1985 (20 July 1990) and *Randolph Barrett and Clyde Sutcliffe*, Communication Nos 270/271/1988 (30 March 1992)..."[59] In these cases, the Committee was of the view that a very long period on death row, even if partially due to the failure of the condemned prisoner to assert his or her right to seek a remedy, cannot exonerate the State party from its obligations under the Covenant. Justice Gubbay remarked that "It is this latter that I find the more compelling."[60] Relying partly on these judgments, the Court noted that in the light of the constant fear by the prisoners of being put to death, the mental anguish and suffering endured by them, the death penalty should be set aside. The Court further observed that whether a form of treatment is assessed as inhuman or degrading depends on the exercise of value judgment which has to take account of the emerging consensus of values in the civilised international community, as evidenced by the decisions of other courts. Clearly, these decisions also formed the basis for the Court to hold that the death row was inhuman and degrading.

The decision in *Catholic Commission for Peace and Justice in Zimbabwe v. Attorney-General, Zimbabwe and Others* has a far-reaching significance. It clearly demonstrates the extent to which the Zimbabwean courts are moving away from the classical dualistic approach of treating international human rights law and national law of Zimbabwe as two distinct legal regimes each having a separate sphere of application. By relying actively and rigorously on international human rights law and sources, the Zimbabwean courts recognise the significant role of this law in municipal law. This approach is fully in line with international obligations of Zimbabwe to outlaw any inhuman or degrading treatment or practice.

---

[59]   Ibid., at 264.

[60]   Id.

Civil imprisonment The notion of civil imprisonment is another problematic issue which has arisen in Zimbabwe with respect to prohibition of inhuman or degrading punishment or treatment. The question is, does civil imprisonment amount to an inhuman or degrading punishment or treatment? Civil imprisonment is flatly proscribed under international human rights law.[61] Article 11 of the ICCPR categorically and unambiguously provides that "No one shall be imprisoned merely on the ground of inability to fulfil a contractual obligation." This clause is comparable to Article 1 of the Fourth Protocol to the ECHR which stipulates that "No one shall be deprived of his liberty merely on the ground of inability to fulfil a contractual obligation." These provisions prohibit positively and mandatorily any incarceration of an individual for inability to perform a contractual obligation or civil debt. They constitute the basis for protection from civil imprisonment at international level. They contain additional restrictions of the executive powers of the state authorities to deprive a person of his/her physical liberty. These provisions cover any contractual obligation, namely, the payment of debts, performance of services, or the delivery of goods. This right is non-derogable.[62]

The protection does not, however, cover criminal offences related to civil-law debts or obligations of public interest, which were imposed by statute or court order such as payment of maintenance under family law and detention for fraud. A person convicted of these offences may be punished with imprisonment even when he is able to pay his debts.[63]

As indicated above in relation to the right to personal liberty, civil imprisonment in Zimbabwe is authorised by Section 13(2)(c) of the Constitution. Moreover, in terms of Section 27 of the Magistrates Court Act (Cap 18) "The Court may, upon the return of the summons

---

[61] Nowak, *U.N. Covenant*, at 193-6; Van Dijk and Van Hoof, *European Convention*, at 488-9; Dinstein, "Life, Physical Integrity and Liberty," in Henkin, *International Bill of Rights*, at 135-6.

[62] Nowak, *U.N. Covenant*, at 193; Van Dijk and Van Hoof, *European Convention*, at 489.

[63] Nowak, *U.N. Covenant*, at 194; Dinstein, "Life, Physical Integrity and Liberty," in Henkin, *International Bill of Rights*, at 135.

and whether the judgment debtor appears or not, make a decree of civil imprisonment against such debtor and authorise the issue of a warrant for his arrest and detention in any prison named in the warrant." These provisions constitute the basis for civil imprisonment under municipal law of Zimbabwe. This is in sharp contrast to international law.

However, according to Section 27(ii) of the Magistrates Court Act, civil imprisonment shall not be ordered against a judgment debtor if he/she proves to the satisfaction of the court that he/she has no means of satisfying the judgment debt either wholly or in part and either out of his/her present means or out of future earnings or income. This clause creates an exception to civil imprisonment. It, however, imposes a duty on the debtor to prove that he/she is unable to honour his/her debt. This means that if the debtor fails to discharge this duty or there is sufficient evidence that he/she is able to pay but decides not to pay or divests himself/herself of all his/her property, he/she is liable to civil imprisonment.[64] This issue was one of the issues that the Supreme Court of Zimbabwe was invited to adjudicate in the fore-cited *Chinamora v. Angwa Furnishers and Others.* The applicant challenged a decree of civil imprisonment ordered against him on the basis, inter alia, that the imprisonment contravened the constitutional prohibition on inhuman or degrading treatment or punishment. He argued that if he were imprisoned for inability to pay his debt, this would amount to an infringement of his immutable right not to be subjected to an inhuman or degrading treatment or punishment. However, evidence on record indicated that the applicant was able to pay his debt but he decided to divest himself of his property so as to avoid payment.

In resolving this issue, the Supreme Court of Zimbabwe made eloquent reference to international human rights instruments and sources dealing with imprisonment for inability to pay a debt or contractual obligation such as Article 11 of the ICCPR, Article 1 of the Fourth Protocol to the ECHR and Article 7(7) of the ACHR. The Court emphasised the point that under each of these instruments, the implication is that only the impecunious judgment debtor is protected. They do not protect the debtor who has the means to pay the debt but obdurately declines to do so. According to the Court, the purpose of these instruments is to protect the individual against imprisonment for

---

[64] Dinstein, "Life, Physical Integrity and Liberty," in Henkin, *International Bill of Rights*, at 135-36; Van Dijk and Van Hoof, *European Convention*, at 488.

debt in circumstances where there is a genuine inability to pay. Relying on these instruments, the Court finally held that the imprisonment of the applicant was ordered not as a punishment but for wilful refusal to fulfil an obligation by divesting himself of his property. He was able to pay his debt but clandestinely decided not to do so. Accordingly, since the choice whether to undergo or avoid the indignity and humiliation of incarceration rested with the debtor, the procedure of civil imprisonment did not contravene the constitutional prohibition on inhuman or degrading treatment or punishment. It was perfectly in order for the Magistrate Court to issue a warrant of civil imprisonment against him.

It is submitted that the Court's utilisation of international human rights law and sources to broadly interpret the Zimbabwean national law on civil imprisonment is a sound one. The interpretation ensures that only people who are unable genuinely to honour their debts are protected. It does not protect fraudulent or malicious debtors. This approach challenges the Zimbabwean classical dualist theory with respect to conventional international law. It seeks to bring the Zimbabwean protective clause in line with international human rights regime.

Non-discrimination

The principle of non-discrimination is recognised and protected under the municipal law of Zimbabwe. It is outlawed in two provisions of the Constitution. Section 11 thereof, which is exactly the same as the Botswana clause, provides that, "Whereas every person in Zimbabwe is entitled to the fundamental rights and freedoms of the individual, that is to say, the right whatever his race, tribe, place of origin, political opinions, colour, creed or sex, but subject to respect for the rights and freedoms of others and for the public interest..." Section 23 entitled 'Protection from Discrimination on the Grounds of Race, etc' provides in paragraph (1) that "Subject to the provisions of this section - (a) no law shall make any provision that is discriminatory either of itself or in its effect; and (b) no person shall be treated in a discriminatory manner by any person acting by virtue of any written law or in the performance of the functions of any public office or any public authority." This clause is also analogous to Section 15 of the Constitution of Botswana. It reinforces Section 11 by protecting non-discrimination in greater detail. It prohibits any law that is discriminatory either of itself or in its effect. It also outlaws discrimination of any person by a person acting in accordance with any written law or in performance of public function or authority.

These clauses correspond to Articles 2 and 7 of the UDHR, Article 14 of the ECHR, Articles 14(1) and 26 of the ICCPR and Articles 2 and 3 of the ACHPR. Section 11, in particular, corresponds to Article 14 of the ECHR despite the fact that it omits concepts of religion, language, birth or other status embodied in this instrument. It clearly reveals the influence of the European non-discrimination clause. It also slightly resembles the ACHPR clause. The international clauses firmly enshrine the principle of non-discrimination. They mandatorily prohibit, broadly and variously, discrimination on such grounds as race, sex, language, religion, ethnic origin, political or other opinion.[65] These instruments constitute the cornerstone of non-discrimination at universal level.

Thus, in line with international human rights treaties, the Zimbabwean non-discrimination clauses outlaw discrimination based on whatever ground. Both clauses outlaw discrimination in mandatory terms, positively and without exceptions. Moreover, every person in Zimbabwe has an inherent right not to be discriminated against. Theoretically, these clauses internally incorporate non-discrimination norms encapsulated in, and prohibited by, these treaties. The form and content of this right correspond to international human rights standards.

The enumerated grounds of discrimination in the Zimbabwean clause are wide-ranging. However, most of these grounds are yet to be a subject of litigation in Zimbabwean courts. For instance, notwithstanding the fact that racialism engulfed Zimbabwe during colonial rule, it has not attracted much judicial attention. But it is doubtless that should racialism arise in future court proceedings, the courts will express their revulsion against the practice. The Zimbabwean courts especially the Supreme Court has exhibited a proactive stance in favour of human rights protection in issues like corporal punishment. However, one issue that has occupied a focal point in the courts of Zimbabwe is sex discrimination. It is thus appropriate to examine how the Zimbabwean courts have treated it and

---

[65] Generally, see Vierdag, *Discrimination,* at 86-95.

whether in so doing they have sought guidance from international human rights standards.

Sex discrimination   It is significant to note that, as in Botswana, Section 23 of the Constitution of Zimbabwe does not include sex as a ground of discrimination. Sex appears only in Section 11. However, both the High Court and the Court of Appeal in Botswana in the *Unity Dow* case conclusively held that Section 15 of the Constitution was not restrictive and definitive, unless this was the intention of the Legislature. Rather, it is merely explanatory of the word discrimination. It also outlaws sex discrimination. By analogy, Section 23 of the Constitution of Zimbabwe also outlaws any discrimination or differential treatment of individuals on the basis of sex.

Discrimination on the ground of sex has arisen mainly with respect to discrimination against the female sector of the society, or rather women's equality with men. This is a pivotal issue on discourses on sex discrimination in Zimbabwe. In this vein, according to Article 18(3) of the ACHPR, Zimbabwe is legally obliged, as a State party to this Convention, to ensure the elimination of every form of discrimination against women.

Discrimination against women arises in two senses. First, the customary law perspective. Secondly, legislation which adversely affect the status of women. In both these areas, there is a body of legal norms which discriminate against women.

First, customary practices. One of the features of the dual legal system in Zimbabwe: customary law and general law, is that there is an entire system of customary practices interacting with general rules which discriminate against women in areas such as succession and family law, property, finance and contracts. For instance, customary law of succession does not recognise the rights of female children to succeed to their father's property on his death. Similarly, where the father dies intestate, his property devolves only upon his eldest son but not other children. Where there is no eldest son, the property devolves upon the younger son even where he has older sisters. Moreover, unless the husband makes a specific bequest to his wife, she does not inherit from his estate. The estate devolves upon the eldest son.[66]

---

[66] May, *Zimbabwean Women*, at 65-9; Holleman, *Customary Law*, at 318-77.

However, these practices are yet to be tested in Zimbabwean courts in order to determine whether, in line with international human rights norms, they are permissible under Zimbabwean municipal law.

It is submitted that on strict application of Article 18(3) of the ACHPR, these customary practices constitute discrimination against women. They are incompatible with the non-discrimination norms especially in so far as they accord women less favourable treatment as compared to their male counterparts. They are not only unreasonable as the High Court of Botswana observed in *Unity Dow* case but are also utterly discriminatory, in content and effect. They need to be corrected and modernised to effectuate universal standards.

On the second question of national legislation and sex discrimination, there is a body of laws which limits equality of women with men. Legislation according unequal status to women in Zimbabwe continues to exist. Women married in community of property still require their husband's consent to acquire, cede or dispose of immovable property. According to Sections 5 and 6 of the Constitution of Zimbabwe, the acquisition of Zimbabwean citizenship by descent or birth depends on the status of the child's father whether he is a citizen of or lawfully and ordinarily resident in Zimbabwe, but not on the mother's status except where the child is illegitimate. Thus the child cannot assume its mother's citizenship. Moreover, women married to citizens of Zimbabwe are entitled to be registered as citizens but not vice versa.[67]

The Zimbabwean Parliament has, however, introduced reforms to ensure that the law gives equal protection to women. The Legal Age of Majority Act, No. 15 of 1983 and Matrimonial Causes Act, No. 33 of 1985 are examples. Both acts of legislation aim at alleviating inequality against, and unfavourable treatment of, women. The Legal Age of Majority Act sets the legal age of majority at eighteen years and extends it to customary law. The Matrimonial Causes Act gives married women the right to institute proceedings in Court without the assistance of the husband where he is domiciled abroad. In essence, both Acts give women the right to transact in their own names.[68]

---

[67] Rowland, "Legislation Dealing with Women," at 16.

[68] For discussion of these legislation, see generally Rowland, "Legislation Dealing with Women," at 16; Gubbay, "Women's Rights," at 3-11.

The Zimbabwean Parliament approach towards discrimination against women has been augmented by the courts. Sex discrimination was one of the issues to be resolved by the Supreme Court in *Rattigan and Others v. Chief Immigration Officer and Others.*[69] In resolving this issue, the Court made reference to and relied upon international human rights law and sources particularly the ECtHR and HRC judgments, and the ICCPR. The Court was faced with three applicants all of whom were Zimbabwean citizens. Each of them was married to a non-citizen who had been refused a permit by the Department of Immigration to reside in Zimbabwe. In an application to the High Court of Zimbabwe to have the decision of the Chief Immigration Officer refusing their husbands residence in Zimbabwe to be declared unconstitutional, they relied on two clauses of the Constitution, viz, Section 11 on non-discrimination and Section 22(1) on freedom of movement. As regards the former, they argued that the refusal by the Chief Immigration Officer to issue residents permit to their foreign husbands was discriminatory. In other words, the alien status of their husbands constituted an impediment to enjoy their freedom of movement. They were discriminated against purely on the basis of sex.

Relying on the ECtHR decisions in *Abdulazia Cabales and Balkandali v. United Kingdom* (1995) 7 EHHR 471 and *Berrehab v. Netherlands* (1989) 11 EHHR 322 interpreting Article 8 of the ECHR on the right to family life,[70] the Supreme Court held that the constitutional right to freedom of movement of a female citizen is contravened if her alien husband is not permitted to reside with her in Zimbabwe. A decision or law that forbids her husband from residing with her while allowing wives of Zimbabwean men to reside with their husbands in Zimbabwe is discriminatory. The Court concluded that Section 5 of the Immigration Act allowing wives of Zimbabwean men to reside in Zimbabwe should also apply to women. Their husbands should be allowed to reside with them in Zimbabwe.

Moreover, relying on these judgments, the Court emphasised that Section 11 is not merely a guide to the intention of the framers or a

---

[69] 1995 (2) S.A. 182 (ZSC). For an analysis of this case, see Madhuku, "The Impact of European Convention," at 941-2; Gubbay, "Fundamental Human Rights," at 242-3.

[70] 1995 (2) S.A. 182 (ZSC) at 190.

preamble to the chapter on fundamental human rights and freedoms. It confers substantive rights on individuals. According to the Court, Section 11 is "'the key or umbrella provision' in the Declaration of Rights under which the rights and freedoms are subsumed, and.. it encapsulates the sum total of the individual's rights and freedoms in general terms, which may be expanded upon in the expository, elaborating or limiting ensuing ss 12-23."[71] The Court allowed the application. The above ECtHR judgments formed the basis of its decision. They influenced the Court to adopt a liberal and broad construction of Section 11 thereby ensuring that the applicants be accorded maximum protection in fundamental justice.

Property Rights

Property rights in Zimbabwe are elaborately recognised and protected in two clauses of the Constitution. In terms of Section 11(c), every person in Zimbabwe is entitled to the "protection for the privacy of his home and other property and from the compulsory acquisition of property without compensation." Section 16(1), which constitutes the main property clause, provides that "No property of any description or interest or right therein shall be compulsorily acquired except under the authority of a law..." These clauses are similar to Article 17(1) of the UDHR which guarantees to everyone "the right to own property either alone as well as in association with others." Paragraph (2) thereof prohibits arbitrary deprivation of property. They also resemble Article 14 of the ACHPR according to which "the right to property shall be guaranteed." They are analogous to Article 1 of the First Protocol to the ECHR. These provisions constitute the legal basis for the protection of property rights at international level.[72]

However, the main Zimbabwean property clause, Section 16(1), does not employ the language of the international human rights instruments and formulate the individual right to property in positive prescriptive terms. It protects property in a negativist manner by merely prohibiting its arbitrary deprivation or compulsory acquisition.

---

[71] Ibid., at 186. See also In re Munhumeso and Others 1995 (1) S.A. 551 (ZSC).

[72] Alfredsson, "Article 17," in Eide, *Human Rights*, at 225-62; Harris et al, *European Convention*, at 516-38; Ankumah, *TheAfrican Commission*, at 142.

Moreover, property rights under this clause are not inherent in human beings. However, unlike the international human rights instruments, this clause goes further to protect interest or right in property from compulsory acquisition.

Nevertheless, in terms of substantive content, the Zimbabwean property clause is largely in line with international human rights law. It protects any property from unlawful deprivation whether owned under the common law or customary law. This clause recognises everyone's right to own property or interests therein irrespective of the manner of acquisition. Under this clause, every person has the right to own or hold any property lawfully acquired and to dispose of such property. It constitutes the legal basis for the protection of individuals' right to property in the country.[73]

The term "property" in this context is all-encompassing. It covers both movable and immovable property. Moreover, in *Hewlett v. Minister of Finance and Others*[74] it was held that a debt or compensation provided under the Government scheme for the benefit of victims of terrorism was property within the meaning of Section 16(1) of the Constitution.

Critical but controversial issues associated with the right to property in Zimbabwe are expropriation and compensation. Both issues are inter-connected. These issues have preoccupied the attention of the Zimbabwean courts since independence. It is significant to examine whether in an attempt to resolve these issues, the Zimbabwean courts have made use of international standards for the protection of the right to property.

Expropriation of property The general rule that States have a sovereign right in contemporary international law to expropriate or compulsorily acquire property either of its citizens or foreigners[75] is

---

[73] Ncube, "Land Tenure System," at 26-39; Hlatshwayo, "Land Expropriation Laws," at 41-58; Naldi, "Land Reform," at 78-91.

[74] 1982 (1) S.A. 490 (ZSC).

[75] Mapp, *Iran-US Claims Tribunals*, at 170; Brownlie, *Principles*, at 531-8; the Charter of Economic Rights and Duties of States, 1974, GA Res. 3281(XXIX), Article 2(2)(c). *Reprinted* in 14 ILM 251(1975). See also the ACHPR, Articles 14 and 21(2); First Protocol to ECHR, Article 1; UDHR, Article 17(2).

also embraced by Zimbabwean municipal law. Section 16(1) of the Constitution of Zimbabwe gives the government executive powers to compulsorily acquire property of any description or interest or right in property. This clause constitutes the legal basis for expropriation of property in Zimbabwe.

The enumerated purposes for which property may be expropriated are detailed in Section 16(7)(1) (a) to (o) of the Constitution. This clause requires property or interest or right therein to be expropriated if, for example, it is in a dangerous state or prejudicial to the health or safety of human beings, animals or plants; to satisfy any tax or rate; by way of penalty for breach of the law whether under civil process or after conviction for a criminal offence and to prevent removal or attempted removal of property out of or into the country in contravention of any law and in the general public interest.

In addition, property may be expropriated for purposes of securing the development or utilisation of mineral resources. This limitation broadens areas in which the authorities may compulsorily acquire individual property in order to meet special economic needs of Zimbabwe whose economy thrives partly on mineral resources. It is a reasonable exception to the protection of the right to property. These exceptions serve an obvious, albeit significant, societal need. They are in stark accord with general international law. States have a sovereign right to acquire property for public purposes. This principle now forms part of customary international law.[76]

The sovereign right of the government of Zimbabwe to acquire property for public purposes should, however, be reconciled with the fundamental right of individuals to own property.[77] It must be balanced against the welfare and interest of individuals to own and be in continued, undisturbed and peaceful enjoyment of their right to property. In this regard, Section 16(1) of the Constitution requires that expropriation of property should be under the authority of a law. It

---

[76] The case concerning certain German interests in Polish upper Silesia P.C.I.J (1926), Ser A, No 7 at 22. See also Shaw, *International Law*, at 520; Hlatshwayo, "Expropriation laws in Zimbabwe," at 50; Brownlie, *Principles*, at 537-8; Mapp, *Iran-United States Claims Tribunal*, at 175. See also Resolution on Permanent Sovereignty Over Natural Resources of 1962 GA Reso. 1803 (XVII), Article 4.

[77] Sporrong and Lonnroth v. Sweden (1984) 7 E.H.R.R. 256.

should not be discriminatory or arbitrary. This safeguard ensures legality in expropriation of property.

An opportunity to test Zimbabwe's expropriation laws arose in the fore-cited *Hewlett v. Minister of Finance and Others*.[78] The Court was asked to determine, inter alia, whether compensation awarded to Mr Hewlett under the pre-independence Victims of Terrorism (Compensation) Act, but not paid out, and later frozen by the new War Victims Compensation Act No. 2 of 1980 was compulsorily acquired by the State for the purposes of Section 16(1) of the Constitution.

The Court interpreted Section 16(1) in order to find out whether freezing of compensation by the State amounted to compulsory acquisition of property. In doing so, it did not only seek guidance and inspiration from comparative national judicial decisions. In the process, it also drew inspiration from the ECHR and UDHR. After referring to *Minister of Home Affairs (Bermuda) and Another v. Collins MacDonald Fisher and Another* 1980 AC 319 at 328-9 dealing with principles governing the interpretation of the provisions of the Constitution on the Bill of Rights, the Court said, "It is known that this chapter, as similar portions of other constitutional instruments drafted in the post-colonial era, ...was greatly influenced by the European Convention for the Protection of Human Rights and Fundamental Freedoms (1953) (Cmd 8969). That Convention was.. applied to dependent territories including Bermuda. It was in turn influenced by the United Nations' Universal Declaration of Human Rights of 1948."[79] According to the Court, per Fieldsend, C.J., as he then was, "These antecedents, and the form of chap 1 itself, call for a generous interpretation avoiding what has been called 'the austerity of tabulated legalism.'"[80] However, the Court held that jurisprudentially, the State did not acquire Mr Hewlett's property as contemplated by Section 16(1) although it had benefited from the debt owed to him. Notwithstanding this conclusion, the significant point to emphasise is that the Court informed its decision with these human rights instruments.

---

[78]   1982 (1) S.A. 490 (ZSC).

[79]   Ibid., at 495.

[80]   Id.

In *Minister of Home Affairs v. Bickle and Others*[81] involving confiscation of Mr Bickle's immovable property, who was in exile in South Africa, pursuant to the Emergency Powers (Forfeiture of Enemy Property) Regulations, the State asked the Court to uphold the confiscation order as a valid exercise of powers conferred under Section 16(8)(b) of the Constitution. This clause provides for the vesting or administration of 'enemy' property. The Court rejected the argument that the word "enemy" should be brought under Section 16(8)(b) on the basis that Bickle was not an enemy of Zimbabwe. It held that no state of war existed between Zimbabwe and South Africa despite their hostile relation. Thus Section 16(8)(b) could not be a basis for confiscating Mr Bickle's property.

The Court interpreted the word "enemy" by relying, inter alia, on international law. It said, per Georges, C.J., as he then was, that "None of the cases cited by Mr Blom-Cooper casts any doubt on the general proposition that in public international law the term "enemy" can only have meaning in the context of a declared state of war or of armed conflict of a character which can be categorised as a state of war."[82]

The Court then proceeded to examine whether the State could confiscate the applicant's property or derogate from the protection of his right to property assuming a state of war existed between Zimbabwe and South Africa. The Court examined this issue by referring to the ECHR and the judgments of the ECtHR in the *Cyprus case* and *Lawless case* dealing with state of emergencies. It then held that there being no state of war between the two countries which could justify the state of emergency necessitating expropriation of the applicant's property, the Emergency Powers (Forfeiture of Enemy Property) Regulations were unconstitutional and thus null and void.

By contrast, in *May v. Reserve Bank Zimbabwe,*[83] the High Court of Zimbabwe held that compulsory acquisition of external shares by the Government pursuant to Section 12A (6) of the Exchange Control Regulations 399 of 1977 amounted to expropriation of

---

[81]   1984 (2) S.A. 431 (ZSC).

[82]   Ibid., at 450.

[83]   1986 (3) S.A. 107 (ZSC).

property in terms of Section 16(1) of the Constitution without making any specific and express reference to international law sources or standards. However, the Court approvingly relied on *Hewlett v. Minister of Finance and Others* in which the ECHR and UDHR were consulted when interpreting Section 16(1) to include compensation.[84]

The determination of Zimbabwean courts to invoke and rely on international human rights norms to construe national human rights law was amply demonstrated in *Nyambirai v. National Social Security Authority and Others*.[85] The applicant, a professional assistant in a firm of legal practitioners, challenged the National Social Security Authority (Pensions and Other Benefits Scheme) Notice issued by the Ministry of Public Service, Labour and Social Services compulsorily requiring employees and employers to contribute three percent of their salaries and wages to a Pensions and Other Benefits Scheme aimed at providing benefits to employees. Section 4(1) of the Notice provided that all working persons between sixteen and sixty years of age were obliged to register and contribute as employees to the Scheme. The applicant contended that Section 4(1) infringed his right not to have property of any description compulsory acquired in terms of Section 16(1) of the Constitution of Zimbabwe. The respondents argued that the mandatory contributions were not unconstitutional. They were reasonably justifiable in a democratic society and in satisfaction of a "tax" in terms of 16(7)(a) of the Constitution. Both instances justified derogation from the applicant's right to property.

It was common cause between the parties that the contributions amounted to compulsory acquisition of property in terms of Section 16(1). The contentious issues were whether they were reasonably justifiable in a democratic society and in satisfaction of a "tax." As regards the latter issue, the Court had to construe the word "tax" in order to determine whether it covered the contributions in question. In doing so, it relied, inter alia, on the ECtHR decision in *James v. United Kingdom* and the ECHR and ICESCR. The Court discerned several features which designate a tax. One of these features, according to the Court, is that the revenue from tax should be utilised to provide services for the general public. The applicant disputed this feature

---

[84] Ibid., at 122 and 129.

[85] 1996 (1) S.A. 636 (ZSC).

arguing that the Notice provides for no direct benefit to members of the public in general. The benefits under it derive only for employees. In determining whether the scheme was aimed at the general public, the Court took into account the social and economic policies which prompted the Government to design the compulsory contribution scheme such as provision of adequate social security for employees upon retirement and in old age.

Most significantly for the present study, the Court also took into account Zimbabwe's international obligation under the ICESCR, as a state party, to set up a social security scheme. Gubbay, C.J., as he then was, said that, "... it is of significance that Zimbabwe has acceded to the International Covenant on Economic, Social and Cultural Rights of 1966. By its accession, the Government undertook an international commitment to establish and maintain a system of social security for its people."[86] Justice Gubbay concluded that the passing of the National Social Security Act fulfils that obligation.

Furthermore, relying on the ECtHR decisions in *James v. United Kingdom* and *Mellacher v. Austria*, the Court was of the view that the determination of whether or not a particular service or programme promotes public interest is a matter for the national authorities which should be respected by the courts. It observed that the courts "will not intrude but will allow a wide margin of appreciation, unless convinced that the assessment is manifestly without reasonable foundation. See *James v. United Kingdom* (1986) 8 EHHR 123 at para 46; *Mellacher v. Austria* (1989) 12 EHHR 391 at para 51.[87] The Court further noted that it had to respect the Ministers' assessment that the scheme provides a service in the public interest and it is not manifestly without reasonable foundation. Accordingly, the Court concluded that the contributions made payable under the authority of Section 4 of the National Social Security Authority Notice were in satisfaction of a "tax."

---

[86] Ibid., at 644. Article 6 of the ICESCR states that "The State Parties to the present Covenant recognise the right of everyone to social security, including social insurance." The Court also cited the First Protocol to the ECHR, Article 1(b) which expressly reserves the right of a State "to enforce such laws as it deems necessary... to secure the payment of taxes or other contribution in the public interest."

[87] 1996 (1) S.A. 636 (ZSC) at 644.

Respecting the question of whether the "tax" was reasonably justifiable in a democratic society, Justice Gubbay's answer was "emphatically in the affirmative." He was influenced not only by the fact that most developed and lesser developed countries operated the social security scheme but by the fact that "the right to social security and social insurance is embodied in several international instruments... especially art 22 of the Universal Declaration of Human rights, 1948, and art 9 of the International Covenant on Economic, Social and Cultural Rights, 1966. In addition, there are about 20 International Labour Organisation Conventions dealing variously with medical care, old age, invalidity, survivors, employment injury and unemployment benefits. See, in particular art 57 of Convention 102 (27 April 1955) and Convention 157 (11 September 1986)."[88] According to the Court, "the internationally recognised right to social security in the wide sense and the extent to which that obligation has been implemented throughout the world offers cogent evidence of the Government's objective in establishing the Pensions and Other Benefits Scheme in 1993 as one sufficiently important to justify the imposition of the tax."[89] Finally, the Court dismissed the application.

It is demonstrably clear that international human rights treaties and decisions of the ECtHR played a central role in the Court's decision. It is important to observe that the Court's reliance on international sources did not end with the UDHR and ICESCR, and decisions of the ECtHR. It also drew inspiration from international instruments adopted within the auspices of the International Labour Organisation (hereafter ILO) to further reinforce its reasoning. Reliance on ILO conventions widens the scope of the Court's utilisation of international human rights standards and sources. It constitutes a firm challenge to Zimbabwe's classical dualist theory regarding the status and role of conventional international law in its municipal law.

The concept of expropriation of property in Zimbabwean municipal law has attracted attention particularly in relation to land. In pursuit of its land reform policy due to the problem of landlessness particularly among the African population in the post-colonial context,

---

[88] Ibid., at 647-8.

[89] Ibid., at 648.

the Zimbabwean Parliament amended the property clause to bring it into line with the exigencies of land reform. It enacted the Land Acquisition Act of 1992 to implement the National Land Policy (hereafter NLP).[90] The Act aims at designating, declaring and acquiring derelict immovable property and land compulsorily, and allocate it to landless people. Section 12 of the Act empowers the President to compulsorily acquire land, inter alia, for purpose beneficial to the public generally or to any section of the public. In particular, Section 12(1) authorises the Minister responsible for land to designate *any* area or piece of land as land to be acquired for resettlement purposes. As a consequence, the Government has used this clause to designate pieces of land for resettlement purposes.

The Government land designation action was challenged in *Davies and Others v. Minister of Lands, Agriculture and Water Development*.[91] In April 1993 the appellants, five commercial farmers, were notified that their farms had been designated in terms of Section 12(1) of the Land Acquisition Act, 1992 by the Minister as rural land to be acquired by the President, as the acquiring authority, for purpose of resettling persons. Their written objections failed to persuade the Minister to revoke the designations of the farms in question. They brought an application to the High Court for an order declaring the designations of the six farms in violation of their constitutional rights to property or interest therein and, consequently of no legal force and validity. Having lost the case, they appealed to the Supreme Court. In the Supreme Court, the inquiry revolved around whether or not the act or effect of designation amounted to compulsory acquisition of property or interest or right therein in contravention of Section 16(1).

Unlike in the previous cases, the Court did not expressly invoke international human rights instruments and similar sources to interpret Sections 16(1) in relation to designation of land. It, nonetheless, indirectly utilised these instruments by relying on its

---

[90] Act No. 3/1992, Cap. 20:10. See generally Hlatshwayo, "Land Expropriation Laws," at 41-58; Naldi, "Land Reform," at 78-91. For a discussion of the political and social ramification of land allocation and distribution in Zimbabwe, see generally Moyo, *Land Question*, 1995.

[91] 1997 (1) S.A 228 (ZSC). For an analysis of this case, see Naldi, "Land Reform," at 84-90.

previous decision in the *Hewlett case*[92] wherein it referred to the ECHR and the UDHR in order to determine whether or not 'designation' of land amounts to compulsory acquisition. On the basis of the *Hewlett case*, the Court concluded that the word 'designation' of land does not amount to compulsory acquisition of land. It means identifying specific tracts of land for intended acquisition whose effect is to restrict the owner's power to dispose the land without divesting him with the right of ownership. But compulsory acquisition, according to the Court, signifies the transfer of property or interest therein to the State in the sense of parting with ownership or possession. This occurs with or without the owner's consent. Finally, the Court held that the designation of the six farms did not amount to compulsory acquisition or arbitrary deprivation of property as contemplated by law. It further noted that, in any case, designation was clearly in the public interest. It dismissed the appeal.

Compensation   Once expropriation of property is determined to be lawful compensation follows. However, compensation is the most controversial aspect of the right to property. The initial Section 16(1)(c) of the Lancaster House Zimbabwean Constitution of 1980 required the acquiring authority to effect "prompt payment" of "adequate compensation" for the acquisition of property or interest in property. But the interaction between the Lancaster House property clause and the demand for meaningful land reform necessitated the reformulation of the standard of compensation. Section 16(a) of the new Land Acquisition Act, 1992 only requires "fair compensation."[93] By contrast, as observed elsewhere in this study, the UDHR and the First Protocol to the ECHR neither mention compensation for deprivation of property nor indicate the standard of measurement. Compensation is only mentioned in Article 21(2) of the ACHPR in terms of which "dispossessed people shall have the right to ..an adequate compensation."

As indicated earlier on, the traditional rule generally supported by Western countries is that compensation for compulsory acquisition of property should be prompt, adequate and effective. This rule

---

[92]   1982 (1) S.A. 491 (ZSC).

[93]   Naldi, "Land Reform," at 84-8.

effectively requires full compensation for expropriated property.[94] It has, however, been challenged by developing States as too rigid. They maintain that a less rigid standard of adequate compensation be adopted.[95]

It is clear that the Zimbabwean compensation clause diverges from the prompt, adequate and effective international standards of payment. It has relaxed the standard of measurement to fair compensation. This dichotomy between Zimbabwean local and international standards is aimed at reflecting the country's local conditions which demand the adoption of much lesser strict requirements of compensation assessment.

The question of compensation arose in *Hewlett v. Minister of Finance and Others*.[96] One of the issues to be decided by the Court was whether the debt or compensation owed to the applicant under the War Victims Compensation Act was compensation in terms of Section 16(1) of the Constitution of Zimbabwe. In its construction of Section 16(1), the Court relied on comparative national jurisprudence dealing with the interpretation of constitutional provisions on declaration of human rights in which specific reference was made to the ECHR and UDHR. In particular, it relied on the Privy Council decision in *Minister of Home Affairs (Bermuda) and Another v. Collins MacDonald Fisher and Another* 1980 AC 319 at 328-9 interpreting Section 11(5) of the declaration of human rights in the Constitution of Bermuda dealing with the right of a person to live in Bermuda. This case relied on the ECHR and UDHR to interpret this provision. Finally, the Zimbabwean High Court, per Fieldsend, C.J., as he then was, relied on these authorities and held that the debt owed to the applicant was compensation falling within the framework of Section 16(1) and was as

---

94   Mapp, *Iran-United States Claims Tribunals*, at 177; Harris, D.J. *Cases and Materials on International Law*. 4th ed. (London: Sweet & Maxwell, 1991) at 543; Hlatshwayo, "Expropriation Laws," at 50.

95   United Nations Resolution 3281 of 1974 Article 2(c) G.A. Res. 3281 (XXXIX), 12 December 1974. See also Mapp, *Iran-United States Claims Tribunals*, at 165. This standard seems to have acquired some status of *de lege ferenda*. See Naldi, *Constitutional Rights*, at 83; Texaco v. Libya 17 ILM 1 (1978).

96   1982 (1) S.A. 490 (ZSC). See also May v. Reserve Bank of Zimbabwe 1986 (3) S.A 107 (ZSC).

such a constitutionally enforceable property right. Clearly, the Court was influenced by the Privy Council decision in which it utilised ECHR and UDHR to interpret the right of a person to live in Bermuda under the Constitution of Bermuda. Through this decision, it indirectly used both instruments to broadly and liberally interpret Section 16(1) and unambiguously held that a debt owed to the applicant was compensation.

An opportunity to test the Zimbabwean compensation standard also arose in the fore-cited *Davies and Others v. Minister of Lands, Agriculture and Water Development*.[97] However, the Court did not analyse the notion of fair compensation. Having held that the designation of land did not amount to expropriation and hence not compensable, it was unnecessary for the Court to examine what amounts to fair compensation. But had the issue been pursued actively by the parties, it is entirely possible that in line with its emerging human rights proactiveness, the Supreme Court could have examined the issue and gone further to enlighten its decision with comparative international human rights normative standards.

One important aspect of the Zimbabwean property clause is that it sets a time limit for the payment of compensation. Section 16(1)(c) of the Constitution requires compensation to be made within a reasonable time. This requirement is in line with international law as enunciated in *Erkner and Hofauer v. Austria* where the ECtHR found a violation of human rights when land compensation proceedings had lasted an unreasonable time, more than sixteen years.[98]

Moreover, in order to ensure legality, Section 16(1)(d) of the Constitution of Zimbabwe entitles any person who contests the acquisition of property or the amount of compensation payable to challenge it in court. The claimant may further apply to court for the prompt return of the property if the court does not confirm the acquisition or to appeal to the Supreme Court. It appears that this safeguard was included in the property clause with the principal aim of assuring settler communities that property titles acquired by whatever means during the colonial era would not be arbitrarily repossessed by the new breed of African rulers. Significantly, this mechanism ensures

---

[97]   1997 (1) S.A 228 (ZSC).

[98]   (1987) 9 E.H.R.R 464.

that expropriation be carried out in strict accord with the law. It ensures procedural fairness.

Clearly, the Zimbabwean right to property clause corresponds fully to international standards. It is in line with international standards. Moreover, in practice, judicial pronouncements demonstrate the extent to which the courts increasingly invoke and rely on international human rights standards when interpreting the Zimbabwean right to property clause. The courts in Zimbabwe recognise the sovereign right of the State to use its executive powers to confiscate property but also seek to ensure that these powers are used in accordance with international human rights standards. Thus the courts have relied upon international sources especially the ECHR and judgments of the ECtHR to interpret the word property in Section 16(1) widely and liberally to encompass shares and compensation. They have moved away from the dualistic conception of international and national law in implementing property rights in Zimbabwean domestic law.

Freedom of Movement and its Relation with Protection of the Family

The right to freedom of movement enjoys express constitutional status and recognition in Zimbabwe.[99] Section 22(1) of the Constitution expressly declares that "no person shall be deprived of his freedom of movement, that is to say, the right to move freely throughout Zimbabwe, the right to reside in any part of Zimbabwe, the right to enter and to leave Zimbabwe and immunity from expulsion from Zimbabwe." On the international plane, corresponding safeguards are articulated in Article 13(1) and (2) of the UDHR, Article 12(1) to (4) of the ICCPR and Article 12(1) to (5) of the ACHPR. The latter, additionally includes the right of every individual who is persecuted to seek and obtain asylum in accordance with international conventions.[100]

Thus in line with international human rights instruments, the Zimbabwean clause reflects international standards for the protection

---

[99] See Madhuku, "The Impact of European Convention," at 940-1; Gubbay, "Fundamental Human   Rights," at 242-3.

[100] Ankumah, *The African Commission*, at 139-40. See further Nowak, *U.N. Covenant*, 197-222.

247

of freedom of movement. It enshrines the individual liberty and freedom to move freely and unhindered within Zimbabwe. This freedom includes the right to move unhindered and freely in and out of the country. The clause constitutes the bedrock of the right to freedom of movement in Zimbabwe. It is the fountain of Zimbabwe's legal obligation to protect freedom of movement of the individual. In practice, State authorities recognise and respect individual freedom of movement. Thus this freedom is generally implemented in Zimbabwe.

Several cases have, however, recently come before the Zimbabwean courts based on Section 22(1) of the Constitution. These cases have mainly involved the mobility of women citizens married to aliens. In resolving these cases, the Zimbabwean courts have drawn heavily on international human rights norms and sources particularly the ECtHR judgments and the ECHR. One such case is the fore-cited *Rattigan and Others v. Chief Immigration Officer and Others.*[101] One of the issues to be resolved by the Supreme Court was whether the refusal of the Chief Immigration Officer to grant the applicant's husbands residence in Zimbabwe was unconstitutional in that it infringed Section 22(1) on freedom of movement. The issue was premised on the fact that if their husbands could not stay in Zimbabwe it effectively meant that each of the applicants had also to leave in order to maintain their marital relationships. However, the State argued that freedom of movement of the applicants had not been infringed because they were still entitled to freely move in and out of Zimbabwe. According to the State, the issue of marriage was of no relevance. Their choice to accompany their husbands was unconnected with their freedom of movement.

Although the main issue concerned the infringement of the applicants' freedom of movement, the decision of the Court centred mainly around married life. The Court described marriage as a juristic act *sui generis*. It gives rise to a physical, moral and spiritual community of life - a *consortium omnis vitae*. This analysis of the sanctity of marriage led the Court to refer to international human rights standards particularly respective Articles 8(1) and 17 of the ECHR and ICCPR on the right to family life. The Court noted that "Decisions

---

[101] 1995 (2) S.A. 182 (ZSC). For an analysis of this case, see Madhuku, "The Impact of European Convention," at 941-2. See further in re Wood and Hansard 1995 (2) S.A. 191 (ZSC).

concerning art 17 of the International Covenant on Civil and Political Rights, and art 8(1) of the European Convention on Human Rights, both provisions of which afford protection against interference with family life, lay emphasis upon the importance of preserving well-established family ties."[102] The Court proceeded, relying on the HRC decision, to observe that "In *Aumeeruddy-Cziffra and Others v Mauritius* (1981) 62 International Law Reports 255, the United Nations Human Rights Committee examined the effect of the law passed by the Government of Mauritius which removed the right of alien husbands of Mauritian women citizens to the right of residence and immunity from deportation, and found that it had infringed art 17 of the Covenant."[103]

The Court further referred to and relied on the decisions of the ECtHR, namely, *Abdulaziz Cabales and Balkandi v. United Kingdom, Berrehab v. Netherlands, Moustaquin v Belgium and Beljoudi v. France* all of which concerned the interpretation of Article 8(1) of the ECHR on the right to the family and concluded, per Gubbay, C.J., as he then was, that when Article 8(1) of the ECHR and Article 17 of the ICCPR are taken in conjunction with Section 11 and 22(1) and interpreting all of them generously and liberally, "I reach the Conclusion that to prohibit the husbands from residing in Zimbabwe and so disable them from living with their wives undermine and devalue the protection of freedom of movement accorded to each of the wives as a member of a family unit."[104] It then concluded that the applicants' freedom of movement has been violated. The courts emphasised that it had the duty to preserve family life in line with international human rights standards.

It is submitted that while the decision of the Court may be viewed as extreme judicial activism in the sense that it compared two

---

[102] 1995 (2) S.A. 182 (ZSC) at 189.

[103] Id. When citing the Committee, the Court said that "..the common residence of husband and wife has to be considered as the normal behaviour of a family. Hence, and as the State party has admitted, the exclusion of a person from the country where close members of his family are living can amount to an interference within the meaning of art 17. In principle, art 17(1) applies also when one of the spouses is an alien." Id.

[104] Ibid., at 190.

unrelated provisions of the Constitution,[105] it underscores the extent to which the Zimbabwean courts are prepared to go when invoking and utilising international human rights standards to construe domestic legislation particularly where it diverges from or falls short of meeting international standards. In a way, it demonstrates the extent to which the court is drifting away from the perception that international law and Zimbabwean national law are separate and govern different spheres of conduct. It also underlines how the courts can use international law to complement national law generally and national human rights standards in particular.

Freedom of Expression

According to Section 20(1) of the Constitution of Zimbabwe, "Except with his own consent or by way of parental discipline, no person shall be hindered in the enjoyment of his freedom of expression, that is to say, freedom to hold opinions and to receive and impart ideas and information without interference, and freedom from interference with his correspondence." This clause is similar to Article 19 of the UDHR, Article 19(1) to (3) of the ICCPR, Article 10(1) and (2) of the ECHR and Article 9(1) and (2) of the ACHPR. These clauses positively protect the right to hold opinions and to receive and impart information and ideas without interference by public authorities and regardless of boundaries. They impose a duty on member-states and certainly Zimbabwe to respect and protect individuals freedom of expression. Moreover, state authorities are obliged to respect this freedom.[106]

The Zimbabwean clause, in line with international human rights standards, fully protects freedom of expression. It accords individuals the right to express their views freely subject to the standard limitations of public interest, the protection of the reputation of others, maintenance of the authority and independence of the courts. This clause translates the international normative standards on freedom of expression into Zimbabwean municipal law.

---

[105] Cf Madhuku who argues that this form of judicial activism amounts to an abuse of comparative analysis. See Madhuku, "The Impact of European Convention," at 941.

[106] Nowak, *U. N. Covenant*, at 335-58; Harris, et al, *European Convention*, at 372-416.

Freedom of expression is one of the fundamental human rights norms that have attracted judicial activity in Zimbabwe. It was a point of contention in *Woods and Others v. Minister of Justice, Legal and Parliamentary Affairs and Others*[107] concerning the constitutionality of restricting access to receiving and sending personal letters and correspondences of prisoners. The applicants, described as "Class D Maximum Security Prisoners," were serving life sentences. They were restricted by prison regulations to writing and receiving only one letter every month. They challenged the regulations on the ground that they contravened their constitutional right to freedom of expression.

The Zimbabwean Supreme Court had no difficulty in holding that the regulation was contrary to the Constitution and that it was not reasonably justifiable in a democratic society. The judgments of the ECtHR in *Golder v. United Kingdom and Silver v. United Kingdom* formed, in part, the basis of the Court's decision that a prisoner does not shed his fundamental rights at the prison gate.

Recourse to international human rights norms and sources especially the jurisprudence of the ECtHR was further had in *In re Munhumeso*.[108] The applicants were charged with contravening Section 6 of the Zimbabwean Law and Order (Maintenance) Act, (Cap. 65) in that they staged a public procession notwithstanding refusal of permission by the police. Section 6 gave the police general powers to sanction any public demonstration and to refuse permission without giving reasons. In court, the applicants contended that Section 6 infringed their freedom of expression and assembly. The Court construed Section 6 against Section 20(1) of the Constitution on freedom of expression. It concluded that indeed Section 6 infringed Section 20(1) of the Constitution. The Court did this by invoking and relying on decisions of the ECtHR in *Handyside v. United Kingdom* interpreting the equivalent Article 10(1) of the ECHR. It then, per Gubbay, C.J., observed that "The importance attaching to the exercise of the right of freedom of expression and assembly must never be underestimated. They lie at the foundation of a democratic society and are 'one of the basic conditions for the progress and development of

---

[107] 1995 (1) S.A. 123 (ZSC). See further Madhuku, "The Impact of European Convention," at 941-2; Gubbay, "Fundamental Human Rights," at 243-4.

[108] 1995 (1) S.A. 551 (ZSC).

every man', per European Court of Human Rights in *Handyside v. United Kingdom* 1 EHHR 737 at para 49."[109]

According to the Court, this right is one of the most precious of all the guaranteed freedoms. It serves four broad special purposes, viz., it helps an individual to obtain self-fulfilment; it assists in the discovery of truth; it strengthens the capacity of an individual to participate in decision-making and provides a mechanism by which it would be possible to establish a reasonable balance between stability and social change. In addition, the Court referred to the ECtHR pronouncement in *Klass and Others v Federal Republic of Germany* 2 EHHR 214 at para 48[110] and emphasised that an interpretation of the law that favours the liberty of the individual is to be preferred to the one that interferes with it. In the result, the Court found in favour of the applicants and struck down the relevant provision of the Law and Order (Maintenance) Act restricting public demonstrations.

Freedom of expression was also an issue in *Retrofit Pvt Ltd v. Post and Telecommunications*.[111] The applicant, Retrofit Pvt Ltd, invited the Supreme Court of Zimbabwe to determine whether or not the Postal and Telecommunications Services Act of Zimbabwe abridged its right of freedom of expression by prohibiting it from operating a mobile cellular telephone service. The Act vested in the Postal and Telecommunications Corporation an exclusive monopoly to provide telecommunication services within, into and from Zimbabwe, and so prohibited the establishment by a private company of a mobile cellular telephone service for public use. The Court considered several points. Significantly, in deciding these points, it relied extensively on international comparative judicial pronouncements and international human rights treaties and instruments.

First, *locus standi*. In opposing the application, the respondent had argued that the applicant, as a corporate body, lacked the necessary *locus standi* to challenge the Postal and Telecommunications Services Act in the High Court. The Court held that the applicant had *locus*

---

[109] Ibid., at 557.

[110] Ibid., at 560.

[111] 1996 (1) S.A. 847 (ZSC). Generally, see Gubbay, "Fundamental Human Rights," at 243-4.

standi to challenge the Act. It reached its decision by relying on the judgment of the ECtHR in *Autronic AG v. Switzerland* in which the Court said that the fact that the *Autronic AG* was a limited company and its activities were commercial could not deprive it of the protection of Article 10 of the ECHR on freedom of expression.[112] Freedom of expression is conferred universally, on "everyone", individual and corporate personality alike.

As regards the second point whether the Postal and Telecommunications Services Act breached Section 20(1) of the Constitution, the Court, again relying on international human rights law and sources, concluded that it did. The Court emphasised the fact that the fundamental freedom of expression is 'one always to be jealously guarded by the Courts.' It retorted that, "This approach, which underscores the pre-eminence of freedom of expression as an indispensable condition for a free and democratic society, conforms with what is reflected in international human rights instruments, some of which Zimbabwe has ratified/acceded to. See art 10 of the Universal Declaration of Human Rights; art 19 of the International Covenant on Civil and Political Rights; art 10 of the European Convention for the Protection of Human Rights and Fundamental Freedoms; art 9 of the African Charter on Human and Peoples' Rights; art 4 of the American Declaration of the Rights and Duties of Man; and art 13 of the American Convention on Human Rights."[113] These instruments formed, in part, the basis for the court decision that the Postal and Telecommunications Services Act contravened Section 20(1) of the Constitution and was therefore unconstitutional.

These judicial pronouncements clearly and amply demonstrate the readiness and the extent to which the Zimbabwean courts especially the Supreme Court, as the custodian and protector of fundamental human rights of individuals, invoke and rely on international human rights law embodied in international sources to construe the national human rights norm of expression. Admittedly, courts do not expressly say that the international human rights norms are part of the municipal law of Zimbabwe and should be treated as such. They, however, recognise the significant role that these norms can play in the domestic enforcement of human rights law. The approach of the Zimbabwean

---

[112] 1996 (1) S.A. 847 (ZSC) at 854-5.

[113] Ibid., at 856.

courts does not only depart from the inherited classical dualist theory but also has the beneficial effect of injecting international normative standards on freedom of expression into the national law of Zimbabwe. It has an enriching effect on national human rights standards and jurisprudence.

Conclusion

It is abundantly clear from the fore-going discussion that, by and large, the various human rights norms in the Zimbabwean Bill of Rights, as in Botswana and Namibia, are in line with international human rights standards. The Bill incorporates, albeit implicitly, international human rights standards embodied in major international human rights instruments and treaties into the domestic law of Zimbabwe. The juridical content of the human rights norms in the Bill of Rights is almost similar to rights in international human rights instruments. The derogation and claw-back clauses are also cast in the same terms. Put differently, the Bill of Rights essentially reflects the influence of international human rights standards. The difference pertains only to the formulation of these clauses. Thus most Zimbabwean human rights clauses, unlike the international ones, do not protect these rights in positive terms. Rather, they adopt a negativist approach. Moreover, most clauses do not give the natural-law basis of these rights. They are granted on the basis of the standing of the individual and thus lend themselves to a positivistic approach. Their recognition is dependent upon the positive laws of the state.

Most significantly, the spirit of the Bill of Rights has been expressed and reinforced by the judiciary. Judicial practice indicates that in enforcing national human rights law, the Zimbabwean courts have began to drift away from the apparently dualistic approach inherited from Britain in the way they treat international norms in domestic law. It is evidently clear that when interpreting the various human rights norms in the Bill of Rights, the Zimbabwean courts have actively referred to and relied upon similar provisions in international human rights instruments. Their interpretation has not been solely based on national law particularly the Constitution of Zimbabwe. They have drawn inspiration from international human rights instruments such as the UDHR, ICCPR, ECHR and ACHPR as well as general international human right law. For example, these sources have been relied upon to interpret concepts such as trial within a reasonable time, inhuman and degrading treatment or punishment, the right to property, freedom of expression and freedom of movement. The use of these instruments to construe national human rights law has been consistent and uniform. It has not been merely cursory and intermittent.

Moreover, the courts have not only referred to international human rights norms. They have also invoked and relied actively on these norms to invalidate practices which adversely affect the domestic enforcement of human rights norms. For instance, international human rights norms have been relied on not only to challenge but also to outlaw practices such as adult and juvenile corporal punishment and the "death row" phenomenon as inhuman and degrading treatment and punishment. Courts have been prepared to use norms in international sources such as judgments of the ECtHR and HRC to nullify these practices although their activism has been frustrated by Parliament reversing their decisions, for instance, in juvenile whipping. In other words, the courts have not yielded to national standards especially cultural norms which sanction these practices. In sum, the courts have challenged or tempered with the imposed classical dualistic approach and swayed towards a monistic approach. This approach reinforces the domestic role of international law. It makes international human rights law more effective in national law. It also accords this law a firm place in domestic sphere and enriches national human rights normative standards with international standards. Most significantly, this approach incorporates international human rights law into Zimbabwean national law.

Part V:
General Conclusions

8 Lessons on Monism and Dualism

In the preceding chapters, a number of observations and conclusions have already been made. This chapter is not meant to repeat them but some salient points may be reiterated and stressed, and some lessons, both general and specific, drawn from the classical theories of monism and dualism with respect to the domestic incorporation and role of international human rights law.

The central objective of this study is to examine the process and techniques of incorporating international human rights law into the domestic laws of Botswana, Namibia and Zimbabwe. It examines the status and role of international human rights law in the national laws of these countries. The inquiry involves, in the main, a wider issue of the relationship between international law especially international human rights law and the municipal laws of the three countries. It finds out the extent to which the place and role of international human rights law in these countries can adequately be examined with the aid of the traditional theories of the relationship between international law and municipal law commonly represented by monism on the one hand and dualism on the other. In essence, the study examines the relevance of these theories in the domestic application of international human rights law.

The monist theory, sometimes called the automatic incorporation principle, is based on the natural-law assumption that international law and national law compose a single normative system. It thus assumes that international law is automatically applicable in internal law. It does not require any act of incorporation to be part of national law. The dualist theory, is, on the other hand, predicated on the positivist notion that the two legal regimes are independent of each other and cannot purport to conflict. For international law to have internal effect, it needs a specific act of incorporation. Philosophically, these theories provide clarity and a backdrop of the assessment of the place and role of international law (including international human rights law) in municipal legal order. Also, adherence to or adoption of either of these theories may, by and large, assist in determining the impact and role of international law in municipal law.

General Lessons

Two main general lessons can be drawn from an examination of the incorporation and role of international law (including international human rights law) in national law on the basis of monism and dualism. The first general and main lesson is that these theories only serve as part of the solution to the major debate on the interaction between the international legal regime and municipal normative orders. At a practical level, generally speaking, State practice does not always accord neatly with this theoretical distinction. In some countries, the national Constitution or statutory enactment may assign international law a role in municipal law without necessarily conforming to either the classical dualist or monist theory. In other countries, both or either of these theories may be adopted in the Constitution or statutory enactment. Yet, in other countries the relationship may not even be regulated either by the national Constitution or primary legislation. This diversity of practice is exemplified by the countries under consideration. The three countries have variously embraced different theories on the relationship between international law, customary and conventional, and their national legal systems.

As regards Namibia, it is clear that it has radically departed from the imposed colonial legacy. Under the pre-existing legal order, customary international law (including customary international human rights law) was treated as part of municipal law of Namibia. It was governed by the monistic theory. International agreements or treaties (including human rights treaties) did not have automatic and direct application in national law. They required legislative transformation to be part of municipal law and confer rights and impose duties on individuals. They were governed by the dualist theory. This legal position has been fundamentally altered by the independence Constitution. The Constitution makes both customary international law and treaty law part of municipal law of Namibia. Customary and treaty rules are directly applicable in municipal law. Significantly, these rules are not only assigned statute-like effect in municipal law, they are also accorded a constitutional status. Conceptually, the approach adopted by

Namibia effectively makes it a monist country. Both customary and treaty rules are governed by the monistic theory. The gravamen of this theory is to make international law and Namibian legal order part of a single normative system. It creates unity between the international legal order and national law of Namibia. The two legal orders complement each other.

The Namibian monist approach is further reinforced by the fact that the substantive and juridical content of most of the various human rights norms contained in the Bill of Rights are largely fashioned along similar rights in international human rights treaties and instruments. They reflect the influence of, and are indeed in line with, international human rights standards. Put differently, the Bill incorporates, albeit implicitly, international human rights standards into national law of Namibia.

The Namibian monist strategy has several advantages. In the first instance, it makes the task of Namibian courts relatively easier. If and when the Namibian courts are faced with questions involving rules of international law, and international human rights law for that matter, they do not have to undertake the arduous task of inquiring into whether or not these rules are part of municipal law. In other words, faced with rules of international law, customary or conventional, the Namibian courts do not have to investigate whether the rules in question are governed by classical dualism or monism. According to the Namibian monist strategy, these rules are directly and automatically applicable in national law. Municipal judges can directly invoke and use these rules in domestic legal proceedings. Moreover, individuals are directly accorded rights and obligations recognised and protected by international law. They can directly claim international legal rights embodied in human rights treaties and customary international law since these rights have been integrated into the national legal system. Individuals are rights-holders. This approach further assigns international law a firm and secure place in municipal legal sphere.

In sharp contrast, Botswana and Zimbabwe have left the imposed colonial heritage unaffected. The independence legal order of both countries has not changed the pre-existing legal position of both customary and conventional international law in national law. As regards Zimbabwe, judicial practice, based on the superimposed Roman-Dutch common law approach, established that international agreements were governed by the dualist theory. In terms of this theory, international agreements required specific legislative transformation in order to be integrated into municipal law. Customary international law, on the other hand, was governed by monist theory according to which existing rules of customary international law had automatic and direct application into municipal law. This rule, unlike the one governing treaties, was not established by the courts. Rather, it was discerned, and thus based on, the imposed Roman-Dutch common law.

Significantly, the Roman-Dutch common law has been retained by the Independence Constitution of Zimbabwe. According to this law, the place of international agreements in Zimbabwean municipal law is governed by classical dualism and customary international law by monism. This legal position has been authoritatively confirmed by the Zimbabwean judiciary. Thus the colonial legacy continues to operate in the extant municipal law of Zimbabwe.

In Botswana, the pre-existing domestic legal position of international law, customary and conventional, never received any judicial confirmation. Moreover, the various proclamations decreed for the territory were silent on the matter. The legal position was, as in Zimbabwe, based on the superimposed Roman-Dutch common law approach. According to this approach, the status of treaties in the pre-existing municipal law of Botswana was governed by dualist theory. Treaties required legislation to make them part of national law. The legal position of customary international law in municipal law was, on the other hand, governed by monist theory. This law was directly applicable in municipal law. As in Zimbabwe, this position was not altered at independence. It continues to operate in the present municipal law of Botswana. It has been confirmed not by the independence Constitution but by the judiciary. However, the judiciary has not vigorously, consistently and uniformly acted upon this legal position in order to make it more clear and certain, and define its parameters.

It essentially means, therefore, that Zimbabwe and Botswana have adopted the same approach towards international law. They adhere to the same theories in the way they treat international law in general in municipal law. In both countries, the domestic status of treaties is governed by classical dualism and customary international law is regulated by monism.

The monist approach to customary international law (including customary international human rights law) in both countries has also been underscored by the fact that the content of most of the various human rights norms embodied in the Bills of Rights of both countries largely reflect the influence of international human rights standards. They are in line with similar rights in the main international human rights treaties and instruments. The Bills replicate the standard human rights norms enshrined in these treaties and instruments. As with international human rights instruments, the Bills of Rights protect most human rights norms in a positive and mandatory language. The difference relates mainly to form. For instance, the human rights clauses in the national Bills of Rights are drafted in negativist terms. Further, most of these clauses do not give expression to the natural-law foundation of human rights norms as reflected in the international instruments. They make the protection of these rights depend mainly on the positive laws of the State. But, by and large, these clauses translate the substantive content of international human rights norms into national law. They make these norms easily available to municipal courts and individuals in municipal legal proceedings.

The adoption of the classical dualist theory in Zimbabwe and Botswana with respect to international treaties, on the other hand, essentially means that, in theory, international human rights standards contained in these treaties do not have direct application in municipal law in the absence of an express and specific incorporation by legislation. The internal operation of these standards depends on the positive action of the State. Clearly, the dualist theory limits the domestic operation and role of international law. It minimises the influence of international law in national sphere. This positivistic approach to international law does not embed fully this regime in national law. It reduces the effectiveness of international human rights law in national law. This is especially true with regard to international human rights law. It means that this law is unavailable to the judge in national law unless the national legislature accords it internal status. In principle, national courts may not invoke and utilise this law. Moreover, an individual can only derive rights and incur obligations from treaty standards after parliament has legislated them into law.

The second significant general lesson to be learnt from dualism and monism is that, even in situations where States are prepared to assign international law a place and role in municipal law, they do it cautiously. States do not permit international law an unregulated predominance in municipal legal sphere. They ensure that the domestic operation of rules of international law should give way to internal rules under certain specified and prescribed circumstances in line with the principle of sovereignty. There are some matters that the national legislatures should be able to exclude from the general domain of international law. The approaches adopted by the countries under consideration seek to take account of this practical reality.

In Namibia, the international law clause does not allow international legal norms to operate unsupervised in municipal law of Namibia. The operation of these norms in domestic law is not absolute and unlimited. The Constitution recognises that rules of both customary and conventional international law may be excluded from operating directly and automatically in municipal law by the Constitution or legislation. Thus the Namibian monist approach is subject to constitutional supremacy and legislative sovereignty. A clear and unequivocal constitutional provision supersedes a rule of international law. Further, an unambiguous posterior legislation clearly manifesting the intention of the legislature to disregard international law prevails over a rule of international law.

As regards, Botswana and Zimbabwe, judicial practice also reveals that domestic application of international law particularly the automatic operation of customary international law (including customary international human rights law) is not absolute. It is subject to three main exceptions. Firstly, it may be excluded by the *stare decisis* rule. Second, legislation enacted subsequent to a rule of customary international human rights law may exclude customary international human rights law from operating in national law. Thirdly, the act of state doctrine. Executive actions may operate to exclude automatic operation of customary international human rights law. These are the only three recognised exceptions to the automatic operation of customary international human rights law in municipal law of Botswana and Zimbabwe. These exceptions minimise the role of international law and certainly of international human rights law in domestic law.

But, at the same time these exceptions underline the fact that international law cannot be accorded unlimited and absolute status in national law. National authorities particularly the legislature have residual powers to exclude its operation in national legal sphere. This scenario casts a burden on the national courts to enhance the role of international law in national law by construing a constitutional provision or legislation, case law and executive actions designed to disregard international law in a manner that is consistent with and gives effect to international obligations of these countries. Phrased differently, in applying national legal rules, the courts should ensure that they act in conformity with, and not contrary to, the obligations assumed by these countries in international law. This is in direct accord with the principle that a state cannot invoke its national law as an excuse for failure to carry out its international responsibility.

Specific Lessons

The determination of the incorporation and role of international law (including international human rights law) in national law purely on the basis of these theories also has specific lessons. These lessons become self-evident with respect to the enforcement of human rights law in general and particularly in the countries presently under consideration. These lessons are not mutually exclusive. They are inter-related and cover a wide spectrum of human rights issues. They have a bearing on the actual application of these theories in national legal order.

1. The first lesson relates to divergence of State practice from monism and dualism. The actual practice of States shows that in the specific sphere of the enforcement of human rights norms national courts often diverge from the specific theory embraced by their country. In monist countries, for instance Namibia, courts may sometimes fail to actively give effect to the automatic incorporation theory in interpreting national law. Conversely, in dualist countries such as Botswana and Zimbabwe, national courts may under certain circumstances refer to and draw inspiration from international standards even where there is no express and categorical provision assigning international law a place and role in national law. Practice in dualist countries also varies. In some countries, courts may hold firmly to the classical dualist theory

while in others, through judicial activism, they may directly and actively invoke international law and sources to construe national law thereby challenging the traditional dualist theory. This divergence of practice has evidently been exhibited by courts in the countries in question when interpreting a variety of human rights issues.

The divergence has revealed itself with respect to the death penalty in Botswana and Zimbabwe. The death penalty is a permissible sentence under the municipal laws of both countries and has been carried out in practice even in recent years. Although in Zimbabwe it is yet to be actively challenged in courts, the view of the judiciary is that its constitutionality is unquestionable. This view was expressed by the Supreme Court of Zimbabwe following an enactment of the law by parliament debarring its challenge, that is, the death penalty, in a court of law on the basis that it is unconstitutional.

However, in Botswana, the constitutionality of the death penalty has already been challenged in courts. It has been challenged not only on the basis that it is contrary to the constitutional clause protecting the right to life. International human rights standards have also been utilised and relied upon to challenge it. However, the courts of Botswana have constrained themselves to utilise these standards to determine its constitutionality. Similarly, the courts have been unable to determine the constitutionality of hanging, as a mode of executing the death penalty, on the basis of international human rights standards. In fact, the courts have relied on national law, the Constitution, to hold that they cannot declare both practices unconstitutional because their functions are not legislative but purely adjudicatory. This judicial attitude has reinforced the dualist heritage of Botswana.

In Namibia, the total abolition of the death penalty by the Constitution has meant that the challenge has been directed against life imprisonment. It has been argued that life imprisonment in itself amounts to the death penalty. However, the courts have unambiguously ruled that life imprisonment does not amount to the death penalty. This decision was made on the basis of national law and not international law notwithstanding Namibia's monist approach.

Divergence of practice from these theories has also occurred with respect to the enforcement of fair trial guarantees. Generally, courts in the three countries have implemented fair trial safeguards. They have given life and substance to the constitutional protection of fair trial. However, the extent to which the courts have drawn

266

inspiration from international human rights law has not been strictly in accordance with the theory observed in each country. In Namibia, fair trial attributes which have been the subject of judicial activity include trial within a reasonable time, judicial independence, the right to legal counsel and public trial. In examining these principles, the Namibian courts have mainly relied on the Constitution, national law and jurisprudence as well as judicial decisions from other jurisdictions especially South Africa, United Kingdom and the United States of America. They have not actively informed their decisions with international human rights law and standards. Reference to these standards has been made in few and isolated cases. Even in these cases, recourse to international standards has not been very consistent and uniform. Thus the Namibian courts have neglected to internally effectuate the Namibian monist, or rather the automatic incorporation theory when enforcing the right to fair trial.

In Botswana, judicial interpretation and subsequent enforcement of fair trial guarantees in the Constitution has reinforced the inherited dualist theory. This has occurred notwithstanding the fact that the Interpretation Act of Botswana authorises the courts of Botswana to have regard to treaties when interpreting domestic law. International human rights standards have been referred to in few instances such as in cases dealing with trial within a reasonable time. However, most safeguards such as the right of the accused to have trial conducted in the language that he/she understands, judicial independence and impartiality, the right to legal counsel and public trial have predominantly been construed on the basis of national law and jurisprudence. The courts have not demonstrated any inclination to seek guidance and assistance from international human rights instruments and sources when interpreting these guarantees.

This picture contrasts sharply with the situation in Zimbabwe. The Zimbabwean courts have demonstrated a readiness to invoke and rely on the international human rights standards and sources to construe fair trial clauses of the Constitution notwithstanding Zimbabwe's dualist legacy. This approach has been adopted, for instance, in the interpretation of the content and scope of the right to trial within a reasonable time. Reliance on international human rights sources especially the jurisprudence of the ECtHR to interpret this right is ample demonstration of the preparedness of the Zimbabwean courts to depart from the dualist conception concerning Zimbabwean municipal law and conventional international law. This approach enriches Zimbabwe's national law with international standards.

A radical departure from classical monism and dualism has especially been demonstrated with respect to the enforcement of the prohibition against torture, inhuman and degrading treatment or punishment. This issue has arisen mainly in relation to the institution of corporal punishment. It should be underlined that this is an area where the Namibian courts have given effect to the country's monist theory. The Namibian Supreme Court, in particular, has invoked and relied heavily on international human rights law especially Article 3 of the ECHR on the prohibition of torture and similar conducts and the jurisprudence of the ECtHR to declare unconstitutional corporal punishment of whatever form and irrespective of whomsoever is inflicted. This notwithstanding the fact that Namibia is not, and cannot, be a party to the ECHR due to its geographical limitation. Consequently, corporal punishment of whatever form is unlawful under municipal law of Namibia. Significantly, international human rights standards played a major part in its total abolition.

In Zimbabwe, despite the fact that the country adheres to the classical dualist theory in relation to the treatment of treaties in its municipal law, the Zimbabwean courts have actively relied on international human rights treaties especially Article 3 of the ECHR and the jurisprudence of the ECtHR to declare unconstitutional whipping of both adults and juvenile offenders. Relying on these sources, the courts have stressed that whipping is not only dehumanising and degrading. It is also repugnant to contemporary international civilised standards. But, with respect to juvenile offenders, the Zimbabwean parliament has frustrated the progressiveness of the courts. Parliament has reversed the pronouncements of the courts and made juvenile whipping lawful and barred its challenge on the basis that it is inhuman and degrading. Moreover, the Zimbabwean courts have drawn inspiration from international human rights law to declare that the "death row" practice in Zimbabwe is an inhuman and degrading treatment.

In stark contrast, judicial practice in Botswana has reinforced the dualist approach with respect to the enforcement of prohibition against torture and related conducts. These concepts have arisen mainly in relation to corporal punishment. International human rights standards have been invoked to challenge this punishment. The courts have, however, refused to utilise these standards to declare it unconstitutional. As a consequence, corporal punishment has remained a lawful and permissible punishment in Botswana. The objection of the Botswana courts has mainly been directed against the mode of its execution in a delayed and repeated manner and its combination with other equally severe sentences such as a long term of imprisonment. As an institution, both under traditional customary law and general law, corporal punishment is legally permissible in Botswana. The courts have exercised extreme judicial restraint with respect to pronouncing on its constitutionality. Moreover, Botswana's dualist theory has been enforced in relation to hanging as a mode of carrying out the death penalty. Hanging continues to constitute the only mode of execution despite the fact that both the constitution and international human rights law have been invoked to challenge it as being an inhuman and degrading treatment. Botswana courts have been unable to declare it unconstitutional.

Divergence of practice from these theories has further been demonstrated in relation to discrimination especially sex discrimination. Discrimination against women has for a long period of time been a feature of both traditional law and general law in the countries under consideration. In challenging it before national courts, reliance has been placed not only on the non-discrimination provisions of the Constitution but also on international human rights law particularly human rights treaties. Significantly, the courts have also been proactive in invoking international human rights law and sources to outlaw it. This has been a positive approach especially in Botswana and Zimbabwe despite their adherence to the dualist theory. International human rights law has constituted the basis for removing legal impediments against women resulting in the improvement and enhancement of their legal and social status.

It is important to note that the Namibian government has complemented the proactiveness of the Namibian courts in domestically effectuating the monist theory in the general area of sex discrimination. The realisation of the disadvantageous position that women find themselves in the country has prevailed on the Namibian parliament to outlaw any form of discrimination. Moreover, the government has adopted a policy of affirmative action, or rather positive discrimination in order to address the problem of sex discrimination.

However, sex discrimination is still prevalent in Botswana and Zimbabwe. Women, in particular, continue to be discriminated against under both customary law and formal statutory and common law in areas such as acquisition of property, succession and inheritance in both countries. International human rights law has yet to play a part in enhancing the status of women in this area. It is submitted that these laws should be reviewed and repealed in order to effectuate internally the principle of equality and non-discrimination and bring them in line with current international human rights standards.

2. The other specific lesson concerns consistency, regularity and uniformity in the application of monism and dualism in national law. Judicial practice in the countries in question evidently demonstrates that there is lack of consistency, regularity and uniformity in the application of these theories. For instance, in Namibia, since the adoption of the national Constitution, the courts have not consistently and uniformly invoked and utilised international human rights law, in line with the classical monist theory, when interpreting national human rights law. Human rights issues have basically been resolved by reference to national law and jurisprudence as well as comparative national jurisprudence at the expense of international human rights standards. Quite often, international standards are referred to incidentally and intermittently where constitutional issues touch upon international law. As a result, Namibia's monist theory has been compromised.

Botswana's dualist approach has also not been applied and implemented with any degree of consistency and uniformity. Thus although the courts have outlawed sex discrimination in the country by having recourse to international human rights standards, they have not used the same standards to outlaw corporal punishment. Moreover, inordinate delays in trying the accused have been held to be unconstitutional by relying upon human rights treaty provisions protecting trial within a reasonable time. However, despite recourse having been had to these standards to challenge the death penalty and hanging, Botswana courts have exercised extreme restraints to declare both practices unconstitutional.

It is also evident that despite Zimbabwe's adherence to dualist theory in relation to conventional international law, the courts have been ready to utilise international human rights treaties to declare

270

unconstitutional some national law and practices. For instance, these sources have been relied on to interpret the concept of trial within a reasonable time, freedom of movement and freedom of expression. This approach has, however, not been applied consistently and in all cases. There are still instances where the courts exercise some restraints to interpret national human rights law on the basis of international sources. For instance, in interpreting the constitutional clause on personal liberty, the Zimbabwean Supreme Court has relied on national law and not international law to hold that it is not in every case that failure to accord individuals the right to liberty should be held to be unconstitutional. National law can be relied on to disregard this protection even where international normative standards would be compromised. Consequently, the enforcement of individuals right to personal liberty has been adversely affected especially in relation to preventive detentions which have occurred during state of emergencies.

3. Closely connected with consistency and uniformity is the question of the preparedness of national courts to invoke international normative standards to invalidate practices infringing national human rights norms. The question is, do courts actually or as a matter of fact rely on international human rights standards to invalidate these practices? Judicial practice various from one jurisdiction to another. Again, corporal punishment offers the best example. Whilst in Namibia and Zimbabwe international human rights standards have constituted the basis for outlawing corporal punishment, this has not been the case in Botswana. The courts in Botswana have restrained themselves from invoking and relying on these norms to invalidate corporal punishment despite reliance having been placed on these norms to challenge this practice. Likewise, courts in Botswana have been reluctant to invoke and rely on international human rights norms and sources to declare the death penalty unconstitutional. Courts have adhered strictly to Botswana dualist theory. Thus it is one thing to refer to international law and sources in construing national human rights norms and quite the other to actually rely on and utilise these norms to declare unconstitutional any practice, act or omission that contravenes these norms.

4. Effectiveness of international human rights law in national law. This relates to the extent to which adoption of the monist and dualist theories ensure and enhance the effectiveness of international human rights norms in the enforcement of national human rights norms. It is clear that adherence to classical dualist theory limits and reduces the effectiveness of international human rights law in national law. This is particularly the case where the national courts, as judicial practice in Botswana amply demonstrates, stick to the letter and spirit of this theory. This means that national courts are not able to draw inspiration from international standards to enrich and cross-pollinate national law especially human rights law where it falls below or diverges from international standards.

It is also demonstrably clear that although monism empowers national institutions particularly courts to rely upon international rules when construing national law, its effectiveness in municipal law is lessened and as such compromised if courts do not rigorously act upon it. This is abundantly illustrated by the Namibian situation. The Namibian courts have not rigorously acted on the monist theory so as to firmly confirm its place and effective role in municipal law. The relevance of this theory in the protection of human rights has been minimised.

Thus both instances, that is, strict adherence to classical dualism and lack of judicial activity on monism, have a limiting effect on the role of international law in the domestic protection of human rights. They do not enhance the effectiveness of international human rights norms in the enforcement of human rights at the national level.

5. Last but not least, is the role of the judiciary in the application of monism and dualism in enforcing national human rights law. The judiciary has an immense and pivotal role to play in the internal application and effectuation of these theories. The judicial role divides itself into two major kinds. First, judicial activism. Secondly, is judicial restraint. The latter approach has been exemplified by the judiciary in Botswana and to a lesser degree in Namibia. The courts in both countries have relied extensively on national rules when enforcing human rights law at the expense of international human rights law and sources. They have demonstrated their inclination to maintaining the status quo and have not actively invoked international human rights standards in enforcing national human rights law and, if need be, used

these standards to invalidate practices that minimise the domestic protection of human rights. Thus, in Botswana, this form of extreme judicial restraint has led the courts to reinforce the inherited dualist theory. Similarly, in Namibia, judicial restraint has compromised Namibia's monist theory. As a consequence, the role of international law in general and international human rights law in particular in the enforcement of national human rights laws of both countries has been limited.

The Zimbabwean courts have, on the other hand, shown a certain degree of judicial activism notwithstanding Zimbabwe's dualist legacy and approach to international law. The Zimbabwean courts have actively invoked international human rights law and sources not only to interpret national human rights law but also to invalidate national practices that frustrate the full implementation and enforcement of human rights law. In a great majority of cases, they have disregarded dualism which enjoins the court to apply national, and not international, law in enforcing national law. They increasingly have recourse to international human rights standards in interpreting national human rights law. This approach has enabled the courts to harmonise national legal norms with international norms. It has enabled national courts to depart from the rigid and dogmatic monist-dualist perception and controversy. This approach gives practical effects to international human rights standards in national law.

This approach attracts several advantages. First, it is a positive, pragmatic and progressive approach to the application of international human rights law in municipal law. It is an approach that municipal courts in Botswana and Namibia, and indeed many countries should adopt in order to firmly assign international legal rules both formal and substantive role and validity in the national legal arena. Secondly, this approach does not amount to effectuation of cultural imperialism of universal norms into national law. It is also not judicial legislation on international legal rules by fiat or back-door. Rather, it is a recognition of the vital role that international normative rules can play in the protection of individual human rights in national law particularly where the national rules fall below or diverge from universally recognised standards. Thirdly, in adopting this approach, the courts are effectively fulfilling the international obligations of these countries assumed under existing international human rights law.

273

Fourthly and most importantly, provided it is done within legally permissible limits and reasonably, this form of judicial activism injects, even for classical dualist jurisdictions, universally recognised norms into municipal law. It reinforces the domestic protection of human rights by international standards and gives practical effect to the human rights rhetoric. It also has an incorporative effect of international human rights law into domestic law. It thus makes municipal law international law friendly.

It is demonstrably clear from these lessons that the countries under consideration do not adhere strictly to classical monism and dualism. The courts, in particular, increasingly depart from these theories. Significantly, there is a fledgling judicial trend, which, of course, varies from country to country, of relying on and drawing inspiration from both customary and conventional international law especially international human rights law in interpreting and enforcing national law even in the absence of any specific and express authority. This approach demonstrates the courts' preparedness to make the legal position of international human rights law in particular in national law more homegrown, or rather autochthonous. It also indicates that there is indeed a great potential for the courts in the three countries to integrate international normative standards into national law so that national human rights law and jurisprudence develops *in tandem* with international law.

Recommendations

The fore-going discussion, particularly the lessons on classical monist and dualist theories, clearly lends support for the need especially of Botswana and Zimbabwe, to establish a firm foundation for the operation of rules of international law, customary and conventional, in national law. In this vein, several recommendations and suggestions are in order. These recommendations and suggestions are inter-related and complement each other.

1. First and foremost, Botswana and Zimbabwe, like Namibia, should incorporate international law in general into their national legal systems. They should assign international law (including international human rights law) an explicit and categorical place and role in their respective national laws. This mechanism underscores the willingness of both countries to abide by the commitments and indeed legal obligations they have assumed at international level. In particular, it serves as clear demonstration of both countries to implement the obligations they have undertaken under relevant international human rights treaties to which they are signatories to respect and protect the rights of individuals in their respective territories.

The reform of this kind can be done in several ways. It can be achieved by primary legislation. The national legislatures of both countries should enact legislation assigning both customary and conventional international law (including international human rights law) a precise place and function in municipal law. They should enact a specific legislation, as the United Kingdom has done with the Human Rights Act 1998,[1] directly incorporating rules of both customary and conventional international law into national law. These rules should be incorporated in the main body of the legislation and schedules providing additional detail annexed thereto. Alternatively, and preferably, international law can be incorporated into municipal laws of both countries by a constitutional mechanism. A clause in the national Constitution is a preferable mode of incorporating

---

[1] Cap. 42. The preamble to this Act, inter alia, states thus: "An Act to give further effect to rights and freedoms guaranteed under the European Convention on Human Rights.." Section 1 thereof entitled "Introduction" incorporates the Convention Rights into United Kingdom municipal law.

international law in national law. As a compact that enshrines the wishes and aspirations of the people, a national Constitution commands universal respect of the people. Most crucially, a national Constitution may not be easily alterable so as to advance the whims and narrow interests of the rulers. Consequently, a constitutional clause translating rules of international law in domestic law has the potential of enjoying universal respect from the general public and rulers alike.

A constitutional provision or legislative enactment translating international law into municipal law should be precise as to which rules of international law are being incorporated into municipal law. As regards international treaties, this device needs to be exact with respect to the kinds of treaties or international agreements that are transplanted into national law. Obviously, no country will accept a blanket provision. But, a provision that domestically incorporates any international agreement subject to reasonable exceptions would be acceptable. The legal position of custom in municipal law should also be more precise. For instance, a provision to the effect that customary international law shall subject to precisely defined exceptions be part of municipal law is a preferred one.[2] This approach incorporates rules of customary international law into national law in their entirety be they general, regional or local.

A reform of this nature offers several advantages. An embodiment of international law in the Constitution or legislation gives this law a firm footing in national law. It also accords rules of international law a statute-like effect in national law so that individuals can directly claim rights and incur responsibilities regulated by this law. Moreover, national courts can directly invoke and rely upon this law in national legal proceedings. This mechanism further ensures that the position of international law in national law is clear, certain and predictable. Furthermore, since international law, especially international human rights law, will continue to play pivotal role in the national legal sphere of both countries, it makes it all the more necessary to accord it a clear and categorical place and role in municipal law.

---

[2] This formula has been adopted in Malawi. See the Constitution of Malawi, Section 211(3).

2. In view of the fact that countries, and certainly those under examination, are not prepared to allow rules of international law to operate unsupervised in their municipal legal systems, it is recommended that exceptions to, or limitations of, direct incorporation and application of international law in municipal law should be clearly and expressly defined. The circumstances under which rules of international law may be excluded from operating in national law should be made absolutely clear and be drafted with utmost precision. This enables the various national actors, particularly the courts, to be in no doubt whether or not a particular rule of international law is excluded from operating in national law. For instance, exclusion of the domestic operation of a rule of international law, customary and conventional, by primary legislation should clearly indicate that the exception relates to posterior but not anterior legislation. Most importantly, exceptions to direct operation of international law in municipal law should be narrowed in order to further enhance the influence and operation of international law in national law.

3. It is further recommended that national courts in the countries under consideration should play a major role in injecting international human rights standards into municipal law. The courts should be more proactive, as the Zimbabwean courts have started to become, in extensively relying upon and drawing inspiration from international law, especially international human rights law and sources, in interpreting national human rights law. Moreover, they should also use these sources to outlaw practices which infringe upon and undermine human rights standards. In other words, it would not be enough for the courts to rely on international human rights standards and sources to interpret a national practice, act or omission that infringes human rights norms and standards or limits the enjoyment of human rights, say, for instance, adult whipping or sex discrimination, but the courts should also utilise these standards and sources especially customary international law to actually invalidate any such practice, act or omission. These norms should form the basis for the protection of individual human rights. They should not just be another form of judicial embellishment. Of course, this form of judicial activism challenges classical dualism especially in Botswana and Zimbabwe. Nevertheless, it helps to interlace national law with international human rights standards. It also complements any constitutional or

legislative measures of incorporation suggested above and reinforces the domestic enforcement of human rights law.

4. In order to ensure that the above-mentioned recommendation is effective particularly in the specific area of the protection and enforcement of human rights law, a provision in the Constitutions of these countries or a duly enacted statute enjoining national institutions especially the courts and tribunals with similar trappings to take international law in general and international human rights law in particular into consideration when interpreting national human rights law is recommended. Such a provision should specifically enjoin national institutions to take into account any sources of international human rights law such as decisions of international law tribunals, treaties and custom when determining human rights related issues.[3] This device ensures that the courts and these bodies not only invoke and rely on international human rights law but also adopt a reasonable interpretation that is consistent and compatible with international human rights standards. This device further ensures that national law standards develop alongside international human rights standards. This mechanism provides a legal basis for the judiciary to develop and internalise a culture of utilising international human rights norms in construing national legal rules.

5. It is further recommended that reliance upon international law (including international human rights law) by national courts to construe national human rights law, say, for unreasonableness or ambiguity should be regular, uniform and consistent. International law in general and international human rights law in particular should not be referred to in few and isolated instances, and incidentally in cases touching upon international interests. It should be relied upon more regularly and consistently in order to demonstrate that the judiciary is

---

[3]   Cf the 1996 Constitution of South Africa, Section 39. Paragraph 1(b) thereof states that "when interpreting the Bill of Rights, a court, tribunal or forum must consider international law." See also the Constitution of Malawi, Section 11(2)(c) which provides that "In interpreting the provisions of this Constitution a court of law shall, where applicable, have regard to the current norms of public international law and comparative foreign case law." Further, see United Kingdom Human Rights Act 1998, Sections 2 and 3. Both provisions enjoin the courts or tribunals to interpret primary legislation and subordinate legislation in a way that is compatible with the ECHR.

internalising the function and significance of this law in the domestic protection and enforcement of national human rights law. This approach has the beneficial effect of enriching and cross-pollinating national law and jurisprudence with international human rights standards. Significantly, it drifts away from classical dualist approach to international law in favour of an approach that forges harmony and unity between international law and national law.

Bibliography

General Works

Aguda, Akinola (1972), "Discriminatory Statutory Provisions and Fundamental Rights Provisions of the Constitutions of Botswana, Lesotho and Swaziland," *South African Law Journal*, vol. 89, pp. 299-308.

Aldrich, H. G. (1996), *The Jurisprudence of the Iran-United States Claims Tribunal*, Clarendon Press, Oxford.

Alexander, C.H. (1952), "International Law in India," *International and Comparative Law Quarterly*, vol.1 pp.289-96.

Alfredsson, Gudmundur (1992), "Article 17", in Asbjørn Eide et al, (eds), *The Universal Declaration of Human Rights: A Commentary*, Scandinavian University Press, Oslo, pp.255-62.

Allot, A. N. (1962), *Judicial Decisions and Legal Systems in Africa*, Butterworths, London.

Amankwah, H. Alex (1988), "Constitutions and Bills of Rights in Third World Nations: Issues of Form and Content", *Comparative and International Law Journal of Southern Africa*, vol. 21, pp. 190-211.

Amankwah, H. Alex (1989), "Fundamental Human Rights: Roots, Fruits, Myths and Realities", *Zambia Law Journal*, vol. 21, pp. 51-75.

Ankumah, A. Evelyn (1996), *The African Commission on Human and Peoples' Rights: Practice and Procedures,* Martinus Nijhoff, The Hague.

Barnett, G. LLoyd (1977), *The Constitutional Law of Jamaica*, Oxford University Press, Oxford.

Barry, D. Donald and Eric J. Williams (1997), "Russia's Death Penalty Dilemmas", *Criminal Law Forum*, vol. 2, pp. 231-58.

Beddard, Ralph (1967), "The Status of the European Convention of Human Rights in Domestic Law", *International and Comparative Law Quarterly*, vol. 16, pp. 206-17.

Beyani, Chaloka (1994), "Toward a More effective Guarantee of Women's Rights in the African Human Rights System", in Roberta Cook (ed), *Human Rights of Women: National and International Perspective*, University of Philadelphia Press, Philadelphia, pp. 285-306.

Beyleveld, Deryck (1995), "The Concept of a Human Right and the Incorporation of the European Convention on Human Rights", *Public Law,* pp. 577-99.

Bingham, T. H. (1993), " The European Convention on Human Rights: Time to Incorporate", *Law Quarterly Review,* vol. 109, pp. 390-400.

Bix, Brian and Adam Tomkins (1992), "Unconventional Use of the Convention", *Modern Law Review*, vol. 55, pp. 721-6.

Blix, H. (1953), "The Requirement of Ratification", *British Year Book of International Law*, vol. 30, pp. 352-80.

Botha, Neville (1995), "Incorporation of Treaties under the Interim Constitution: A Pattern Emerges?", *South African Year Book of International Law*, vol. 20, pp. 196-204.

Bridge, J. W. (1971), "The Relationship Between International Law and the Law of South Africa", *International and Comparative Law Quarterly*, vol. 20, pp. 746-9.

Brierly, J. L. (1963), *The Law of Nations: An Introduction to the International Law of Peace*, 6th ed, Sir Humphrey Waldock (ed), Clarendon Press, Oxford.

Brierly, J. L. (1935), "International Law in England", *Law Quarterly Review*, vol. 51, pp. 24-35.

Brownlie, Ian (1990), *Principles of Public International Law*, 4th ed. Clarendon Press, Oxford.

Brownlie, Ian (1995), *Basic Documents in International Law,* 4th ed. Clarendon Press, Oxford.

Burgenthal, Thomas (1965), "The Effect of the European Convention on Human Rights on the Internal Law of Member States", *International and Comparative Law Quarterly*, pp.79-106.

Burman, B. Sandra and E. Barbara Harrell-Bond (eds) (1979), *The Imposition of the Law*, Academic Press, New York.

Butler, W. E. (1985), "Comparative Approaches to International Law", *Recueil Des Cours*, vol. 190, pp. 9-90.

Byre, D. Angela and Beverley Y. Byfield (1991), *International Human Rights Law in the Commomwealth Caribbean*, Martinus Nijhoff, Dordrecht.

Cassese, A. (1985), "Modern Constitutions and International Law", *Recueil Des Cours*, vol. 192, pp. 331-476.

Charney, I. Jonathan (1986), "May the President Violate Customary International Law?", *American Journal of International Law*, vol. 80, pp. 913-22.

Clapham, Andrew (1993), *Human Rights in Private Sphere*, Clarendon Press, Oxford.

Coccia, Massimo (1985), "Reservations to Multilateral Human Rights Treaties," *California Western International Law Journal*, vol. 15, pp. 1-51.

Collier, J. G. (1989), "Is International Law Really Part of the Law of England?", *International and Comparative Law Quarterly*, vol. 38, pp. 924-35.

Commonwealth Secretariat (1988), *Judicial Colloquium in Bangalore: Developing Human Rights Jurisprudence - The Domestic Application of International Human Rights Norms*, Human Rights Unit, London.

Commonwealth Secretariat (1995), *Judicial Colloquium in Bloemfontein: Developing Human Rights Jurisprudence - The Domestic Application of International Human Rights*, vol. 6, Interights, London.

Crawford, James (1974/5), " Decisions of British Courts During 1974-75 Involving Questions of Public and Private International law", *British Year Book of International Law*, vol. 47, pp. 355-61.

Crawford, James (1979), " The International Law Standard in the Statutes of Australia and the United Kingdom", *American Journal of International Law*, vol. 73, pp. 628-46.

Crawford, James (1993), "Democracy and International Law", *British Year Book of International Law*, vol. 64, pp. 113-33.

Cunningham, J. Andrew (1994), "The European Convention of Human Rights, Customary International Law and the Constitutions", *International and Comparative Law Quarterly*, vol. 43, pp. 537-67.

Deener, R. David (1951), "International Law Provisions in Post-World War II Constitutions", *Cornell Law Quarterly*, vol. 36, pp. 503-33.

Demerieux, Margaret (1992), *Fundamental Rights in Commonwealth Caribbean Constitutions*, University of the West Indies, Bridgetown.

de Smith, S.A. (1964), *The New Commonwealth and its Constitutions*, Stevens and Sons, London.

de Smith, S.A. (1961), "Fundamental Rights in the New Commonwealth", *International and Comparative Law Quarterly*, vol. 10, pp. 83-102.

Devine, J. Dermont (1995), "The Relationship Between International Law and Municipal Law in the Light of the Interim South African Constitution 1993", *International and Comparative Law Quarterly*, vol. 44, pp.1-18.

Dinstein, Yoram (1981), "The Right to Life, Physical Integrity, and Liberty", in Louis Henkin (ed), *The International Bill of Rights: The Covenant on Civil and Political Rights*, Columbia University Press, New York, pp.114-37.

Drzemczewski, Z. Andrew (1983), *European Convention of Human Rights in Domestic Law: A Comparative Study*, Clarendon Press, Oxford.

Duffy, P.J. (1980), "English Law and the European Convention on Human Rights", *International Comparative Law Quarterly*, vol. 29, pp. 585-618.

Dugard, C.J.R. (1966), "Consular Immunity", *South African Law Journal*, vol. 83, pp.126-32.

Dugard, C.J.R. (1971), "International Law is Part of Our Law," *South African Law Journal*, vol. 88, pp.13-15.

Dugard, C.J.R. (1983), "International Human Rights Norms in Domestic Courts: Can South Africa Learn from Britain and the United States," in E. Kahn (ed), *Fiat Iustitia: Essays in Memory of Oliver Deneys Schreiner*, Juta, Cape Town, pp. 221-43.

Dugard, C.J.R. (1994), *International Law: A South African Perspective*, Juta, Kenwyn.

Dugard, C.J.R. (1996), "The Influence of International Human Rights Law on the South African Constitution", *Current Legal Problems*, vol. 49, pp. 304-24.

Eze, C. Osita (1982), *Human Rights in Africa: Some Selected Problems*, Macmillan (Nigeria), Lagos.

Ezejiofor, Gaius (1964), *The Protection of Human Rights Under the Law*, Butterworths, London.

Fawcett, J.E.S. (1963), *The British Commonwealth in International Law*, Stevens and Sons, London.

Fawcett, J.E.S. (1969), *The Application of the European Convention on Human Rights in Domestic Law*, Clarendon Press, Oxford.

Forer, Norman (1979), "The Imposed Wardship of American Indian Tribes: A Case Study of the Prairie Band Potawatomi", in B. Sandra Burman, and E. Barbara Harrel-Bond (eds), *The Imposition of Law*, Academic Press, New York, pp. 89-114.

Francis, G. Jacobs and Robin C. A. White (1996), *The European Convention on Human Rights*, Clarendon Press, Oxford.

Franck, M. Thomas (1992), "The Emerging Right to Democratic Governance", *American Journal of International Law*, vol. 86, pp. 46-91.

Franck, M. Thomas (1995), *Fairness in International Law and Institutions*, Clarendon Press, Oxford.

Gittleman, Richard (1982), "The African Charter on Human and People's Rights: A Legal Analysis", *Virginia Journal of International Law*, vol. 22, pp. 667-714.

Golsong, H. (1962), "European Convention on Human Rights Before Domestic Courts", *British Year Book of International Law*, vol. 38, pp. 445-56.

Hailley, William, Malcolm (1953), *Native Administration on the British African Territories; the High Commission Territories: Basutoland, the Bechunaland Protectorate and Swaziland*, Part 5, Her Majesty's Stationery Office, London.

Hannum, Hurst (ed) (1992), *Guide to International Human Rights Practice*, 2nd ed. University of Pennsylvania Press, Philadelphia.

Harris, David (1967), "The Right to a Fair Trial in Criminal Proceedings as a Human Right", *International and Comparative Law Quarterly*, vol.16, pp. 352-78.

Harris, D.J, M. O'Boyle and C. Warbrick (1995), *The Law of the European Convention on Human Rights*, Butterworths, London.

Henkin, Louis (1991/92), "The United States Bill of Rights and its International Significance", *Zimbabwe Law Review*, vol. 9, pp. 14-30.

Heyns, Christof (1995), "African Human Rights Law and the European Convention", *South African Journal of Human Rights,* vol. 2, pp. 252-63.

Hogg, W. Peter (1992), *Constitutional Law of Canada*, 3rd ed. Carswell, Toronto.

Holdsworth, W. S. (1942), "The Treaty-Making Power of the Crown", *Law Quarterly Review*, vol. 58, pp. 175-83.

Holloway, Kaye (1967), *Modern Trends in Treaty Law*, Stevens and Sons, London.

Hudson, O. Manley (1948), "Integrity of International Instruments", *American Journal of International Law*, vol. 42, pp. 105-8.

Hudson, O. Manley (1950), "Charter Provisions on Human Rights in American Law", *American Journal of International Law*, vol. 44, pp. 543-8.

Humphrey, John (1989), *No distant Millennium: The International Law of Human Rights*, Paris, UNESCO.

Hyde, Charles, Cheney (1937), "The Supreme Court of the United States as an Expositor of International Law", *British Year Book of International Law*, vol. 25, pp. 1-16.

Hyde, N. James (1959), "The Act of State Doctrine and the Rule of Law", *American Journal of International Law*, vol. 53, pp. 635-8.

Jackson, H. John (1992), "Status of Treaties in Domestic Legal Systems: A Policy Analysis", *American Journal of International Law,* vol. 86, pp. 310-40.

Jennings, Robert and Arthur. Watts (1992), *Oppenheim's International Law*, 9th ed. vol. 1, Longman, London.

Kamminga, T. Menno (1992), *Inter-state Accountability for Violations of Human Rights*, University of Pennsylvania Press, Philadelphia.

Kanyeihamba, W. George (1975), *Constitutional Law and Government in Uganda*, East African Literature Bureau, Nairobi.

Kelsen, Hans (1945), *General Theory of Law and State*, Harvard University Press, Cambridge.

Kelsen, Hans (1966), *Principles of International Law*, 2nd ed, Holt, Rinehart and Winston, New York.

Kopelmanas, Lazare (1937), "Custom as a Means of Creation of International law", *British Year Book of International Law*, vol. 18, pp.127-51.

Kunz, Joseph, Laurenz (1953), "The Nature of Customary International law", *American Journal of International Law*, vol. 47, pp.662-69.

Kunz, Joseph, Laurenz (1968), *The Changing Law of Nations: Essays on International Law*, Ohio State University Press, Toledo.

Lauterpacht, Hersch (1939), "Is International Law a Part of the Law of England?" *Transactions of the Grotius Society*, vol. 25, pp. 51-88.

Lauterpacht, Hersch (1973), *International Law and Human Rights*, Garland, New York.

Lillich, B. Richard (1982), "The Promotion of Human Rights by Domestic Courts: A Comparative Approach", in Peter N. Takirambudde (ed), *The Individual under African Law - Proceedings of the First All African Law Conference 11-16 October 1981*, Swaziland Printing and Publishing, Kwaluseni, pp.160-79.

Lillich, B. Richard (1989), "The Constitution and International Human Rights", *American Journal of International Law*, vol. 83, pp. 851-63.

Lillich, B. Richard (1992), "The Role of Domestic Courts in Enforcing International Human Rights Law", in Hurst, Hannum (ed), *Guide to International Human Rights Practice*, 2nd ed, University of Pennsylvania Press, Philadelphia, pp.228-46.

Lindholt, Lone (1997), *Questioning the Universality of Human Rights: The African Charter on Human and People's Rights in Botswana, Malawi and Mozambique*, Ashgate, Dartmouth.

Makua wa Mutua (1995), "The Banjul Charter and the African Cultural Fingerprint: An Evaluation of the Language of Duties", *Virginia Journal of International Law*, vol. 35, pp. 339-80.

Maluwa, Tiyanjana (1993), "Human Rights and Refugees in Southern Africa", *Heidelberg Journal of International Law*, vol.1, pp. 89-102.

Maluwa, Tiyanjana (1993/94), "International Human Rights Norms and the South African Interim Constitution," *South African Yearbook of International Law*, vol.19, pp. 14-42.

Maluwa, Tiyanjana (1996), " The Role of International Law in the Protection of Human Rights under the Malawian Constitution of 1995", *African Year Book of International Law*, pp. 53-79.

Maope, K.A. (1986), *Human Rights in Botswana, Lesotho and Swaziland Survey*, Institute of Southern African Studies, Maseru.

Mapp, Wayne (1993), *The Iran-United States Claims Tribunal - The First Ten Years 1981-1991: An Assessment of the Tribunal's Jurisprudence and its Contribution to International Arbitration*, Manchester University Press, Manchester.

McKean, Warwick (1983), *Equality and Discrimination Under International Law*, Clarendon Press, Oxford.

McNair, D. Arnold (1928), "When Do Treaties Involve Legislation?" *British Year Book of International Law*, vol. 9, pp. 59-68.

Meena, Ruth (ed), (1992), *Gender in Southern Africa: Conceptual and Theoretical Issues*, Southern African Political Economy Series, Harare.

Morgenstern, Felice (1950), "Judicial Practice and the Supremacy of International Law", *British Year Book of International Law,* vol. 27, pp. 42-92.

Neff, Stephen (1984), "Human Rights in Africa: Thoughts on the African Charter on Human and Peoples' Rights in the Light of Case Law from Botswana, Lesotho and Swaziland", *International and Comparative Law Quarterly,* vol. 33, pp. 331-47.

Neff, Stephen (1986), *Human Rights in Botswana, Lesotho and Swaziland: Implications of Adherence to International Human Rights Treaties,* Institute of Southern African Studies, Maseru.

Nettheim, Garth (1988), "'Peoples' and 'Populations'- Indigenous Peoples and the Rights of Peoples", in Crawford, James (ed), *The Rights of Peoples,* Clarendon Press, Oxford, pp.107-26.

Ng'ong'ola, Clement (1992), "The Post-Colonial Era in Relation to Land Expropriation Laws in Botswana, Malawi, Zambia and Zimbabwe", *International and Comparative Law Quarterly,* vol. 41, pp. 117-36.

Nobel, Peter (1978), "National Law and Model Legislation on the Protection of Refugees in Africa" in Gøran Melander and Peter Nobel (eds), *African Refugees and the Law,* Scandinavian Institute of African Studies, Uppsala, pp. 58-76.

Nowak, Manfred (1993), *U.N. Covenant on Civil and Political Rights: CCPR Commentary,* Kehl and Rhein, Strasbourg.

Nwabueze, B.O. (1964), *Constitutional Law of the Nigerian Republic,* Butterworths, London.

O'Connell, D. P. (1970), *International Law,* 2nd ed, Stevens and Sons, London.

Obadina, Derek (1997), "The Right to Speedy Trial in Namibia and South Africa", *Journal of African Law,* vol. 41, pp. 229-38.

Odumosu, Oluwole Idowu (1963), *The Nigerian Constitution: History and Development,* Sweet and Maxwell, London.

Okoth-Ogendo, H.W.O. (1979), "The Imposition of Property Law in Kenya", in Sandra B. Burman and Barbara E. Harrell-Bond (eds), *The Imposition of Law*, Academic Press, New York, pp.147-65.

Okoye, Chuks Felix (1972), *International Law and the New African States*, Sweet and Maxwell, London.

Oppenheim, L. (1935), "Is International Law Part of Our Law?" *Transactions of Grotius Society*, vol. 25, pp. 51-9.

Pain, J.H. (1978), "The Reception of English and Roman-Dutch law in Africa with reference to Botswana, Lesotho and Swaziland", *Comparative and International Law of Southern Africa*, vol.11, pp. 137-67.

Partsch, Karl Joseph (1981), " International Law and Municipal Law", in R. Bernhardt (ed), *Encyclopedia of Public International Law*, vol. 10, North-Holland, Amsterdam, pp. 238-57.

Paust, J. Jordan (1988), "Self-executing Treaties", *American Journal of International Law*, vol. 80, pp. 760-81.

Peaslee, J. Amos (1966), *Constitutions of Nations: Europe*, vol.3, 3rd ed, Martinus Nijhoff, The Hague.

Potter, B. Pitman (1925), "Relative Authority of International Law and National Law in the United States", *American Journal of International Law*, vol.19, pp. 314-26.

Preis, S. Ann-Belinda (1996), "Human Rights as Cultural Practice: An Anthropological Critique", *Human Rights Quarterly*, vol.18, pp. 286-315.

Preuss, Lawrence (1950), "The Relation of International Law to Internal Law in the French Constitutional System", *American Journal of International Law*, vol. 44, pp. 641-69.

Radipati, B.D.D. (1995), "Legal Semiotics and Normative Imposition in an African Context: The Case of the San/Bushmen", in Roberta Kevelson (ed), *Conscience, Consensus and Crossroads in Law: Eighth Round Table on Law and Semiotics*, Peter Lang, New York, pp. 261-70.

Robertson, A. H and J. G. (1989), Merrills. *Human Rights in the World: An Introduction to the Study of the International Protection of Human Rights*, 3rd ed, Manchester University Press, Manchester.

Rupp, G. Hans (1976), " International Law as Part of the Law of the Land: Some Aspects of the Operation of Article 25 of the Basic Law of Germany", *Texas International Law Journal*, vol. 11, pp. 541-7.

Rupp, G. Hans (1977), " Judicial Review of International Agreements: Federal Republic of Germany", *American Journal of Comparative Law*, vol. 25, pp. 286-302.

Sanders, A.J.G.M. (1974), "Transformation of Treaties", *Tydskrif Vir Hedendaagse Romeins-Hollandse Reg*, vol. 37, pp. 365-71.

Sanders, A.J.G.M. (1977), "The Applicability of Customary International Law in Municipal Law- South Africa's Monist Tradition", *Tydskrif Vir Hedendaagse Romeins-Hollandse Reg*, vol. 40, pp. 147-55.

Sanders, A.J.G.M. (1978), "The Applicability of Customary International Law in South African Law: The Appeal Court has Spoken", *Comparative and International Law Journal of Southern Africa*, vol.1, pp. 198-207.

Schachter, Oscar, Mahomed Nawaz and John Reid (1971), *Toward Wider Acceptance of UN Treaties*, Arno Press, New York.

Schaffer, P. Rosaile (1983), "The Inter-relationship Between Public International Law and the Law of South Africa: An Overview", *International and Comparative Law Quarterly*, vol. 32, pp. 277-315.

Schermers, H.G. (1977), "The Namibia Decree in National Courts", *International and Comparative Law Quarterly*, vol. 26, pp. 81-96.

Schreuer, C. Christoph (1978), "The Relevance of United Nations Decisions in Domestic Legislation", *International and Comparative Law Quarterly*, vol. 27, pp. 1-17.

Schreuer, C. Christoph (1981), *Decisions of International Institutions Before Domestic Courts*, Oceana, London.

Schwelb, Egon (1972), "The International Court of Justice and the Human Rights Clauses of the Charter", *American Journal of International Law*, vol. 66, pp. 337-51.

Scott, James. Brown (1907), "The Legal Nature of International Law", *American Journal of International Law*, vol. 1, pp. 831-66.

Singh, Gurdip (1988), "Status of Human Rights Covenants in India", *India Journal of International Law*, vol. 28, pp. 16-21.

Starke, J.G. (1936), "Monism and Dualism in the Theory of International Law", *British Year Book of International Law*, vol. 16, pp. 66-81.

Takirambudde, Peter (1983), "External Law and Social Structure in an African Context: An Essay about Normative Imposition and Survival in Swaziland", *Comparative and International Law of Southern Africa*, vol.16, pp. 209-28.

Van Panhuys, H.F. Jonkheer (1964), "Relations and Interactions Between International and National Scenes of Law", *Recueil des Cours*, vol. 112, pp. 1-87.

Vasak, Karel (1963), "The European Convention on Human Rights Beyond the Frontiers of Europe", *International and Comparative Law Quarterly*, vol. 12, pp. 1206-31.

Vasak, Karel (1982), *The International Dimensions of Human Rights*, vol. 2, Greenwood Press, Westport.

Vierdag, E. W. (1973), *The Concept of Discrimination in International Law with Special Reference to Human Rights*, Martinus Nijhoff, The Hague.

Vitanyi, Bela (1977), "Some Reflections on Article 25 of the Constitution of Germany", *Netherlands International Law Review*, vol. 24, pp. 578-88.

Watson, S. Cary (1977), "The European Convention on Human Rights and the British Courts", *Texas International Law Journal*, vol.12, pp. 61-73.

Westlake, J. (1906), "Is International law Part of the Law of England?" *Law Quarterly Review*, vol. 22, pp.14-26.

Wildhaber, Luzius (1971), *Treaty-Making Power and Constitution: An International and Comparative Study*, Helbing and Lichtenhahn, Basel.

Williams, S.A and A.L.C. de Mestral (1987), *An Introduction to International Law: Chiefly as Interpreted and Applied in Canada*, 2nd ed, Butterworths, Toronto.

Wilson, R. Robert. et al. (eds) (1966), *The International Law Standards and the Commonwealth Developments*, Duke University Press, Durham.

Wright, Quincy (1951), "National Courts and Human Rights - The Fujii Case", *American Journal of International Law*, vol. 41, pp. 62-82.

Yadin, U. (1962), "Reception and Rejection of English Law in Israel", *International and Comparative Law Quarterly*, vol. 11, pp. 59-88.

Zander, Michael (1959), "The Act of State Doctrine", *American Journal of International Law,* vol. 53, pp. 826-52.

Botswana

Aguda, Akinola (1973), "Legal Development in Botswana from 1885 to 1966", *Botswana Notes and Records*, vol. 5, pp. 52-63.

Bishop, Kristyna (1998), "Squatters on their Own Land: San Territoriality in Western Botswana", *Comparative and International Law Journal of Southern Africa*, vol. 31, pp. 92-121.

Brewer, I. G. (1974), "Sources of Criminal Law of Botswana", *Journal of African Law*, vol. 18, pp. 24-36.

Coldham, Simon (1992), "Human Rights in Botswana: Unity Dow v. Attorney-General (Botswana)", *Journal of African Law*, vol. 36, pp. 91-2.

Commonwealth Relations Office (1960), *Bechuanaland Protectorate: Constitutional Proposals*, HMSO, London.

Commonwealth Relations Office (1964), *Bechuanaland: Constitutional Proposals*, HMSO, London.

Danevad, Andreas (1995), " Responsiveness in Botswana Politics: Do Elections Matter?" *Journal of Modern African Studies*, vol. 33, pp.381-402.

Dow, Unity and Alice Mogwe (1992), *The Convention on the Rights of the Child and the Legal Status of Children in Botswana: A Consultancy Report For UNICEF*, Women and the Law in Southern Africa, Gaborone.

Edwards, H. Robert (1967), "Political and Constitutional Change in the Bechuanaland Protectorate", in J. Butler and A. A. Castagno (eds), *Transition in African Politics*, Praeger, New York, pp.135-165.

Forster, Bankie (1981), "Introduction to the History of the Administration of Justice of the Republic of Botswana", *Botswana Notes and Records*, vol. 13, pp. 89-100.

Good, Kenneth (1996), "Towards Popular Participation in Botswana", *Journal of Modern African Studies*, vol. 34, pp. 53-77.

Granberg, Per and J. R. Parkinson (eds), (1988), *Botswana: Country Study and Norwegian Aid Review*, CHR, Michelsen Institute, Bergen.

Holm, John and Patrick Molutsi (1989), *Democracy in Botswana*, Macmillan (Botswana), Gaborone.

Joint Advisory Council Constitutional Committee (1958), *Report on the Establishment of Legislative Council and Executive Council for the Bechuanaland Protectorate*, HMSO, London.

Mbao, M. L. B. (1990), "Constitutional Government and Human Rights in Botswana", *Lesotho Law Journal*, vol. 6, pp. 179-206.

Molokomme, Athaliah (1985), "The Reception and Development of Roman-Dutch Law in Botswana", *Lesotho Law Journal*, vol. 1, pp. 121-34.

Ng'ong'ola, Clement (1989), "Compulsory Acquisition of Private Land in Botswana: The Bonnington Farm Case", *Comparative and International Law Journal of Southern Africa*, vol. 22, pp. 298-317.

Ng'ong'ola, Clement (1997), "Land Rights for Marginalised Ethnic Groups in Botswana, with Special Reference to the Basarwa", *Journal of African Law*, vol. 41, pp.1-26.

Nsereko, Daniel D. Ntanda (1988), "The Right to Legal Representation in Botswana", *Israel Year book of Human Rights*, pp. 211-27.

Nsereko, Daniel D. Ntanda (1991), "Extenuating Circumstances in Capital Offenses in Botswana", *Criminal Law Forum*, vol. 2, pp. 236-59.

Nsereko, Daniel D. Ntanda (1992), " Religious Liberty and the Law in Botswana", *Journal of Church and State*, vol. 34, pp. 843-62.

Otlhogile, Bojosi (1994), *A History of Higher Courts in Botswana: 1912-1990*, Mmegi, Gaborone.

Otlhogile, Bojosi (1994), "Judicial Intervention in the Electoral Process: Botswana's Experience", *Comparative and International Law Journal of Southern Africa*, vol. 27, pp. 222-33.

Penna, David. R. (1994), "Continuity and Change in Human Rights Protection in Botswana: Political Participation and Personal Security", in Eileen McCarthy-Arnolds, et al (eds), *Africa, Human Rights and the Global System: The Political Economy of Human Rights in a Changing World*, Greenwood Press, Westport, pp. 211-24.

Picard, A. Louis (ed), (1985), *The Evolution of Modern Botswana: Politics and Rural Development in Southern Africa*, Rex Collings, London.

Quansah, E. K. (1992), " Unity Dow v. Attorney-General of Botswana - One More Relic of a Woman's Servitude Removed", *African Journal of International and Comparative Law*, vol. 4, pp. 195-204.

Quansah, E. K. (1995), " Is the Right to Get Pregnant a Fundamental Human Right in Botswana?" *Journal of African Law*, vol. 39, pp. 97-102.

Rembe, N.S. (1990), "Emang Basadi: Women, Sex Discrimination and the Constitution of Botswana", *Lesotho Law Journal*, vol. 6, pp. 155-65.

Sanders, A.J.G.M. (1983), "Constitutionalism in Botswana: A Valiant Attempt at Judicial Activism", *Comparative and International Law Journal of Southern Africa*, vol. 16, pp. 351-73.

Sanders, A.J.G.M. (1984), "Constitutionalism in Botswana: A Valiant Attempt at Judicial Activism - Part Two", *Comparative and International Law Journal of Southern Africa*, vol. 17, pp. 49-64.

Sanders, A.J.G.M. (1985), Legal Dualism in Botswana, Lesotho and Swaziland: A General Survey", *Lesotho Law Journal*, vol. 1, pp. 47-67.

Sanders, A.J.G.M. (1990), "Sekgoma Lesholathebe's Detention and the Betrayal of a Protectorate", *Comparative and International Law Journal of Southern Africa*, vol. 23, pp. 348-60.

Schapera, I. A. (1955), *Handbook of Tswana Law and Custom*, 2nd ed, Oxford University Press, London.

Secretary of State for Colonies (1966), *Official Report of the Bechuanaland Independence Conference 1966*, HMSO, London.

Sillery, Anthony (1976), "Comments on Two Articles", *Botswana Notes and Records*, vol. 8, pp. 292-5.

Sillery, Anthony (1965), *Founding a Protectorate: History of Bechuanaland Protectorate 1885-1895*, Mouton, London.

Sillery, Anthony (1974), *Botswana: A Short Political History*, Methuen, London.

Takirambudde, Peter (1996), "Botswana", in Peter Baehr, et al (ed), *Human Rights in Developing Countries: Yearbook 1995*, Kluwer Law International, The Hague, pp. 129-51.

Tshosa, B. Onkemetse (1994), "Freedom of Political Activity: Law and Practice in Botswana", *Comparative and International Law Journal of Southern Africa*, vol. 27, pp. 371-83.

Van Niekerk, B. J. (1970), "Customary Law in Botswana: Substitution or Adaptation?" *Comparative and International Law Journal of Southern Africa*, vol. 3, pp. 242-7.

Vengroff, Richard (1977), *Botswana Rural Development in the Shadow of Apartheid*, Fairleigh Dickinson University Press, Rutherford.

Zetterquist, Jenny (1990), *Refugees in Botswana in the Light of International Law*, The Scandinavian Institute of African Studies, Uppsala.

Namibia

Becker, H. (1997), " Women and Land Rights", in J. Malan, and M. O. Hinz (eds), *Communal Land Administration: Second National Traditional Authority Conference - 28 September, 1997*, Centre for Applied Sciences, Windhoek, pp. 56-63.

Bruwer, J.P. van S. (1966), *South West Africa: The Disputed Land*, Nasionale Boekhandel, Cape Town.

Carpenter, Gretchen (1991), "The Namibian Constitution - ex Africa Aliquid Novi after All", in D. Wyk et al (eds), *Namibia: Constitutional and International Law Issues*, Centre for Public Law Studies, Pretoria, pp. 22-64.

Cleary, M. Sean (1988), "A Bill of Rights as a Normative Instrument: South West Africa/Namibia 1975-1988", *Comparative and International Law of Southern Africa*, vol. 21, pp. 291-355.

Cliffe, Lionel. et al (1994), *The Transition to Independence of Namibia*, Lynne Reinner, Boulder.

Cockram, G. Gail-Maryse (1976), *South West African Mandate*, Juta, Cape Town.

Cottrell, Jill (1991), "The Constitution of Namibia: An Overview", *Journal of African Law*, vol. 35, pp. 56-78.

Diescho, Joseph (1994), *The Namibian Constitution in Perspective*, Gamsberg Macmillan (Namibia), Windhoek.

Erasmus, Gerhard (1989/90), "The Namibian Constitution and the Application of International Law", *South African Year Book of International Law*, vol. 15, pp. 81-110.

Fourie, N. Frederick (1990), "The Namibian Constitution and Economic Rights", *South African Journal of Human Rights*, vol. 6, pp. 363-79.

Harring, L. Sidney (1996), "The Constitution of Namibia and the 'Rights and Freedoms' Guaranteed Communal Land Holders: Resolving the Inconsistency Between Article 16, Article 100, and Schedule", *South African Journal on Human Rights*, vol. 12, pp. 467-84.

Hatchard, John (1992), "The Fall of the Cane Again: Corporal Punishment in Namibia", *Journal of African Law*, vol. 36, pp. 81-5.

Imishue, R.W. (1965), *South West Africa: An International problem*, Pall Mall, London.

International Society for Human Rights (1986), *Human Rights in Namibia: An In-depth Analysis of Human Rights in Namibia - Includes Namibia Human Rights Report*, British Section, London.

Kaela, C. W. Laurent (1996), *The Question of Namibia*, Macmillan, London.

Katjavivi, H. Peter (1988), *A History of Resistance in Namibia*, UNESCO, Paris.

Mbuende, Kaire (1986), *Namibia, The Broken Shield: Anatomy of Imperialism and Revolution*, Liber Forlog, Malmo.

Mtopa, M. Arnold (1990/91), "The Namibian Constitution and the Application of International Law - A Comment", *South African Year Book of International Law*, vol. 16, pp. 105-12.

Naldi, J. Gino (1994), "Some Reflections on the Namibian Bill of Rights", *African Journal of Comparative and International law*, vol. 6, pp. 45-58.

Naldi, J. Gino (1995), *Constitutional Rights in Namibia: A Comparative Analysis with International Human Rights*, Juta, Kenwyn.

Namibia Human Rights and Documentation Centre (1995), *Human Rights Education and Advocacy in Namibia in the 1990s: A Tapestry of Perspectives*, University of Namibia, Windhoek.

National Society for Human Rights (1996), *Namibia: Human Rights Report 1995*, National Society for Human Rights, Windhoek.

Parker, C. (1991), "Legal Aspects of Access to Land and Tenure in Namibia: A Case of Social Inequality Supported and Regulated by Law", *Lesotho Law Journal*, vol. 7, pp. 93-107.

Richardson, Henry Jr. (1984), "Constitutive Questions in the Negotiations for Namibian Independence", *American Journal of International Law*, vol. 78, pp. 76-120.

Rukuro, Vekuii (1995), "The Constitution as a Vehicle for the Protection of Human Rights: The Southern African Experience - Namibia", *Legal Forum*, vol. 7, pp. 35-9.

Serfontein, J. H. P. (1976), *Namibia?* Rex Collings, London.

Wellington, John. H. (1967), *South West Africa and its Human Issues*, Clarendon Press, Oxford.

Wiechers, Marinus (1991), "Namibia: The 1982 Constitutional Principles and their Legal Significance", in D. Wyk, et al (eds), *Namibia: Constitutional and International Law Issues*, Centre for Public Law Studies, Pretoria, pp. 1-21.

Wyk, Dawid (1991), "The Making of the Namibian Constitution: Lessons for Africa", *Comparative and International Law Journal of Southern Africa*, vol. 24, pp. 341-51.

Zacklin, Ralph (1981), "The Problem of Namibia in International Law", *Recueil des Cours*, vol.171, pp. 225-339.

Zimbabwe

Austin, Reginald (1968), *The Character and Legislation of the Rhodesian Front*, London, Africa Bureau.

Christie, Michael John (1972) *Rhodesia: Proposals for a Sell-out*, Southern African Research Office, London.

Chung, Fay and Emmanuel Ngara (1985), *Socialism, Education and Development: A Challenge to Zimbabwe*, Zimbabwe Publishing House, Harare.

Devine, D. J. (1973), " The Status of Rhodesia in International Law", *Acta Juridica*, pp. 1-171.

Feltoe, G. (1989), "Fair Trials for Those Who Cannot Afford Lawyers to Defend Them", *Legal Forum*, vol. 1, pp. 10-17.

Foreign and Commonwealth Office (1980), *Southern Rhodesia: Report of the Constitutional Conference*, HMSO, London.

Foreign and Commonwealth Office (1977), *Rhodesia: Proposals for a Settlement*, HMSO, London.

Gubbay, R. Anthony (1989), "Women's Rights", *Legal Forum*, vol.1, No.3, pp. 3-10.

Gubbay, R. Anthony (1997), "The Protection and Enforcement of Fundamental Rights: The Zimbabwean Experience", *Human Rights Quarterly*, vol. 19, pp. 227-54.

Hatchard, John (1986), "Emergency Powers in Zimbabwe: An Overview of Post-Independence Development", *Zambia Law Journal*, vol. 18, pp. 35-70.

Hatchard, John (1988), "The Right to Legal Representation in Africa: The Zimbabwean Experience", *Lesotho Law Journal*, vol. 4, pp. 135-49.

Hatchard, John (1991), "The Fall and Rise of the Cane in Zimbabwe", *Journal of African Law*, vol. 35, pp. 198-204.

Hatchard, John (1993a), "Delay and the Death Sentence: The Zimbabwean Approach", *Journal of African Law*, vol. 37, pp. 195-207.

Hatchard, John (1993b), *Individual Freedoms and State of Emergency in the African Context: The Case of Zimbabwe*, Baobab, Harare.

Hlatshwayo, Ben (1993), "Land Expropriation Laws in Zimbabwe and their Compatibility with International Legal Norms", *Zimbabwean Law Review*, vol. 2, pp. 41-58.

Holleman, J. F. (1969), *Shona Customary Law with Reference to Kinship, Marriage, the Family and the Estate*, Manchester University Press, Manchester.

Human Rights Watch (1989), *Zimbabwe: A Break with the Past? Human Rights and Political Unity*, Africa Watch Committee, New York.

International Defence and Aid Fund (1969), *Rhodesia: Why Minority Rule Survives*, Christian Action Publications, London.

Madhuku, Lovemore (1996), "The Impact of the European Court of Human Rights in Africa: The Zimbabwean Experience", *African Journal of International and Comparative Law*, vol. 8, pp. 932-43.

May, Joan (1983), *Zimbabwean Women in Customary and Colonial Law*, Holmes McDougal, Edinburgh.

Naldi, J. Gino (1998), "Constitutional Challenge to Land Reform in Zimbabwe", *Comparative and International Law Journal of Southern Africa*, vol. 31, pp. 78-91.

Ncube, Welchman (1987), "The Constitutional Recognition and Popular Enjoyment of Human Rights in Zimbabwe", *Zimbabwe Law Review*, vol. 5, pp. 54-94.

Ncube, Welchman (1994), "Review of Electoral Laws and Institutions in Zimbabwe", *Legal Forum*, vol. 6, pp. 17-27.

Nherere, Pearson (1995), " How Can a Bill of Rights Best be Protected Against Undesirable Erosion and Amendment?" *Legal Forum*, vol. 7, pp. 40-7.

Nkala, Jericho (1985), *The United Nations, International Law and The Rhodesian Independence Crisis*, Clarendon Press, Oxford.

Palley, Claire (1966), *Constitutional History and the Law in Southern Rhodesia 1888-1965 with Special Reference to Imperial Control*, Clarendon Press, Oxford.

Patel, B. (1991), "Effect on Domestic Law of Treaties to which Zimbabwe is a Party", *Legal Forum*, vol. 3, pp. 26-9.

Rowland, John Reid (1994), "An Outline of Zimbabwean Legislation Dealing with Women", *Legal Forum*, vol. 6, pp. 14-16.

Tshuma, Lawrence (1987a), "The Lancaster House Constitution and the Legal Transformation: A Case Study of the Criminal Law in Zimbabwe", *Zimbabwe Law Review*, vol. 5, pp. 195-201.

Tshuma, Lawrence (1987b) "Spare the Rod and Spoil the Child: Is Juvenile Whipping Constitutional? *Zimbabwe Law Review*, vol. 5, pp. 214-18.

Zacklin, Ralph (1974), *The United Nations and Rhodesia: A Study in International Law*, Praeger, New York.

Zimmerli, Christopher H. (1971), "Human Rights and the Rule of Law in Southern Rhodesia", *International and Comparative Law Quarterly*, vol. 20, pp. 239-300.

Zvobgo, Jonas Rugano (1985), *Transforming Education: The Zimbabwean Experience*, College Press, Harare.

International Instruments

United Nations

Brownlie, Ian (1992) *Basic Documents on Human Rights,* 3rd ed. Clarendon Press, Oxford.

Charter of the United Nations, 26 June, 1945.

International Covenant on Civil and Political Rights, Res. G.A. 2200 A (XX1), 16 December 1966, 6 ILM 368 (1967); 999 U.N.T.S. 171.

International Covenant on Economic, Social and Cultural Rights, Res. G.A. 2200 A (XX1), 16 December 1966, 6 ILM 360 (1967); 993 U.N.T.S. 3.

United Nations. *Multilateral Treaties Deposited with the Secretary General: Status as at 1 December 1995*, New York: Treaty Section, 1996.

Universal Declaration of Human Rights, Res. G.A. 217 A (111), 10 December, 1948.

Vienna Convention on the Law of Treaties, 22 May 1969, 8 ILM 679 (1969); 1155 U.N.T.S. 331.

Regional Instruments

The Charter of the Organisation of African Unity, 15 May 1963, 2 ILM 766 (1963).

The African Charter on Human and People's Rights, 27 June 1981, 21 ILM 58 (1982).

Treaty of the Southern African Development Community, Windhoek (Namibia), 17 August 1992, 32 ILM 116 (1993).

Cases

Permanent Court of International Justice and International Court of Justice

Asylum Case (Peru v. Columbia) 1950 I.C.J. Rep. 266.

Barcelona Traction Case (Belgium v. Spain) 1970 I.C.J. Rep. 3.
Case Concerning Certain German Interests in Polish Upper Silesia (Germany v. Poland) 1926 P.C.I.J Series A, No 7.

Exchange of Greek and Turkish Populations, 1925 P.C.I.J. Series B, No. 10.

Free Zones of Upper Savoy and the District of Gex (France v. Switzerland) 1932 P.C.I.J. Ser. A/B, No. 46.

Greco-Bulgaria "Communities" Case (Bulgaria v. Greece) 1930 P.C.I.J. Ser. B, No. 17.

Jurisdiction of the Courts of Danzig 1928 P.C.I.J. Series B, No. 15.17.

Military and Paramilitary Activities in and against Nicaragua Case (Nicaragua v. United States of America) Merits, 1986 I.C.J. Rep. 14.

Nationality Decrees in Tunisia and Morocco Case (Great Britain v. France) 1923 P.C.I.J. Series B, No. 4.

Nottebohm Case (Liechtenstein v. Guatamala) 1955 I.C.J. Rep .4.

North Sea Continental Shelf Cases (Federal Republic of Germany v. Denmark; Federal Republic of Germany v. The Netherlands) 1969 I.C.J. Rep. 13.

South West Africa Cases (Liberia and Ethiopia v. South Africa) 1966 I.C.J. Rep. 6.

Treatment of Polish Nationals and Other Persons of Polish Origin or Speech in the Territory of Danzig 1931 P.C.I.J. Series A/B, No. 44.

Regional Tribunals

Costello-Roberts v. United Kingdom Appeal (1993) 19 E.H.R.R. 112.

Engel v. The Netherlands (No. 1) (1976) 1 E.H.R.R. 647.

Erkner and Hofauer v. Austria (1987) 9 E.H.R.R. 464.

Fredin v. Sweden (No. 2) (1991) 13 E.H.R.R. 784.

Free Legal Assistance Group et al v. Zaire, Communication No. 25/1989, I.H.R.R Vol. 4 No. 1 (1997), 89.

Golder v. United Kingdom (1975) 1 E.H.R.R. 524.

Hakansson v. Sweden (1991) 13 E.H.R.R. 1.

Ireland v. United Kingdom (1978) 2 E.H.R.R. 25.

Soering v. United Kingdom (1989) 2 E. H.H.R. 439.

Sporrong and Lonnroth v. Sweden (1982) 5 E.H.R.R. 35.

Sunday Times v. United Kingdom (1979) 2 E.H.R.R. 245.

Texaco v. Libya 17 ILM 1 (1978).

Tyrer v. United Kingdom (1978) 2 E.H.R.R 1.

Velasquez v. Honduras 28 ILM 291 (1989).

Warwick v. United Kingdom, Application No. 9471/81 (1986).

Y v. United Kingdom (1994) 17 E.H.R.R. 238.

National: Botswana, Zimbabwe and Namibia

Botswana

Agnes Bojang v. The State, Miscellaneous Criminal Case No. 6/1993, HC, (unreported).

Ali Khan and Another v. State [1968-70] B.L.R. 4.

Attorney-General of Botswana v. Unity Dow [1992] L.R.C. (Const) 623 (CA).

Desai and Another v. State [1985] B.L.R. 582.

Kgolagano v. Attorney-General (Botswana), Criminal Case No. F. 34/1994 (unreported).

Khoza and Another v. Attorney-General and Another, Civil Case No. 94/1982 (unreported).

Macha v. State [1982] 1 B.L.R. 98.

Moisakamo v. Moisakamo, Matrimonial Cause No. 106/1978 (unreported).

Molale v. State, Criminal Appeal No. 56/1994 (CA) (unreported).

Mosarwana v. State [1985] B.L.R. 258.

Mosotho, Masina and Mogotsi v. State, Criminal Appeal No. 14/1983 (unreported).

Oakametse v. Attorney-General (Botswana), Civil Trial No. (F) 52/1987 (unreported).

Petrus and Another v. The State [1985] L.R.C. (Const) 699.

Pieter Bruwer and Others v. The President of Botswana, Misca. No. 478/96 (unreported) (HC).

R v. Earl Crewe [1910] 2 K.B. 576 (CA).

Raditlhose v. State, Criminal Appeal No. 14/1990 (unreported).

Rapula Sello v. State, Criminal Appeal No. 121/1977 (unreported).

S v. Makwekwe [1981] B.L.R. 196.

S v. Zweiger, Review Case No. 522/1978 (unreported).

State v. Galeboe [1968-70] B.L.R. 364.

State v. Gordon Tokwe, Review Case No. 279/1984, HC, (unreported).

State v. Merriweather Seboni [1968-70] B.L.R. 158.

SRC, Molepolole College of Education v. Attorney-General of Botswana, Civil Appeal No. 13/1994 (unreported).

The President of Botswana and Others v. Pieter Bruwer, Civil Appeal No. 13/1997 (unreported) (CA).

Tshipo v. State, Crminal Appeal No. 171/1984 (unreported).

Unity Dow v. Attorney-General of Botswana [1991] L.R.C. (Const) 574 (HC).

Namibia

Binga v. Administrator - General, South West Africa 1984 (3) S.A. 949.

Binga v. Cabinet for South West Africa, 1988 (3) S.A. 155.

Djama v. Government of the Republic of Namibia 1993 (1) S.A. 387.

De Roeck v. Campbell and Others, 1990 N.R. 353 (Nm HC).

Ex Parte Attorney General, Namibia: In Re Corporal Punishment by Organs of State 1991 (3) S.A. 76.

Freiremar SA v. Prosecutor-General of Namibia, Criminal Case No. Fn 175/1995 (unreported).

Government of the Republic of Namibia and Another v Cultura 2000 and Another 1994 (1) S.A. 407.

Kausea v. Minister of Home Affairs 1995 (1) S.A 51.

Minister of Defence, Namibia v. Mwandinghi 1992 (2) S.A 355.

R v. Goseb 1956 (2) S.A. (SWA) 696.

R v. Mbahapa 1991 (4) S.A. 668.

R v. Nassar 1995 (2) S.A. 82.

S v. Acheson 1991 (2) S.A. 805.

S v. Amujekela 1991 N.R. 303.

S v. Alexander, Criminal Case No. 77/1992 (unreported).

S v. Eliasov 1965 (2) S.A. 770.

S v. Heita and Another 1992 (3) S.A. 785.

S v. Moses, Criminal Case No. 2/1992 (unreported).

S v. Mwambazi 1990 N.R. 353 (Nm HC).

S v. Namseb 1991 (1) SACR 223 (SWA).

S v. Shikongo, 23 October 1991, Nm HC, (unreported).

S v. Tcoeib 1992 N.R. 198.

S v. Tuhadeleni 1967 (4) S.A. 511.

S v. Tuhadeleni and Others 1969 (1) S.A. 153.

S v. Cabinet for South West Africa and Others 1988 (3) S.A. (SWA) 155.

State v. Nehemia Tjijo, No. 4/1991 Nm HC (unreported).

Tittel v. R 1921 (2) S.A. (SWA) 58.

Vaatz v. Law Society of Namibia 1991 (3) S.A. 563.

Zimbabwe

Barker McCormac (Pvt) v. Government of Kenya (1986) L.R.C. (Const) 215.

Barker McCormac (Pvt) v. Government of Kenya 1983 (4) S.A. 817.

Bull v. Minister of Home Affairs [1987] L.R.C. (Const) 547.

Catholic Commission for Peace and Justice in Zimbabwe v. Attorney-General, Zimbabwe 1993 (4) S.A. 239.

Chikweche, In re, 1995 (4) S.A. 284.

Chinamora v. Angwa Furnishers (Pvt) Ltd, Civil Case No. 228/1996, HC, (unreported).

Davies and Others v. Minister of Lands, Agriculture and Water Development, 1997 (1) S.A. 228 (ZSC).

Dlamini and Others v. Carter and Another 1968 (1) R.L.R. 136.

Fikilini v. Attorney-General 1990 (1) Z.L.R. 105 (ZSC).

Hewlett v. Minister of Finance and Another 1982 (1) S.A. 490.

May v. Reserve Bank of Zimbabwe 1986 (3) S.A. 102.

Mharapara v. The State [1986] L.R.C. (Const) 235.

Minister of Home Affairs v. Austin and Another [1987] L.R.C (Const) 567.

Minister of Home Affairs v. Bickle and Others 1984 (2) S.A. 431.

Minister of Home Affairs v. Dabengwa 1984 (2) S.A. 345.

Mlambo, In re, 1992 (4) S.A. 144.

Moll v. Commissioner of Police 1983 (1) Z.L.R. 242.

Munhumeso and Others, In re, 1995 (1) S.A. 551.

Nkomo and Another v. Attorney-General, Zimbabwe 1994 (3) S.A. 34.

Nyambirai v. National Social Security Authority and Another 1996 (1) S.A. (ZSC).

Patriotic Front - ZAPU v. Minister of Justice, Legal and Parliamentary Affairs [1986]   L.R.C. (Const) 672.

R v. Kafakarotwe 1951 S.R. 162.

R v. Muirhead 1954 S.A. (3) 259.

R v. Ncube; S v Tshuma; S v Ndlhovu 1988 (2) S.A. 702.

Rattigan and Others v. Chief Immigration Officer, Zimbabwe 1995 (2) S.A. 182.

Retrofit (PvT) Ltd v. Posts and Telecommunications Corporation 1996 (1) S.A. 847.

S v. A Juvenile 1990 (4) S.A. 151.

S v. Masitere 1990 (2) Z.L.R. 105.

S v. Miller 1973 (2) R.L.R. 387.

S v. Ndhlovu 1981 Z.L.R. 600.

S v. Woods and Another 1993 (2) Z.L.R. 258.

Woods and Others v. Minister of Justice, Legal and Parliamentary Affairs 1995 (1) S.A 123 (ZSC).

Zimbabwe Teachers Association v. Attorney-General, Civil Appeal No. 70/1996 (unreported).

National: other jurisdictions

Alcom Ltd. v. Republic of Colombia and Others 1984 2 W.L.R. 750.

Andrea v. The Republic (1970) E.A. 46.

Attorney-General v. Nissan [1969] 1 All E.R. 629 (HL).

Barker v. Wingo 407 U.S. 514 (1972).

Bell v. Director of Public of Prosecutions of Jamaica and Another [1985] 2 All E.R. 585.

Buttes Gas and Oil Co. v. Hammer (No. 3) [1982] A.C. 888.

Buvot v. Barbuit [1737] case t. Talbot 281.

Christopher McGimpsy and Michael McGimpsy v. Ireland and Others [1988] I.R. 567.

Chung Chi Cheung v. R [1939] A.C. 160.

Cook v. United States 288 U.S. 102 (1933).

Cook v. Sprigg [1899] A.C. 572.

Derbyshire County Council v. Times Newspaper Ltd [1993] A.C. 534 (HL).

Earl Pratt and Another v. Attorney-General for Jamaica [1993] 3 W.L.R. 995.

Elliot Mochochoko v. Regina 1961-62 H.C.T.L.R 42.

Forter v. Nielson 27 U.S. (2 Pet.) 253 [1829].

I Congresso del Partido [1983] 1 A.C. 244.

Inter-science Research and development Corporation Services (Pty) Ltd v Republica Popular Mozambique 1980 (2) S.A. 111.

Johnstone v. Peddlar [1921] 2 A.C. 262.

Luther v. Sagor [1921] 3 K.B. 532.

Maclaine Watson v. Department of Trade and Industry (1989) 3 All E.R. 523.

Mortensen v. Peters [1906] S.L.R. 227.

Musoke v. Uganda (1972) E.A. 137.

Nduli and Another v. The Minister of Justice 1978 (1) S.A. 893.

Over the Top, Case 5 F 2d 842 (1925).

Pan American World Airways Inc. v. South African Fire and Accident Insurance Co. Limited 1965 (3) S.A. 150.

Parkin v. Government of the Republique Democratique du Congo and Another 1971 (1) S.A. 259.

Parlement Belge [1879] 4 P.D. 129.

Pauling v. McEroy 164 F Supp. 390 [1918].

People v. Mcleod 25 Wend, 843 [N.Y. 1843].

R v. Camborne Justices, Ex parte Pearce [1955] 1 Q.B. 41.

R v. Keyn (The Franconia) (1876) 2 Ex. D. 63.

R v. Merthyr Tydfil, Ex parte Jenkins [1967] 1 All E.R. 636.

R v. Mngomezulu and Others [1978] Swazi. L. R. 159.

R v. Secretary for State for the Home Department, Ex parte, Thakrar [1974] 2 W.L.R. 573.

R v. Sussex Justices, Ex parte McCarthy [1924] 1 K.B. 256.

R v. Zamora [1916] 2 A.C. 77.

Ross-Spencer and Another v. Mater of the High Court (1970-76) Swazi. L.R. 58.

S v. Makwanyane and Another 1995 (3) S.A. 391.

S v. Werner 1980 (2) S.A. 365 (translation).

Salomon v. Commissioner of Customs and Excise [1962] 2 Q.B. 116.

Sei Fujii v. State of California, 38 Cal (2d) 718 [1952].

Sobhuza 11 v. Miller [1926] A.C. 518.

South Atlantic Islands Development Corporation Ltd v. Buchan 1971 (1) S.A 234 (C).

The Paquete Habana, 175 U.S. 667 (1900).

Trendtex Trading Corporation v. Central Bank of Nigeria [1977] 1 All E.R. 881.

Underhill v. Herhandez, 168 U.S. 250 (1897).

Walter v. Collot 2 U.S. (2 Dall.) 247 (1796).

West Rand Central Gold Mining Company v. R [1905] 2 K.B. 391.